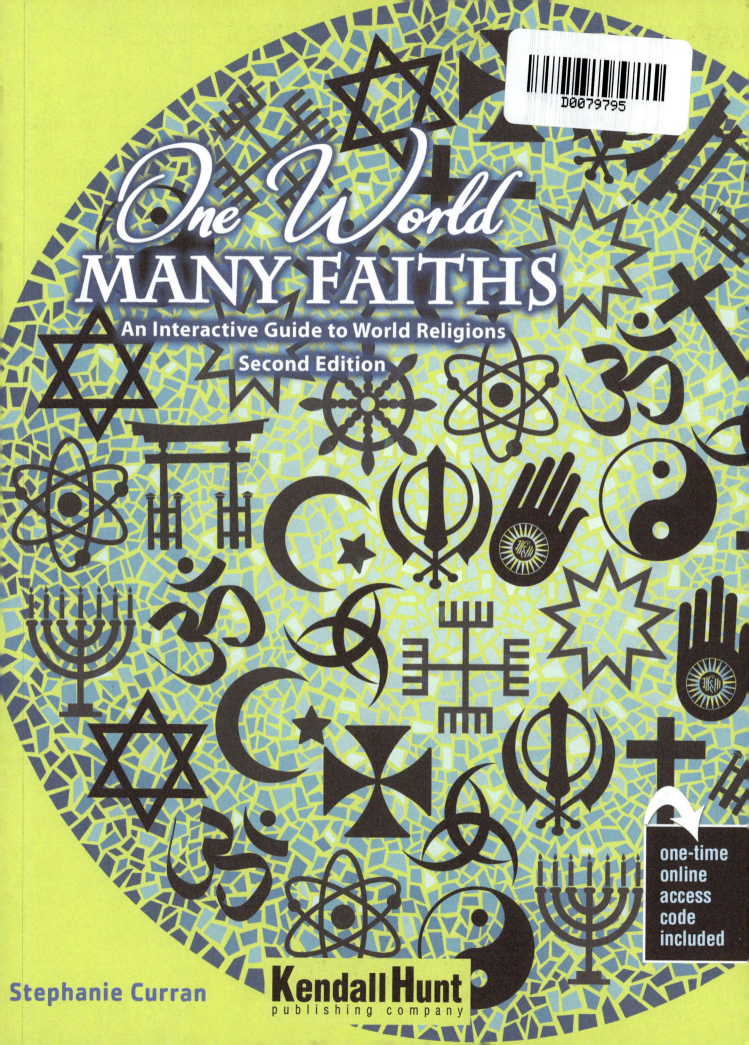

One World MANY FAITHS

An Interactive Guide to World Religions

Second Edition

one-time
online
access
code
included

Stephanie Curran

Kendall Hunt
publishing company

Contents

Part 1: The Origins and Diversity of Religion

CHAPTERS:

Chapter 1: Introduction to Religion and Religious Studies

Chapter 2: Religious Diversity and Religious Pluralism

Chapter 3: Indigenous Religions

TIMELINE OF WORLD'S RELIGIONS

3400 BCE	Early Egyptian and Sumerian religious texts
2000 BCE	Time of Abraham
2000–1500 BCE	Beginning of the Vedic period in Hinduism
1500–1350 BCE	Estimated period of Moses and Zarathustra, the founder of Zoroastrianism
600–400 BCE	Founding of Jainism, Buddhism, Daoism, and Confucianism
100 CE	Christianity separates from Judaism; Shinto develops in Japan
600 CE	Islam is founded
1500 CE	Sikhism is founded
1800 CE	Baha'i is founded

Chapter 1

Introduction to Religion and Religious Studies

Learning Outcomes

By the end of the chapter, students will be able to

- discuss the difficulty of defining religion;
- describe basic elements of religion including creed, code, and cultus;
- identify various definitions of religion offered by scholars from a broad spectrum of disciplines;
- formulate a working definition of religion and analyze its strengths and weaknesses;
- distinguish between religion and spirituality as they are used in contemporary society;
- define key terms associated with the study of religion and the understandings of divinity;
- explain the personal and social needs met by religion;
- discuss contemporary trends in religion particularly the combinative nature of religion and the growth of the nonreligious.

Key Terms

Agnosticism	Incarnation	Rites of passage
Anthropomorphism	Manifestation	Rituals
Atheism	Monotheism	Shopping cart/eclectic
Code	Myth	spirituality
Creed	Nontheistic	Spirituality
Cultus	Pantheism	Theistic
Henotheism	Polytheism	Transcendent
Immanent	Profane	

DEFINING RELIGION

Defining religion has never been more of a challenge than it is today. Some scholars of religion assert that religion cannot be defined. Religion, in their view, is simply a term constructed by scholars to represent a wide diversity of practices in relation to what may be described as sacred, holy, or Other.[1] Religion implies a sense of awe and wonder at the mysteries of life; but, at the same time, it can also reference very specific behavior, institutions, and practices.

For many, religion is a way of life encompassing everything from methods of spiritual practice to style of dress, diet, and social interaction. Some describe their fascination with a television show, football team, or band as their "religion." Du Xin is the owner of the Central Perk Café in Beijing. In 2013, he was interviewed on National Public Radio's (NPR's) program, *All Things Considered* saying, "I'm crazy about *Friends*. For me, it is like a religion. It's my life."[2] Anyone who has driven by a convention center hosting a gathering of Trekkies may also see the resemblance between fandom and religion. Deadheads, Swifties, and other fans of musicians form a communal bond through their devotion. Fans of sports teams can recite statistics, wear "magic" socks on game day, and religiously follow their teams across the country. What, if anything, distinguishes these fascinations and fandoms from religion?

Worship of a higher power is frequently included in definitions of religion, yet there are **nontheistic** religions that do not emphasize a divine being who "saves" its followers. Buddhism, for instance, does not view Buddha as god; rather, he is seen as a teacher or a guide who demonstrates a path to enlightenment. His teachings are not viewed as infallible; rather, the Buddha himself speaks of testing the teachings to see if they prove true in one's own experience. For this reason, some describe Buddhism as a philosophy rather than a religion. However, a visit to a Buddhist meditation center or temple invariably leaves the visitor with the feeling that he or she has been in a sacred space.

Ninian Smart, a noted scholar of religion, describes seven dimensions of religion. While seven is a sacred number, there is no more frequent number than the number three when looking at religion. Muhammad was told to recite three times. In Christianity, the one God is experienced in three persons in the Trinity. In Buddhism, there is the Triple Gem of Buddha, Dharma, and Sangha. For our study, we will narrow the dimensions or components of religion down to three: **creed**, **code**, and **cultus**. Creed refers to doctrines, sacred narratives, or statements of faith. Code involves guidelines for behavior, ethical principles, dress, diet, and so on. Cultus embodies the ritual and communal aspects of the tradition. Festivals, worship, meditation, yogic pathways, and daily prayer are all part of the understanding of cultus.

When exploring these three components, it is easy to see why creating boundaries between religion and other types of devotion (i.e., patriotism or fandom) can be so difficult. "Civil religion" in the United States can be understood through these three components. Here, creed can refer to the Declaration of Independence, the Constitution, and the Bill of Rights. Serving in the military, standing for the Pledge of Allegiance, or putting one's hand over one's heart for the singing of the national anthem can be understood as code. Thanksgiving, Memorial Day, and Fourth of July festivities serve as examples in the category of cultus.

---

[1] For example, see Russell McCutcheon's, *Manufactured Religion*.
[2] For full interview, see http://www.npr.org/2013/01/23/170074762/friends-will-be-there-for-you-at-beijings-central-perk.

Definitions can focus on how a religion is used (functional definitions) or on what constitutes the essence of a religion (substantive definitions). Literally thousands of definitions have been offered by a wide range of scholars. Paul Tillich, a Christian theologian, defines religions as "that which is of ultimate concern." William James, a classical scholar of the psychology of religion, defines it in a more individual way. "Religion, therefore, as I now ask you arbitrarily to take it, shall mean for us the feelings, acts, and experiences of individual men in their solitude, so far as they apprehend themselves to stand in relation to whatever they may consider the divine."[3] In a similar vein, the theologian Friedrich Schleiermacher, emphasizes religion as a "feeling of absolute dependence" on a source outside ourselves. While James and Schleiermacher focus on the individual, the sociologist, Emile Durkheim, emphasizes the importance of community. For Durkheim, "A religion is a unified system of beliefs and practices relative to sacred things, that is to say, things set apart and forbidden—beliefs and practices which unite in one single moral community called a Church, all those who adhere to them."[4] Religion, in Durkheim's view, is a product of social organization. Moreover, some of the negative views of religion in society stem from religion's support of the status quo. For example, Karl Marx viewed religion as the "opiate of the people." By that he meant that religion kept people in their place and supported the hierarchy of social classes.

Religion can be understood as an institution within society, but at the same time, it is also an experience of the sacred. Rudolph Otto and other scholars of the religious experience studied neither the idea of god nor the question of the existence or nonexistence of god, but rather the human reaction to the experience of sacred power and insight.

☯ Look up a variety of definitions of religion (see e.g., http://web.pdx.edu/~tothm/religion/Definitions.htm or http://www.religioustolerance.org/rel_defn.htm#menu). Choose a definition of religion or compose your own definition. What do you like about this definition? What if anything does it lack?

_____

_____

_____

_____

_____

RELIGION AND SPIRITUALITY

In popular culture today, the word **spirituality** is often used in opposition to the term "religion." Spirituality, in this context, refers to the individual experience of the sacred. It is amorphous and noninstitutional. Spirituality is defined primarily by the individual based on how he or she relates to the sacred. We often hear people say, "I'm spiritual, but not religious" as though being religious is a negative. Religion is viewed, in some sectors of our society, as a stale, unwieldy institution that has little relationship to modern life. At

---

[3] William James, *The Varieties of Religious Experience* (New York: Collier Books, 1961), 42.
[4] Emile Durkheim, *The Elementary Forms of Religious Life*, trans. Karen Fields (New York: Free Press, 1995), 44.

the same time, religion assumes an integral role in our culture. We see religious words, ideas, and practices referenced in political speeches, contemporary literature, TV sitcoms, major motion pictures, sporting events, popular music lyrics, and video games. Religion is clearly not dead, but it is in need of reform. Dale Wright, a professor of religious studies and Asian studies at Occidental College, writes:

> "Important religious leaders in all traditions are reformers. They cultivate the religious dimension of life by opening up new possibilities for what it might mean to be religious in their time. If we allow religion to be identified exclusively with a particular form that it took in the past, something that will always be inadequate to the present, we fail to take our own moment in time seriously and surrender the opportunity for renewal and reform."[5]

Religious practice is a way for us to connect to one another and to the higher self that is our goal, particularly when it is approached with humility and openness.

PERSONAL AND SOCIAL NEEDS MET BY RELIGION

Religion meets a variety of personal and social needs. All societies from the earliest recorded history have established systems of religious thought and practice. What is it about social groupings that seem to inspire the need for religion?

☯ As you reflect on the role religious faith fulfills in your life or your community, what are some of the needs you see religion addressing?

_____

_____

_____

_____

There are many needs met by religion and no right or wrong answers to the question of the role of religion within society. Some of the needs most commonly mentioned include dealing with our mortality, guidelines, or ethical principles of "right" conduct, answering life's big questions (such as the search for meaning or the nature of evil). Religion also provides a sense of belonging or community; it is even said to enhance our physical and emotional well-being.

Sadly, religion has also been a negative force; at times, driving a wedge between people and promoting social injustice. Many wars are fought in the name of religion. Interestingly, while religion is used as a tool to motivate people to fight, it is often political power or control of natural resources (i.e., access to water, oil) that is the root of the conflict. Religion has also been used to justify slavery, the oppression of women, and the presence of poverty.

---

[5] Dale Wright, "*Religion Resurrected, Tricycle*," Summer 2015, accessed July 20, 2015, http://www.tricycle.com/feature/religion-resurrected.

❧ Is it human nature, religious teaching, or some combination of both that causes mistreatment of others in the name of religion? Do you think negative perceptions of religion influence the growth of the nonreligious today?

_____

_____

_____

_____

VIEWS OF THE SACRED

Great diversity exists in the way the sacred is viewed by individuals, communities, and religious movements. Terms that are often viewed as simple and straight forward are not nearly so when we look at them in practice. For example, monotheism is the belief in one god and polytheism, the belief in many. Right? When explored in practice, the terms are more like a continuum than an either/or. Hinduism is often said to have 330 million gods (polytheism) indicating the infinite number of forms the divine can take. However, in Hinduism there is only one divine essence, Brahman, (monotheism) which takes these various forms. Is Hinduism monotheistic or polytheistic? Other religious traditions are very clear in their insistence that there is one god that cannot be divided in any way (e.g., Judaism and Islam). On the other hand, Greek, Egyptian and Norse pantheons are examples of strict polytheism.

In addition to the views of monotheism and polytheism, additional understandings of the sacred pervade religious traditions. Some traditions are pantheistic. Pantheism is the belief that all is god and god is in everything. Some indigenous religions, like Shinto, are pantheistic. Another alternate view of the sacred is henotheism, which is the belief that there are many gods/many forms of god but that one is superior to all others. In Hinduism, for example, the one supreme lord is known as **param brahma,** who is superior to all other forms. For many, the divine is a personal being that is often depicted as having human qualities and characteristics, **anthropomorphism**. Examples of this approach can include describing god as a parent or as jealous or angry. Some even view god as an old man with a long beard.

Religious traditions that view a personal relationship with a divine being as the goal of practice are theistic. Those religions/philosophies that view religion as an individual practice (albeit still as a part of a community) engaged in to achieve one's own enlightenment or liberation are **nontheistic**. It is important to note that nontheism is not the same as atheism. **Atheism** is the denial of any divine reality or supernatural element beyond the physical world in which we live. Nontheism does not deny deities exist. Rather, the nontheist does not believe that those divine beings can "save" us. In nontheistic religious traditions, like Jainism and Buddhism, individuals are responsible for reaching their own spiritual goals. While atheists assert that there are no supernatural phenomena, the agnostic says that humanity is incapable of knowing of the existence or nature of god(s).

Sacred reality can be understood as manifest in the created world (immanent) or separate from the created world (transcendent). In most religious traditions, the view of divinity is a combination of the two. There is some sense in which the sacred is wholly other while at the same time manifesting itself in the world around us. Some traditions emphasize the transcendent nature of God more heavily

Figure 1   Picture from Sri Shiva Vishnu Temple in Lanham, MD taken by Stephanie Curran on October 16, 2015. The first four avatars of Vishnu can be seen in this photo from Sri Shiva Vishnu Temple in Lanham, MD. On one side of the foyer in the temple all of the forms of Vishnu are depicted; while, on the other side, attention is given to the forms of Shiva.

(particularly Judaism, Christianity, and Islam); and, others stress immanence more strongly, particularly in the form of nature spirits and ancestors.

In some religious traditions, the divine becomes visible in order to interact with and call followers to faithfulness. In Hinduism, Vishnu has taken nine different forms, or **avatars**. Some of these forms are **incarnations** (i.e., Krishna and Rama) in which the divine takes human form. Others are **manifestations** by which the sacred is manifest in nonhuman form. At various times, Vishnu took the form of a boar, a fish, or a turtle. Sometime in the future, Vishnu will take a tenth and final form (Figure 1).

UNDERSTANDINGS OF TIME

Understandings of time characterize most religions. These views guide the scheduling of religious festivals, influence moral action, and manifest in particular views of the afterlife. Religious festivals, pilgrimages, and sacred days mark religious time. In some traditions, a particular day of the week is sacred while in others there is no separation between the sacred and **profane** (pertaining to ordinary life). Religious festivals also tend to follow the cycles of the seasons or a worship calendar in which specific celebrations occur at a similar time each year. Many religious traditions follow a lunar-based calendar so the dates vary from year to year and don't neatly match the solar or Gregorian calendar to which Western culture is accustomed. Ramadan, the Muslim month of fasting, falls on a different date each year. Over time, Ramadan occurs in summer then cycles through and falls in the winter months. Rituals and myths are often intertwined within religious traditions with rituals enacting sacred narratives.

RITUALS

Rituals are ceremonial acts that connect people to sacred reality. Some rituals mark the seasons in the agricultural cycle. Other rituals are ways to atone for wrongs committed against the spirits or ancestors. Everyone in the community can participate in some ceremonial acts, while religious leaders must conduct other sacred rites. All religions have some type of ritual whether it is prayer, meditation, offerings, or sacrifice. In addition, most religions include rites of passage, rituals that mark significant events in human life such as birth, puberty, marriage, and death helping an individual transition from one stage of life to the next.

Another form of ritual found in many religious traditions is that of **pilgrimage** to holy sites. Devotees will often travel long distances to visit temples, shrines, **stupas**, sacred mountains, or rivers. A common practice at pilgrimage sites is circumambulation. **Circumambulation** involves walking around a site usually in clockwise fashion while praying, meditating, or chanting. Some pilgrimages are internal. Walking the labyrinth is a form of virtual or inner pilgrimage. A labyrinth is a path that takes you to the center and back out again. It is not a maze in which one becomes lost; rather, it is a symbolic journey to the center of oneself (Figure 2).

Francesca Scatena/Shutterstock.com.

Figure 2 Labyrinth carved in stone.

SYMBOLS

Symbols are physical artifacts that point to a sacred reality. Religious symbols convey meaning and often depict important beliefs or practices in a given tradition. For example, the symbol of the yin and yang convey the balance and complementarity of elements and energies that are often viewed as opposites (Figure 3).

Some symbols transcend a specific religion and generally share meaning across cultures. For example, water and fire often symbolize purification and divinity. Prayer beads (Figure 4) are also used by many different religions to count prayers or mantras.

The same symbol can have different meanings depending on the cultural and religious context. For example, the swastika is an ancient symbol of well-being in Eastern religions, such as Hinduism, Buddhism and Jainism. However, when people from Europe and the United States see the symbol, they typically associate it with Nazi Germany and white supremacist movements.

Figure 3 Yin and Yang symbol.

MYTHS

Myths are sacred narratives that convey truths about the relationship between human beings and the sacred, between human beings and each other, and between human beings and the created world. They often explain the divine origin of creation as well as the reason evil exists in the world. Joseph Campbell describes myths as fulfilling four different functions. The first is mystical. Myths evoke a sense of wonder, awe, and mystery in the face of the unknown spiritual realities of our world. The second is cosmological; that is, myths explain the sacred nature of how the world came to be. Myths also have a sociological function offering a sense of social order and a guide for proper conduct. Finally, myths serve a psychological function helping individuals realize their human potential, on the one hand, while coping with fear, death, and guilt on the other. In some religious traditions, myths are primarily oral passed down from generation to generation through storytelling, art, and dance. In other traditions, myths are written texts that

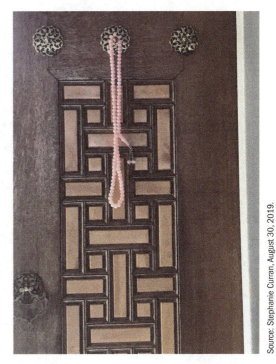

Figure 4 Picture of prayer beads hanging on a door of the Turkish American Cultural Center in Lanham, MD.

Source: Stephanie Curran, August 30, 2019.

are studied, read, and interpreted. Even in many traditions with written texts, there is an oral component. The words of sacred text are chanted, sung, or read aloud in the context of communal worship.

CONTEMPORARY TRENDS IN RELIGION

The one constant in life is change. Nothing stays the same, including religion. It constantly changes and adapts to the contemporary setting as well as the cultural context. Buddhism in Japan is different from Buddhism in the United States. Christianity in the United States is not the same as Christianity in Ethiopia. Islam in Indonesia differs from Islam in Saudi Arabia (Figure 5).

The global context has also changed religion in many ways. As a religious tradition moves to another cultural setting, the religion and cultural traditions blend in a wide variety of ways. For example, ancestor reverence mixes with Christianity; divination blends with Islam.

Combinative Nature of Religion

One of the major trends in religion today involves the combinative realities that result from globalization, individualism, and cultural relativism. Some of these combinations are a result of missionary religions encountering indigenous religions and leaving both practices forever changed. Numerous examples exist around the world. The Native American Church is a blending of Christianity and indigenous practices, particularly the use of peyote and other entheogenic plants (i.e., San Pedro cactus, Ayahuasca) as a sacrament. Peyote is a hallucinogenic cactus that is believed to open the worshiper to the spirit and bring healing, both physical and spiritual.

Figure 5   Ark of the covenant church in Axum, Ethiopia.

Shopping cart or eclectic spirituality are terms to describe a growing trend in the United States and other Western countries. Individuals blend practices and beliefs from various religious traditions into their own customized form of spirituality. These individuals usually practice alone and only join with religious communities for special occasions such as a retreat or blessing ceremony. As we explore the various religious traditions, keep an eye out for examples of combinative spirituality.

Women in Religious Traditions

The history of women and religion is extremely complex. Ancient religious traditions often included the role of both male and female aspects of divinity. Some of the most ancient images found are of a mother goddess. The role of women in giving birth has inspired a view of the sacred power of women as well as any number of taboos related to menstruation and childbirth (Figure 6).

Figure 6   Minoan snake goddess.

In the development of religious traditions women often play a prominent role. However, as emerging movements become more institutionalized, women's roles decrease. For example, in Buddhism, women were early members of the **Sangha** (community of monks and nuns). Yet, as Buddhism spread and became more established a century or two after the time of Siddhartha, the number of nuns drastically decreased. Likewise, in Christianity women had a very prominent role in the early Christian community serving as disciples, apostles, deacons, abbesses, and missionaries. After Christianity became the official religion of the Roman Empire, the voice and power of women was diminished. As each religious tradition is explored in detail, the role of women will be included in the discussion.

Today, religious traditions that provide leadership and equality for women are on the rise. One growing religious tradition is neo-paganism, a collection of earth-based movements which have always included male and female deities as well as women in positions of leadership.

Another interesting phenomena is the global reality of more women adherents to religious traditions than male adherents. In March 2016, the Pew Forum issued a report on the global "gender gap" in religion. In many countries around the world, including followers of all the major religious traditions, women outpace men in religious practice by a minimum of 2%. Religious practice includes affiliation with a religion, attendance at religious services, and daily prayer. In none of the 192 countries represented did men have a 2% or higher affiliation rate than women. In Christianity (particularly in the West), women are more likely than men to practice their faith; while in Islam, men and women are equally likely to practice their faith on a regular basis.

☯ Check out the Gender Gap report from the Pew Forum at http://www.pewforum.org/2016/03/22/ the-gender-gap-in-religion-around-the-world/, http://www.pewforum.org/2016/03/22/theories-explaining-gender-differences-in-religion/. What statistic or statement of analysis most intrigued you? What do you wish you knew more about?

_____

_____

_____

_____

Growth in Numbers of Nonreligious Today

Another contemporary trend is the move away from religious traditions. Atheism, **agnosticism**, and skepticism are on the rise. Not all nonreligious identify as atheists or agnostics. Some continue to believe in a sacred reality beyond the physical world but have been turned off by organized religions. Others, however, only believe in what they can see, test, and verify to be true. Just as diversity of interpretation exists in all of the major world religions, a range of views can be found among atheists as well. According to Common Sense Atheism[6], no less than (and very likely more than) 17 varieties of atheism can be identified, sometimes even overlapping in the same person.

While it may seem counterintuitive and logic defying, there is a debate among atheists and non-atheists alike over whether atheism is a religion. Without a doubt, a desire for community has resulted in the creation of various "churches" made up of atheists, agnostics, skeptics, humanists, etc. From the Church of the Flying Spaghetti Monster (Pastafarianism) and the United Church of Bacon to Dudeism and the Church of Cannabis, movements are springing up around the globe to meet the relational needs of those who have no need for deities, afterlife and other theological trappings.

---

[6] For a full listing of the 17 types, see http://commonsenseatheism.com/?p=6487

WEB RESOURCES FOR FURTHER STUDY

http://atheistspirituality.net/some-definitions/—A forum for exploring the connections between atheism and spirituality.

http://guides.nyu.edu/c.php?g=276742&p=1848187—A summary of some of the major sociological theories of religion and the works that describe them.

http://www.pbs.org/moyers/faithandreason/perspectives3.html—Three brief articles on women in Christianity, Islam and Goddess-centered spirituality.

https://news.osu.edu/the-psychology-behind-religious-belief/—Archived article on Reiss' theory that humans are drawn to religion as a result of 16 different needs.

http://web.pdx.edu/~tothm/religion/Definitions.htm—List of some common definitions of religion.

https://brill.com/view/journals/rag/rag-overview.xml—Excellent, open access (archives), peer-reviewed journal on issues of religion and gender.

https://thepsychologist.bps.org.uk/volume-24/edition-4/cognitive-science-religion—Great article on the cognitive science of religion.

Chapter 2
Religious Diversity and Religious Pluralism

Learning Outcomes

By the end of the chapter, students will be able to

- describe religious diversity in America;
- define approaches to religious diversity including exclusivism, inclusivism, and pluralism;
- distinguish between pluralism and simple tolerance as well as between pluralism and inclusivism;
- explain and identify examples of the interfaith movement; and
- analyze challenges and opportunities of living in a religiously diverse society.

Key Terms

Ecumenism
Exclusivism
Inclusivism
Interfaith Dialogue

Interfaith Movement
Job Ben Solomon
Pluralism
September 11, 1893

Touro Synagogue
World's Parliament of Religions

GLOBAL RELIGIOUS DIVERSITY

The chart on p. 14 from The Pew Forum demonstrates religious diversity on a global scale. The results in the diagram represent a person's self-designation in response to questions from a survey. Christians make up just less than a third of the world's population. However, this includes a broad range of groups: African Initiated Churches, Christian Science, Church of Jesus Christ of Latter Day Saints, Eastern Orthodox, Jehovah's Witnesses, Non-Chalcedonian (i.e., Coptic Orthodox or Ethiopian Orthodox), Nondenominational, Pentecostal, Protestant, Roman Catholic, and so on. The category of "other religions" is also very broad including ancient traditions like Jainism, Daoism, or Zoroastrianism as well as more recent religious traditions such as the Church of Scientology, Rastafarianism, or Sikhism. Folk religionists are generally those who identify with an indigenous religion such as Hmong, Lakota, or Australian Aboriginal.

☯ As you look at the chart of the world's population by religion, what surprises or interests you? What questions do you have?

_____

_____

_____

_____

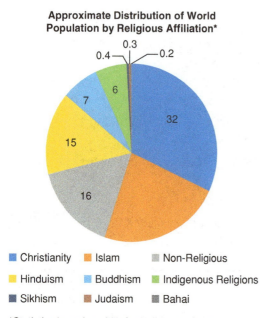

Approximate Distribution of World Population by Religious Affiliation*

- ■ Christianity
- ■ Islam
- ■ Non-Religious
- ■ Hinduism
- ■ Buddhism
- ■ Indigenous Religions
- ■ Sikhism
- ■ Judaism
- ■ Bahai

*Statistics based on data from www.pewforum.org and http://www.worldometers.info/world-population/#religions; percentages are rounded and based on self-description.

**Christianity includes Non-Chalcedonian Churches (i.e. Coptic, Ethiopian and Syrian Orthodox), Eastern Orthodox (Greek, Russian, etc.), Roman Catholic, Protestant, Pentecostal, African Independent Churches, Church of Jesus Christ of Latter Day Saints, Jehovah's Witnesses, etc.

***Indigenous Religions include Native American, traditional African, Aboriginal, Polynesian, Inuit, etc.

****Non-Religious includes theists who identify as none, atheists, humanists, agnostics, etc.

HISTORY OF RELIGIOUS DIVERSITY IN THE UNITED STATES

Religious diversity in the United States is nothing new. From before the founding of this nation, religious diversity was present. Prior to colonization, a diversity of Native American traditions was practiced across the continent. As new peoples began to arrive, they brought with them various forms of Christianity, Judaism, Islam, and traditional African religions. Some suggest that the first visitors to North America were the Vikings as early as 1,000 CE. More controversial claims, most notably by Gavin Menzies, suggest the Chinese discovered North America in 1421.[1]

Whoever was first to reach the Americas was certainly not the last. By 1654, there was a small Jewish community in what is now New York City (then New Amsterdam). Several years ago, the 250th anniversary of the longest standing Jewish synagogue, **Touro Synagogue**, was celebrated in Newport, Rhode Island. It opened on the second day of Hanukkah in 1763.[2]

Many think the arrival of Islam in the United States came with the Immigration Act of 1965, but that is far from accurate. The first Muslims in North America arrived with the slave trade. Ayuba Suleiman Diallo (known as **Job Ben Solomon** by his captors) arrived in Annapolis, MD in 1730. From Senegal, West Africa, he is the first known follower of Islam in what became the United States.[3] Diaries and autobiographies of slaves give firsthand accounts of the struggle to maintain faith in captivity.[4] It wasn't until

[1] For Menzies' theory, see Gavin Menzies, *1421: The Year China Discovered America* (New York: Harper Collins, 2002).

[2] http://www.tourosynagogue.org/history-learning/synagogue-history.

[3] Edward E. Curtis IV, *Muslims in America: A Short History* (New York: Oxford University Press, 2009).

[4] For example, see the autobiography of Omar ibn Sayyid, a slave in North Carolina. http://nationalhumanitiescenter.org/pds/maai/community/text3/religionomaribnsaid.pdf.

1929 that the first formal mosque was built in America; Lebanese Syrians built it in Ross, North Dakota. Though it is no longer standing, a monument marks its location.

While appreciation of diverse religious traditions has not always been evident in our culture, the ideal of religious freedom is a part of the very fabric of our nation. Many of those who came to colonize this land were themselves in search of religious freedom. William Penn, the founder of the colony of Pennsylvania, advocated freedom of conscience. Roger Williams, who established the colony of Rhode Island, was the first advocate of separation of church and state. He was not opposed to the unity of church and state on political grounds but rather religious. He asserted, "Mixing church and state corrupted the church, that when one mixes religion and politics, one gets politics."[5]

RELIGIOUS FREEDOM AND THE CONSTITUTION

Though the language of separation of church and state is not in the constitution, the freedom of religion is guaranteed in the First Amendment to the Constitution. This freedom is addressed in two ways. The first is the Establishment Clause prohibiting "the government from 'establishing' a religion."[6] It was Thomas Jefferson who during his presidency, "coined the phrase 'a wall of separation between Church and State'"[7] in a letter written in 1802. In a 1947 Supreme Court case, *Everson v. Board of Education*, Jefferson's letter was used as part of the justification for the unanimous court decision affirming the separation of church and state. The model of keeping a "wall of separation between Church and State" continues to be tested in the courts and remains controversial in some sectors of society.

The second clause related to religious freedom is the Free Exercise Clause that allows an individual to freely practice his or her faith. Historically, the conditions placed on this clause are that one's free exercise cannot violate established laws or social norms. Therein, lies the controversy. For example, should polygamy be allowed if it is part of your religious or cultural practice? Should it be legal for an individual to use plant-based hallucinogens as part of religious practice? Is it permissible to perform animal sacrifice for religious rituals? Can parents refuse lifesaving medical treatment for a child based on their religious beliefs? The courts are charged with navigating the murky waters of nonestablishment and free exercise.[8]

☯ As you reflect on the role of religion in public life, what are your thoughts about the privilege and challenge of religious freedom in the United States?

_____

_____

_____

_____

[5] John Barry, "God, Government, and Roger Williams Big Idea," accessed October 4, 2015, Smithsonian.com, http://www.smithsonianmag.com/history/god-government-and-roger-williams-big-idea-6291280/#V7mRFCWVr8VO8cYc.99.

[6] http://www.uscourts.gov/educational-resources/educational-activities/first-amendment-and-religion.

[7] http://www.pbs.org/now/politics/churchandstate.html.

[8] If you are interested in some of the Supreme Court cases related to religion, see http://millercenter.org/debates/religion/supreme-court. The Miller Center is a nonpartisan center affiliated with the University of Virginia that explores the intersection of the presidency, policy, and political history.

In Chapter 1, we explored the idea of civil religion as demonstrating aspects of creed, code, and cultus. The connections between god and country have long been part of our cultural heritage. Much debate surrounds the phrase, "under God" in the Pledge of Allegiance. This phrase was not original to the pledge but was added in 1954 through the encouragement of President Eisenhower. Eisenhower and members of Congress saw this as one way to counteract the perceived threat of communism and its antireligious sentiments.

TRENDS IN RELIGIOUS DIVERSITY IN THE UNITED STATES TODAY

While Christianity makes up one third of the world's population, the majority of people in the United States identify Christianity as their religion. At the same time, religious diversity continues to increase in the United States, as does the number of religiously unaffiliated. This graph from The Pew Forum demonstrates changes in the religious landscape between 2007 and 2014. Fewer people stay with the denomination or even religious tradition in which they were raised. Those who identify themselves as "none" on a religious survey now outnumber both Catholics and mainline Protestants (i.e., Presbyterian, Methodist, Lutheran, United Church of Christ).[9] Even Evangelical Protestants who remain a large group within Christianity in the United States today are down roughly 1%. A 2019 update of these numbers demonstrates the same trends are continuing with decreases in both Catholicism and Protestantism and increases in the "nones." For more detail, see https://www.pewforum.org/2019/10/17/in-u-s-decline-of-christianity-continues-at-rapid-pace/

Changing U.S. Religious Landscape

Between 2007 and 2014, the christian share of the population fell from 78.4% to 70.6%, driven mainly by declines among mainline Protestants and Catholics. The unaffiliated experienced the most growth, and the share of Americans who belong to non-Christian faiths also increased.

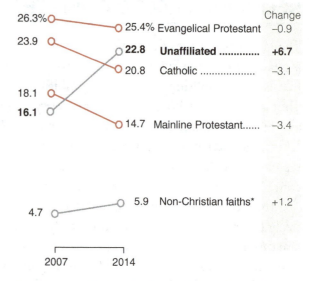

	Change
26.3% — 25.4% Evangelical Protestant	–0.9
23.9 — **22.8 Unaffiliated**	**+6.7**
20.8 Catholic	–3.1
18.1	
16.1 — 14.7 Mainline Protestant	–3.4
4.7 — 5.9 Non-Christian faiths*	+1.2

2007   2014

*Includes Jews, Muslims, Buddhists, Hindus, other world religions and other faiths. Those who did not answer the religious identity question, as well as groups whose share of the population did not change significantly, including the historically black Protestant tradition, Mormons and others, are not shown.

Source: "America's Changing Religious Landscape," Pew Research Center, Washington, DC (May, 2015).

http://www.pewforum.org/2015/05/12/americans-changing-religious-landscape/.

☯ Explore the links: http://www.pewforum.org/2015/05/12/new-pew-research-center-study-examines-americas-changing-religious-landscape/, http://www.pewforum.org/religious-landscape-study/ and https://www.pewforum.org/2018/06/13/the-age-gap-in-religion-around-the-world/. To what do you attribute changes in the religious landscape?

_____

_____

_____

_____

---

[9] http://www.pewforum.org/2015/05/12/americas-changing-religious-landscape/.

APPROACHES TO RELIGIOUS DIVERSITY

Religious diversity offers unique challenges and opportunities. Some people celebrate the diverse expressions of religion, not only in our culture, but also around the world. Others approach it as an opportunity for evangelism; still others find it unsettling at best. Religious fundamentalism and acts of terror in the name of religion taking place around the world can increase the unease over such diversity. Three main approaches to diversity include exclusivism, inclusivism, and pluralism.

Exclusivism is the view that there is only one way to believe. Relationships between diverse religious or nonreligious perspectives are avoided. In most cases, adherents to this approach believe that there is only one truth and all other beliefs (often including other interpretations of their own religious tradition) are false. While this view suppresses religious dialogue, except for the purpose of conversion, it does maintain the integrity and uniqueness of individual religious traditions.

Inclusivism, an approach that seems to be more open to others on the surface, is often very similar to exclusivism. With inclusivism, one is saying that all religions are basically the same and all contain truth. Often what is meant is that the truth found in other religions represents those beliefs and practices that are similar to "my religion." Inclusivism also falls prey to the tendency not to appreciate the genuine differences that exist between religions and to suggest that they are unimportant. To summarize, the inclusivist view is that in essential matters all religions are the same. In the book, *God Is Not One*, Stephen Prothero, asserts that all religions are not the same. While there are similarities in ethics, ritual use of water, and sacred narratives, the differences among religions are important to the integrity and practice of the faith. Religion helps us explore life's big questions and each religion asks slightly different ones. "Only religions that see God as all good ask how a good God can allow millions to die in tsunamis. Only religions that believe in souls ask whether the soul exists before you were born and what happens to it after you die."[10] Is it possible to celebrate both the similarities and the peculiarities of religious traditions? Can we discuss religious differences in the context of mutual respect seeking to understand one another? Can we hold our belief to be true while still being in relationship with someone whose beliefs differ from our own?

WHAT IS PLURALISM?

The perspective of pluralism seeks to answer all of those questions in the affirmative. Religious diversity is all around us, yet religious illiteracy remains high. There is a lack of understanding and a proliferation of stereotypes. Religious pluralism promotes engagement rather than simple coexistence. Diana Eck, a professor of religious studies at Harvard University, began the Pluralism Project (www.pluralism.org) in 1991. The project not only celebrates religious diversity but also seeks to engage people of diverse backgrounds in dynamic and active relationship with one another. Pluralism is active engagement between those of diverse religious beliefs in a respectful way while promoting mutual understanding and cooperation. Eck asserts that the achievement of pluralism involves four main components

---

[10] Stephen Prothero, *God Is Not One* (New York: HarperCollins, 2010), 24.

- ◆ energetic engagement with diversity;
- ◆ active seeking of understanding across lines of difference;
- ◆ an encounter of commitments; it is not relativism; and
- ◆ based on dialogue.[11]

Dialogue is two-way communication that requires the building of relationships. The mutuality of pluralism requires at least two parties that are equally committed to the task of understanding and cooperation. Interfaith dialogue is just one example of pluralism in action. Many may be surprised to discover that the first interfaith dialogue occurred in 1893.

THE WORLD'S PARLIAMENT OF RELIGIONS AND THE INTERFAITH MOVEMENT

The World's Parliament of Religions was the first great interfaith gathering in history. Charles Carroll Bonney and John Henry Barrows organized this first of its kind event. When the gathering was announced, there was both excitement and opposition. Some of those who looked forward to it hoped it would encourage the study of comparative religion. However, others hoped that it would demonstrate the supremacy of Christianity over other religions. In an era in which the theory of evolution was beginning to emerge, these folks understood Christianity to be the most highly evolved religious tradition. Opposition came from those who said that if other religions were given a platform, the implication would be that they were on equal standing with Christianity.

The meeting opened at 10:00 a.m. on September 11th, 1893 with the tolling of the Columbian Liberty Bell ten times to signify the ten great religions of the world: Confucianism, Daoism, Shintoism, Hinduism, Buddhism, Jainism, Zoroastrianism, Judaism, Christianity, and Islam. Part of the ethnocentricity of the

[11] From "What is Pluralism?" by Diana L. Eckk. Copyright © 2006 by the President and Fellows of Harvard College and Diana Eck. Reprinted by permission.

Parliament was that indigenous religions, including Native American religions, were not considered part of the great religions of the world. Again, this reflected the understanding of the evolution of religion that was prominent at the time. Each day began with worship and a recitation of the Lord's Prayer, which in Barrow's words was the "universal prayer."

While a number of religious traditions were represented, the majority of the papers presented came from Christian traditions (152 of the 194). However, there were three speeches from the Indian spiritual leader, Swami Vivekananda. For the first time, Americans heard from a Hindu guru, and many Americans were entranced. The American public thus began its fascination with Eastern philosophy and spirituality.

The sense of superiority that, in practice, came from many Christian leaders was not reflected in the ten purposes for the Parliament conveyed by John Barrows in his 1891 Preliminary Address to the planning committee for the Parliament. Those purposes can be paraphrased as follows

1. To bring together leaders of the major world's religions.
2. To explore the truths these religions have in common.
3. To promote fellowship between people of different religions without creating a false unity.
4. To proclaim the truths which make these religions distinct from one another.
5. To counteract the influence of materialistic or humanistic philosophies which do not stress the belief in Divinity;
6. To enable people of other religions to accurately portray their cultural and religious understandings.
7. To discover what each religion can offer to the other religions of the world.
8. To give a picture of the state of religion in the world.
9. To see what religions have to say about the social issues of the day including Temperance; and
10. To facilitate peace.[12]

The Parliament had a tremendous impact on American culture. Seven thousand people attended the closing ceremonies. World's Parliament of Religions gatherings continue to be held, with the most recent being in Toronto in 2018. These events are examples of the interfaith movement promoting cooperation and dialogue between people of various religious traditions. Hans Küng, one of the foremost theologians of the twentieth century, wrote in his book, *Christianity: Essence, History, Future*, there will be "No peace among the nations without peace among the religions. No peace among the religions without dialogue between the religions. No dialogue between the religions without investigation of the foundation of the religions."[13] In interfaith gatherings, there is both the determination to understand and respect one another as well as the desire to work to solve common problems facing the community. Interfaith groups work together to secure affordable housing, alleviate hunger, and promote the rights of minority communities. Interfaith groups also seek to break down stereotypes that inhibit people from engaging in honest dialogue about very real differences between religions.

---

[12] Purposes paraphrased from Joas Adiprasetya, "The 1893 World's Parliament of Religions," The Boston Collaborative Encyclopedia of Modern Western Theology, 2004. http://people.bu.edu/wwildman/WeirdWildWeb/courses/mwt/dictionary/mwt_themes_707_worldparliamentofreligions1893.htm.

[13] Hans Küng, *Christianity: Essence, History, Future* (Continuum, 1995).

PLURALISM IN ACTION

Interfaith dialogue is only one aspect of pluralism. A growing example of pluralism in action can be found in many of our families where religious diversity is becoming very common. Paul Chaffee, the founding director of the Interfaith Center at the Presidio, describes performing a wedding between a Southern Baptist and Muslim in *American Pluralism: Nurturing Interfaith Dialogue.*[14] Religious diversity in families can be, but is not always, a positive example of pluralism in action.

Conversation cannot move to dialogue without establishing relationships of trust and respect. Engagement with one another can begin with something as simple as a block party or potluck dinner between a church, a synagogue and a masjid. From there, participants can move to the more sensitive ground of discussing beliefs and practices or engaging in dialogue about sensitive political or economic issues in our world. Cooperation and dialogue between various branches of Christianity is usually referred to as ecumenism rather than pluralism.

Often pluralism arises when people of faith as well as people of no faith see a need and respond to alleviate human suffering. After a natural disaster, a fire, or a mass shooting, people of various faiths hold interfaith prayer services to support those who are suffering. People of all religious perspectives sometimes join together to build safe, affordable housing; to feed those who are hungry; and, to work for peace and justice.

☯ Explore www.pluralism.org, http://www.interfaithcenterpa.org/#!what-we-do/c3gn, http://interfaithwichita.org/programs, and local interfaith ministries and news outlets for examples of pluralism in action. Be ready to share examples of what you discover.

_____

_____

_____

_____

WEB RESOURCES FOR FURTHER STUDY

Religious Diversity in America:
Five Myths about Mosques in America http://www.washingtonpost.com/wp-dyn/content/
    article/2010/08/26/AR2010082605510.html.
Pluralism:
    www.pluralism.org.
Interfaith Centers:
    http://www.interfaithcenterpa.org.
    http://interfaithwichita.org.
World's Parliament of Religions:
    https://www.youtube.com/watch?v=19Ph8YkqpiE
    http://www.parliamentofreligions.org/.

_____

[14] Film Media Group, "American Pluralism: Nurturing Interfaith Dialogue," *Beyond Theology,* 2007.

Chapter 3
Indigenous Religions

Learning Outcomes

By the end of this lesson, students should be able to

- identify recurring themes in indigenous religions;
- demonstrate knowledge of roles fulfilled by spiritual specialists in indigenous religions;
- explain general characteristics of Native American, Aboriginal and Indigenous African Religion (IAR);
- describe the roles of sacrifice in religion; and
- discuss issues surrounding the use of peyote and the free exercise of religion.

Key Terms

Ancestor Reverence	Magic	Sacrifice
Animism	Myth	Shaman
Chanunpa	Native American Church	Smudging
Divination	Orisha	Spirit helpers
Dreaming	Peyote	Storyteller
Fetish	Popol Vuh	Taboo
Healer	Priest	Totem
Imitative magic	Rite of Passage	Tricksters
Kwanzaa	Sacred dancers	Vision Quest

CHALLENGES IN STUDYING INDIGENOUS RELIGIONS

These religions have been called by a variety of names: indigenous religions, traditional religions, basic religions, primal religions, or oral religions. Some of the titles, such as basic, primitive, or primal have negative connotations implying that these religious traditions are not as fully developed as others. Sadly, as was noted in the last chapter, such thinking kept these religious traditions from being represented at the first major interfaith gathering, The World's Parliament of Religions, in 1893. Because of these negative connotations, the terms used in this text are indigenous and oral as they represent important characteristics of these traditions. "Indigenous people are descendants of the original inhabitants of lands now controlled by political systems in which they have little influence."[1] The beliefs of these traditions are often tied to the land from which they originated and are therefore not easily exported. People who leave their ancestral land often have a difficult time practicing their faith. The second term, "oral religions," refers to the fact that most of these traditions have been passed down orally with no written texts or scriptures. Of course, in modern times, many of the sacred narratives and practices of these traditions have now been recorded by sociologists, anthropologists, and modern practitioners of the faiths. Ultimately, the terms "indigenous" or "oral" religions are umbrella terms for a wide variety of sacred traditions including Aboriginal, Inuit, Native American, Polynesian, and Indigenous African Religion (IAR).

Another challenge to the study of these traditions is that they have been influenced by colonialism and forced conversions producing various forms of combinative spirituality. As discussed in Chapter 1, hybrids have developed that are a blend of an indigenous tradition and a missionary-based religion such as Christianity, Islam, or Buddhism.

Thousands of distinct indigenous religions exist throughout the world. And while each is unique, there are a few general characteristics that are common across traditions. As we explore religious traditions in this book, you will notice that many of these characteristics are also present in national indigenous religious traditions, such as Shinto.

GENERAL CHARACTERISTICS OF INDIGENOUS RELIGIONS

This chapter explores some of the characteristics most indigenous religions share. Where there are exceptions, they will be noted. In addition, after exploring these common characteristics, the unique features in some specific regions of the world will be explored.

Views of Divinity

Indigenous religions generally hold a belief in **animism**. In these traditions, all living things are imbued with spirit and are spiritually interrelated. Rocks, trees, animals, water, people, mountains, and so on are all viewed as having a spirit that is to be honored and respected. Everything in nature is dependent on each other and is sacred, with no distinction between the sacred and the mundane.

In addition, the view of the sacred can be represented by a triangle. The creator deity is transcendent and often seen as somewhat removed from the day-to-day lives of people. The high god or creator deity is honored and revered but is generally only called upon by a shaman or other "spiritual specialist."

---

[1] Mary Pat Fisher, *Living Religions*, 3rd ed. (Upper Saddle River, NJ: Prentice Hall, 1997).

Ancestor Reverence

Ancestors function as guides, warriors, and healers. These roles are not mutually exclusive of each other. A given ancestor may act in any number or combination of these capacities. It depends on what the person was like during her lifetime and on what work she was doing in the spirit world.

Was your grandmother a seamstress? Then take her shopping with you. She'll lead you to the best bargain on attractive, durable, and low-cost clothing. You'll have to acquaint her with your style and color preferences, but you should also pay attention to hers. Was papa a handy man? Then take him with you when you go house hunting. He can sense the bad wiring, leaky pipes, and deteriorating foundation of the place. He'll steer you toward a better house and then suggest ways to make the necessary repairs. Having trouble dieting? Perhaps your great-aunt realizes now that her heart attack was due to wrong diet. Perhaps she will help you keep to your diet as part of her work in the spirit world. You do not know how much they are willing to help you until you contact them.

—from *Ancestor Reverence* by **Luisah Teish**

From *Jambalaya by Luisah Teish*. Copyright © 1985 by Luisah Teish; published by Harper & Row, Publishers, Inc.

On the other hand, ancestors and spirits are often called upon to help with day-to-day hopes and struggles. Ancestors are particularly important in indigenous African and Asian religions. As they have the power to bless or curse the living, those who have died are to be remembered and respected.

The other aspect of immanence is spirits. In West African and Caribbean traditions, the lesser spirits are often known as **orisha**. In these traditions, the world is full of spirits who also must be treated with respect.

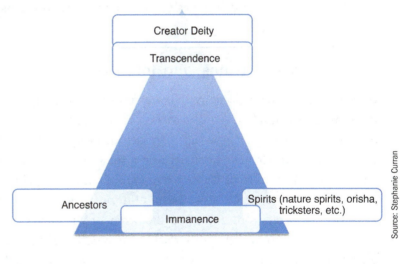

Source: Stephanie Curran

One way of showing respect to both ancestors and spirits is to present them with **sacrifices** and offerings. Another means of staying in right relationship is to observe certain guidelines for behavior. A third important means of evoking blessing and avoiding curse is to engage in rituals that seek to influence the spirits.

Role of Sacrifice

Sacrifices and offerings perform an important function in all religions. From slaughtering a goat to making a monetary donation, there are a variety of ways to please the deities and spirits. One of the first things that people think of when they hear the word "sacrifice" is the human sacrifice practiced by the Aztecs. While some ancient cultures practiced this very dramatic and gory ritual, it was rare. Sacrifice is understood as a gift, a way to show adoration and appreciation. Gifts of tools, weapons, ornaments, money, incense, food, water, rice, tea, or even tobacco are left in sacred places, such as altars or shrines. Those seeking healing in a San Pedro cactus ritual in Peru may bring offerings that symbolize their pain and suffering.[2]

Communities and individuals, at times, miss the mark. Perhaps, they fail to show proper respect or they break a social norm. One way of handling a broken taboo or an unhappy spirit is through sacrifice. Sacrifices may serve to appease the gods or spirits, atone for a misdeed, and help restore right relationship.

In many indigenous religions, the spirit world is viewed on a parallel plane with the physical world. When people die, their spirits must be ushered into the afterlife. In some cultures, such as the Torajans of Indonesia, the spirits of the dead make the journey to the spirit world riding on animals that have been slaughtered for that purpose. In other indigenous religions, ancestors and spirits have the same needs in the spirit world as human beings need in the physical world. Food, beverages, weapons, and tools may be sent to the ancestor or spirit through offerings and sacrifices. Fire and smoke are often means of carrying these items to the spirit world. A **libation** is a drink offering poured on the ground. Drink offerings are particularly characteristic of IAR.

The offering of a sacrifice establishes a bond between an individual or community and the spirit world. Often, the gathered community partakes in food offered to the ancestors or spirits. By eating food that has been offered and blessed, a sacred connection is made between the spirits of the living and the spirits of the dead.

Magic, Taboos, Fetishes, and Totems

An important element in many religious traditions is magic. Magic has been defined in various ways. At its most basic level, **magic** is a way of influencing the sacred. It is the art of causing change in ways that science cannot explain. Magic can include everything from the waving of a particular tree branch, arranging a set of elements, or chanting a mantra to praying for help from a god, ancestor, or spirit. Some rituals are a form of **imitative magic** in which participants dramatize a desired outcome. Some dances, for example, depict a successful hunt or battle.

Taboos are rules forbidding specific behavior with regard to certain objects, people, animals, days, or phases of life. They frequently relate to avoidance of the handling of blood; blood is seen as a life force with mysterious power. A whole chapter could be devoted to religious and cultural taboos related to menstruation and childbirth; however, we will settle for just a few examples. In many indigenous religions, women are separated from the community while they are menstruating as well as for a specific time period after giving birth. Often, there are rituals that must be performed by these women before full participation in the life of the community is possible. Taboos may also deal with sexuality and birth. Twins may be seen as a positive or negative taboo depending on the culture. Taboos may also relate to handling of the dead, social behaviors (particularly how to act in the presence of a community or religious leader), sacred sites, or food (Figure 1).

Fetishes, or talismans, are objects used in a magical fashion to bring good fortune or ward off evil. Examples of such items exist in all cultures including the United States. Items from a lucky rabbit's foot

---

[2] For details of the ceremony, see *Cactus Drug* video from National Geographic at https://www.youtube.com/watch?v=SkQMfLCcNVg.

Figure 1 Native American dream catcher.

to a special jersey that must be worn during the big game are thought to bring luck. In some Native American traditions, the dream catcher is an example of a fetish (Figure 1). Bones, cloth, herbs, shells, and other items can be endowed with special significance because of their relationship to a positive event in the life of the community. **Totems** are similar to fetishes in that they are objects, plants, or animals whose spirits protect families and communities. They can also serve as a mark of identification for a family group. A close link often exists between a tribal group and a particular animal such as a bear, a wolf, or a fish. In addition, individuals may have **spirit helpers**, an animal they feel related to who serves as a guide or protector. A **shaman** usually has a spirit helper to guide his or her travels between the physical and spiritual world.

Divination

Closely related to magic is the practice of **divination**. Divination is seeking the will or the guidance of the spirits. It may involve reading signs in nature such as the flight patterns of birds or the tracks of animals. Other methods of divination consist of heating bones or tortoise shells and reading the cracks formed as the material splits. In addition, divination may involve contacting the spirits through a **medium** who serves as a channel for the spirits to communicate with people. Occasionally, divination seeks to predict the future. Will there be a good harvest or a successful hunt? Is the community going to prosper or suffer in the coming year? Individuals may use divination as a way to discern whether to marry, take a new job or venture out on a voyage. Naturally, astrology (studying the movements of planets, constellations, etc.) is a form of divination with some cultures using such heavenly signs to discern what is the most auspicious (or favorable) time for planting crops, marrying, or holding a festival.

Sacred Narratives

Most indigenous religions have no written sacred text. The most well-known exception to this is the Mayan text, the Popol Vuh. The Popol Vuh is a four-part narrative that tells of the attempts by the gods to successfully create human beings to worship them. Animals, mud, and wood proved to be ineffective materials for creating humans, but finally the gods successfully create people from corn.

While written texts do not feature prominently in indigenous religions, sacred stories serve an important role. The stories are passed on from generation to generation through storytelling, dance, and art. They are not taken literally but interpreted and cherished as sacred. These sacred narratives also confer identity on a particular group of people as well as illustrate acceptable behavior. Historically, many Western missionaries and explorers disparaged these oral narratives as though they were not as durable or "accurate" as written narratives. However, oral histories and sacred stories have a profound impact on the identity and empowerment of indigenous peoples. These narratives are cherished and passed reverently from one generation to the next. The loss of these narratives and traditions represents extinction; special care is often taken to preserve them.

Sacred narratives explain the origins of creation as well as the relationship between humans, the gods, and the rest of the created world. Sacred narratives also teach acceptable and unacceptable practices. A role in some sacred narratives is that of the trickster. The trickster is often an animal or mischievous spirit who behaves badly and plays tricks on the gods, other animals, or humans. Trickster narratives make us laugh, but they also serve as inventive ways to call for overturning the social order.

☯ Read one of the trickster narratives from the following link: http://americanfolklore.net/folklore/tricksters/. What story did you choose? Briefly describe it. What is the role of the trickster in the story?

_____

_____

_____

_____

_____

Spiritual Specialists

In oral religions, religious leaders carry out numerous tasks. A single person or a group of individuals, depending on the structure of a given cultural community, may fulfill these roles. Typical roles include that of storyteller, sacred dancer, priest, healer, diviner, and shaman.

Because of the oral nature of indigenous religions, the role of storyteller and sacred dancer are extremely important. Storytellers may be all elders of a community or the role may be assigned to specific individuals. Stories are told around the campfire, during particular sacred rituals, or at times of transition from youth to adulthood. Storytellers may add their individual flair to the telling of the story but the message always remains the same. In the same way, dance often tells a story or ritually enacts a desired outcome. Because of the sacred purpose of dance, the movements are often clearly prescribed. The dance is not random movement to a beat but carefully choreographed steps in specific dress to set music. The whole community performs some dances; while others are only for men or only for women. **Sacred dancers** are those who have been trained and blessed to carry out the important function of enacting the story or generating spiritual energy and directing that energy toward a desired goal (health, fertility, etc.).

In those religious traditions in which sacrifice is a prominent aspect of worship, the role of **priest** or **priestess** is significant. Officiating over sacrificial rituals is the primary function of the priest. However, priests and priestesses may also serve in a similar capacity as shaman as an intermediary between the people and the spirits or gods.

The **healer** works to bring about physical, emotional, and spiritual healing for individuals and communities. In IAR, the healer fulfills an important function in the community. Moreover, physical illnesses are believed to have spiritual causes. To bring about healing, the root cause must be discovered. The healer often serves as a **diviner** consulting the spirits to determine the cause of sickness, depression, death, and other difficulties. The diviner may also contact ancestors for advice on behalf of a family or community. To consult with the spirits or ancestors, the diviner will enter a trance-like state through drumming, rattling a divining gourd, or consuming hallucinogenic plants, roots, or barks. Once the cause of the sickness is determined, various methods can be prescribed for healing. Sweat lodges, sacrifices, medicinal plants, and smudging are examples of indigenous healing practices. Smudging involves burning specific plants and using the smoke or ash to heal or clear away negative energy.

The **shaman** often combines the role of priest, healer, and diviner. Sometimes, indigenous religions are referred to as Shamanism because of the central role embodied by such spiritual leaders. This word comes from the language of the Evenk, a small group of reindeer herders in Siberia; and, is sometimes erroneously used interchangeably with the terms "sorcerer" or "medicine man." In the strictest sense, it refers to a "practitioner who can will his or her spirit to leave the body and journey to upper or lower worlds."[3] Shamans may heal using herbs, diet, sweat baths, massage, and so on. Many of these healing methods rely on the building up of group energy through chanting or drumming. Shamans are said to have the gift of communicating with plants or animals, controlling weather, prophesying, and divination. The role may be hereditary or may come about because of recognition by the community that one has a special gift. Others become shaman as a result of a dramatic, often near death, experience such as being struck by lightning. Once one has received the "call," training is rigorous. The shaman-in-training ritually undergoes a spiritual or psychological death and rebirth. Many shaman have a power animal or "spirit helper" who enables them to travel between the physical and spiritual worlds. For instance, a shaman's spirit helper may be an eagle who helps her soar or a fish that helps him dive into the depths of the spirit world. They enter altered states of consciousness through a variety of techniques that are the same worldwide: sitting in darkness for prolonged periods, drumming, fasting, chanting, dancing, and in some cases the use of hallucinogens (i.e., peyote, cannabis, opium, and certain mushrooms). The goal of this altered state is to open "the doorway of the heart," the channel of divine power.[4]

---

[3] Piers Vitebsky, "What is a Shaman?" *Natural History* 106 no. 2 (1997): 34–35.
[4] Ibid, 34–35.

RITUALS IN INDIGENOUS RELIGIONS

Through group rituals, traditional people not only honor the sacred but also affirm their bonds with each other and all of creation. They enact sacred narratives through ritual as well as seek the spirits' blessing for health, success, and fertility. Nearly all traditions honor rites of passage (rituals surrounding key points in a person's life, such as birth, death, marriage, puberty). Other rituals are for group survival, pilgrimages to sacred places, or dealing with crises or natural disasters. Seasonal festivals mark the agricultural cycle in many indigenous traditions as they are deeply rooted in the land.

☯ Explore a specific indigenous religion (i.e., Zulu, Iroquois, Cherokee, Aztec, Australian Aboriginal, Polynesian, Yoruba). Write down one new fact you learned about this religion.

_____

_____

_____

NATIVE AMERICAN RITUALS

Great diversity exists between the religious traditions of various indigenous American communities; however, some things are held in common. Animism or the spiritual connection between all living things, honoring ancestors, sacred dance, and traditional healing methods are characteristics shared by many Native American communities.

Native American group rituals often include dancing, chanting, drumming, and the use of a strong tobacco smoked in a pipe called a chanunpa. A chanunpa is a long sacred pipe used for smoking a special tobacco. Tobacco is thought to cleanse and purify.

One of the oldest healing rituals in North America is the sweat lodge ceremony. The ceremony heals mind, body, and spirit and is practiced by the Algonquin, Cherokee, Lakota Sioux, and Navajo among others. Participation in the sweat lodge is for purification, spiritual guidance, or healing.

The ritual takes place in a specially built dome-shaped structure with a pit in the middle to hold the hot stones. The frame is generally built with branches tied together. Historically, animal hides were used to cover the dome, but today blankets are more common (Figures 2 and 3).

Contributed by Cynthia Baush. Copyright © Kendall Hunt Publishing Company.

Figure 2   Image of a family sweat lodge in Maryland without the draping. The colored ties represent individuals prayers, sacred elements and the four directions.

Prior to the sweat bath, participants typically fast and pray in preparation. They may also bring a symbol of their intentions or hopes for the sweat bath experience. The ceremony itself begins with smudging for purification. Herbs such as sweetgrass and sage are most commonly used. A fire tender leads the ceremony and oversees the process by waving purifying smoke over participants, heating the stones, and placing them in the pit in the middle of the lodge. Four distinct rounds typically form the ritual, each lasting around 30 minutes. Each round can involve chanting, meditating, praying, and/or storytelling.

Figure 3 Image of a family sweat lodge in Maryland.

Another important Native American ritual, particularly among the communities of the Great Plains, is the **Sun Dance**. The term, Sun Dance, comes from the Sioux name for the ritual, *Wi wanyang wacipi*, which translates as "sun gazing dance."[5] The ceremony has a sacrificial character and is performed for the well-being of the whole community. Some groups, such as the Sioux, Arapahoe, and Cheyenne, pierce their skin before dancing; however, others focus on fasting only prior to the dance. In

Figure 4 Shoshone Sun Dance, circa 1925.[6]

preparation for the dance, a circle is created around a central pole, often a cottonwood tree (Figure 4).

Today, many gatherings are inter-tribal promoting friendship and the preservation of Native American culture. A common example of this is the **powwow** in which people from diverse tribes gather for singing, dancing, fellowship, eating traditional foods, and celebrating traditional crafts. Powwows are a great opportunity for outsiders to learn about the culture and practices of indigenous people.

An individual observance common in the Native American tradition is the vision quest. A **vision quest** is a **rite of passage** undergone in puberty by young boys (and sometimes girls) as they transition to adulthood. After a period of preparation and purification, an individual goes alone to a remote location, abstains from food and often water, and awaits a vision. The vision quest is most often a rite of passage, but can also be undertaken when an important decision needs to be made or when one is preparing to become a shaman.

---

[5] Dale Stover, "Sun Dance," http://plainshumanities.unl.edu/encyclopedia/doc/egp.rel.046.
[6] U.S. National Archives and Records Administration [Public domain].

THE NATIVE AMERICAN CHURCH

The Native American Church is the result of a blend of Christianity with indigenous Native American religion. Quanah Parker founded the Church in the 1890s. He was given peyote to treat wounds sustained in a battle with government troops. During the peyote experience, he received a vision from Jesus Christ. Following that experience, he promoted the peyote way. In 1918, the Native American Church was incorporated; its first president was Frank Eagle. There are over 100 different branches of the church and about 500,000 members in 24 states.[7] One of the hallmarks of the church is the use of peyote as a sacrament. Peyote is sometimes referred to as "medicine" and is believed to have healing power. Studies indicate it can be an effective tool in the cure for alcoholism. The Native American Church is only one of several traditions that view the ingesting of peyote as a sacrament. A sacrament is a visible object or action that is believed to have spiritual power. It is a connection between ordinary and extraordinary in that an ordinary object or action becomes a link with the extraordinary world of the spirit. Peyote is a cactus that when eaten intensifies the religious experience. In a typical religious ceremony, only a few tablespoons of the cactus are ingested, less than 100 mg of mescaline.[8] Although it is considered a controlled substance, there is nothing to suggest that it is addictive and its use seems to have no negative long-term effects.

The Native American Church is one of several different movements that use peyote as part of their religious ceremonies. The usage of peyote has not been without controversy. Because peyote is a controlled substance it was declared illegal in 1970. At issue is whether the free exercise clause of the constitution protects religious groups and practitioners who violate state or federal law. Limited federal legality provides for the use of peyote by members of the Native American Church. In 2004, the Utah Supreme Court upheld the right of a Native American Church (including its nonnative members) to use peyote for bona fide religious rituals.

Peyote grows naturally in a geographic area encompassing parts of Mexico and Southern Texas. Some legalized peyote growers are registered in South Texas. In addition, *peyoteros* are legally authorized to harvest the indigenous cacti. In addition to peyote, there are other indigenous groups in the Americas who use other mescaline-containing cacti such as the San Pedro Cactus predominantly used in Peru. In addition to cacti, indigenous groups use other hallucinogenic plants. Ayahuasca is a vine used in South America in a healing ritual. Controversy continues to surround the use of these naturally occurring hallucinogens in religious ceremonies.

AUSTRALIAN ABORIGINAL RELIGIONS

The term **aboriginal** can be used synonymously with indigenous. However, our focus here will be on the term as characteristic of the indigenous people of Australia. As with Native American religions, there are diverse practices and **myths** among the Aboriginal communities. For example, the Torres Strait Islanders have different creation narratives than the Aboriginal Australians. However, common characteristics do exist among them.

---

[7] http://www.nativeamericanchurch.us/argument9thcircuitcourt.html.
[8] http://discovermagazine.com/2003/feb/featpeyote.

The **Dreaming** is an English translation of an aboriginal word that cannot be clearly translated by the term, Dreaming. The Dreaming refers to the period of creation, the world of ancestral and spirit beings, and the guidelines for the relationship between the creation and the spirit world. Dreaming stories passed from generation to generation are the foundation of aboriginal belief and practice.

The myth of the Rainbow Serpent tells of the origins of the land and has many variations (Figure 5).[9] The version displayed here is one of the most common. The aboriginal groups of Australia are unique from other indigenous groups in that they do not traditionally hold to a belief in animism. While they do not believe that a rock, mountain, or a river has a spirit, they do believe that the rock, river, or mountain was created by the spirits and is therefore sacred. As they traveled through the land leaving their power in specific places, the ancestral beings created pathways. Aboriginal people travel these sacred pathways and make their living connected to the

The Myth of the Rainbow Serpent

In the beginning, during the time of the Dreaming, the earth was still and sleeping. All the creatures of the earth slept under the ground.

One day, the Rainbow Serpent woke up and thrust her way through the ground pushing aside any rocks in her way. She traveled across the land in every direction. When she was worn out, she slept. Wherever she went, she left the tracks from her belly and the outline of her curled up body.

When she returned to her starting place, she told the frogs to "Come out!" The frogs' bellies were full of water. When the Rainbow Serpent tickled the frogs, they giggled and the water spewed from them and formed the lakes and rivers in the Serpents empty tracks.

As the other animals emerged from the Earth, they all followed the Rainbow Serpent. She created laws that all might live together peacefully. Some disobeyed the laws and were punished by being turned to stone. Others who kept the commands were rewarded, made into humans. They were forever connected to the animal from which they came.

Adapted from *Dreamtime: Aboriginal Stories* by Oodgeroo Nunukul. Copyright © 1999 by Angus & Robertson. Reprinted by permission.

Shanti Shanti/Shutterstock.com.

Figure 5 Rainbow serpent.

---

[9] This version is from http://www.aboriginaldreamtime.net/2011/08/rainbow-serpent.html.

land. They do not believe in controlling the land but living in harmony with it. The elders of the community pass the sacred stories, practices, and survival techniques from generation to generation through stories, ancient wisdom, art, and dance. The ancestral spirits continue to communicate through dreams, visions, and dance revealing knowledge as well as new songs and dances.

Aborigines generally believe in reincarnation. The spirits are reborn and elders can sometimes even identify who the newborn children were in a past life. Funeral and burial practices can vary based on the region. In Northern Australia, burial is in two stages. In the first burial, the body is placed under leaves and branches on a platform and the flesh is left to rot away. Later, the bones are collected and painted with red ochre. Sometimes relatives will carry the bones with them; other times they will be placed in a sacred spot such as a cave or wrapped in bark and buried. Among other aboriginal groups cremation or burial is practiced.[10]

Spiritual power is evident in sacred places and ritual objects. The result of harming a religious site or misusing a sacred object can be death. Sorcerers are said to cause harm to those who desecrate a religious site or misuse a sacred object. Whether sickness or death is a result of the power of suggestion or actual spiritual retribution remains a mystery.

INDIGENOUS AFRICAN RELIGIONS

As with other geographic regions, a diverse range of indigenous religions is practiced in Africa. Some are monotheistic while others are polytheistic. Most honor ancestors as well as nature spirits. Many traditional practitioners offer sacrifices to please the ancestors and spirits and to avoid harm or mischief caused by the spirits. Sacrifices range from slaughtering animals to pouring out liquid offerings, or **libations**, such as water or wine. In eleven different African countries, over 25% of people "say they believe in the protective power of **juju** (charms or amulets), shrines, and other sacred objects."[11] Sacred objects can include skulls, feathers, masks, shells, animal horns, or other items thought to have spiritual power (Figure 6). Furthermore, many followers of IAR believe in the power of evil spirits and the ability of people to curse one another or cast evil spells. Sickness is often viewed as having a spiritual cause, and many consult local healers to discern the cause of their suffering.

Figure 6 Traditional African mask.

ZoneFatal/Shutterstock.com.

[10] David Welch, "Aboriginal Religion and Ceremony," accessed November 1, 2015, http://www.aboriginalculture.com.au/religion.shtml.
[11] http://www.pewforum.org/files/2010/04/sub-saharan-africa-chapter-3.pdf.

Yoruba

The Yoruba tradition of West Africa has a high god, Olodumare, and a large pantheon of deities or energies known as **orisha**. Each orisha has a specific duty and each person has a special relationship with one or more orisha. Divination and individual purpose are intertwined in Yoruba tradition. As with aboriginal faith, the Yoruba believe in reincarnation. Before a soul is reborn, the breath of Olodumare is blown into the person awaiting birth. At this moment, his or her destiny is revealed. Through the birth process, human beings forget their destiny. The practice of Ifa divination, which relies on patterns created by cast shells or nuts and sacred verses, helps individuals discern their destiny and live in harmony with themselves and others. Priests, priestesses, and diviners guide the divination process. Yoruba tradition affirms the leadership of both men and women in sacred rituals. Male priests are called *babalawos*, while female priests are *iyalawos*. Yoruba sacred texts are passed on orally in the form of 256 poems or verses, called *odu*.[12] During the divination process, the priest or priestess will recite a series of poems based on the configuration of sixteen palm nuts that are cast.

Vodou, Santeria, and Candomble

Because of the slave trade, IAR spread to the Americas and the Caribbean. A new form of religious expression emerged through the mixing of Afro-Caribbean traditions and Christianity, particularly Catholicism. The conversion practices of Catholic missionaries led to indigenous traditions disguising the orisha in the guise of Catholic saints. The dominant traditions that emerged are known as Vodou, Santeria, and Candomble. The root meaning of Vodou comes from the Fon word, *Vodun*, best translated as "spirit." Vodou originated in Haiti; Santeria in Cuba, and Candomble in South America, particularly Brazil. Santeria and Vodou can also be found in the United States with particularly active communities in Florida, Louisiana, and New York.

What is often referred to as Voodoo, complete with dolls, zombies, initiation rituals and St. John's Eve, is a commercial invention to draw in the tourist crowd. Much of the healing knowledge passed down through generations of mothers (female elders) is secret. Any "dolls" used in authentic Vodou are focal points of positive energy and love. Much of the practices of these syncretistic traditions focus on divination, spiritual power, and healing.

Kwanzaa

Dr. Maulana Karenga introduced a modern adaptation of an indigenous African festival in the United States in 1966 (Figure 7). The celebration is Kwanzaa (December 26—January 1). The timing of the festival is in part a response to the commercialization of Christmas.[13] Seven principles are emphasized during Kwanzaa: unity (Umoja), self-determination (Kujichagulia), collective work (Ujima), collective economics (Ujamaa), purpose (Nia), creativity (Kuumba), and confidence or faith (Imani). Each night of Kwanzaa a candle is lit and a virtue is highlighted.

---

[12] For a translation and recitation of odus, see http://ask-dl.fas.harvard.edu/odu-ifa compiled by the African Language Program at Harvard University.

[13] http://www.africa.upenn.edu/K-12/Kwanzaa_What_16661.html.

The seven principles of
Kwanzaa

Umoja
Unity

Kujichagulia
Self-Determination

Ujima
Collective Work and
Responsibility

Ujamaa
Cooperative
Economics

Nia
Purpose

Kuumba
Creativity

Imani
Faith

Enraged/Shutterstock.com.

Figure 7   Kwanzaa virtues.

HMONG: AN EAST AND SOUTHEAST ASIAN PEOPLE

An indigenous group widespread throughout East and Southeast Asia are the Hmong. The first Hmong were farmers who settled in southern China along the Yangtze and Yellow Rivers sometime between 4000-3000 BCE. Hmong struggled for independence but failed due to the military might of imperial China. Though many Hmong still reside in China, through migration, they have settled in Laos, Thailand, Vietnam and Myanmar. A sizeable Hmong community is also present in the United States, with the largest group in St. Paul, Minnesota.[14]

---

[14] For an excellent source of information on the history and timeline of Hmong migrations, see https://www.mnhs.org/hmong/hmong-timeline

As with many other indigenous groups, Hmong believe in animism, the idea that all living things have spirit and are spiritually interconnected. They also believe that human beings have multiple souls. If a soul has wandered off or been overtaken by an evil spirit, it can lead to illness in body and spirit. The spiritual specialist in Hmong tradition is the shaman who can be either male or female. One of the most important rituals the shaman performs is the soul calling ritual in which an individual's soul is brought home. Animal sacrifice, chanting, and the use of sacred threads are all part of the soul calling ritual. In some healing rituals, the soul of the animal helps to protect the soul or to bring the soul of a person home.

Music is also important in Hmong culture, particularly for funerals. With the music offering safe passage and the lyrics providing instructions and directions, souls are sung into the afterlife.[15]

☯ Explore the Hmong tradition and summarize your learnings in a minimum of three sentences. Some possible sites to explore include: https://www.mnhs.org/hmong, or http://hmonglessons.com/the-hmong/, or https://www.pbs.org/splithorn/hmong.html

_____

_____

_____

_____

_____

WEB RESOURCES FOR FURTHER STUDY

http://www.americanfolklore.net. This link includes myths of both Native American and African American folklore. There is also a section on the homepage for myths about Tricksters.

http://discovermagazine.com/2003/feb/featpeyote. This article, "Peyote on the Brain" discusses studies done by Dr. John Halpern, of Harvard Medical School, and addresses the possible mental health benefits of peyote use.

https://nativeamericanchurches.org/—This site contains information about the Native American Church and the use of peyote.

http://www.native-languages.org/dreamcatchers.htm. This link gives the background as well as some myths surrounding the Native American symbol of the dream catcher.

http://www.eajournals.org/wp-content/uploads/Ethical-Guidelines-for-Sacrifice-in-African-Traditional-Religion-A-Social-Cultural-Approach.pdf—An interesting and thorough overview of the understanding of and ethical principles involved in sacrifice in traditional African religion.

https://owlcation.com/social-sciences/Indigenous-People-Latin-America—This website offers great general information on indigenous peoples in Central and South America including demographics, specific detail about particular peoples, and contemporary issues facing these communities.

---

[15] To listen to a Hmong funeral song, go to http://hmonglessons.com/traditional-songs/txiv-xaiv/

https://tainomuseum.org/taino/religion/—The Taino Museum offers general information about the history, culture and religion of the Taino people of Puerto Rico.

http://talkingtricksters.com/eshu/—This site offers two specific trickster tales including the story of Eshu, a trickster of the Yoruba tradition.

https://the-singapore-lgbt-encyclopaedia.wikia.org/wiki/Gender_in_Bugis_society—Gender is not binary in Bugis society. In fact, there are five genders. Explore this link for further information.

https://www.thesacredscience.com/the-art-of-smudging/—An excellent resource about the practice of smudging in indigenous religions.

Part 2: Eastern Religions

CHAPTERS:

On the map on next page, see if you can identify Bhutan, Myanmar (Burma), Cambodia, China, India, Indonesia, Japan, North and South Korea, Laos, Mongolia, Nepal, Singapore, Sri Lanka, Thailand, Tibet and Vietnam.

COMPARING EAST AND WEST

Traditionally, significant differences exist between Eastern and Western religious and philosophical traditions. A fundamental difference is monism (the oneness of reality) is prevalent in Eastern views whereas dualism is more common in Western perspectives. Little to no separation between the sacred and the material is present in the East, nor is there a separation between the human soul and Ultimate Reality or God. "In the West the soul is always part of the created order and therefore separate from and subordinate to God. In India, God and the human soul are on the same level, of the same nature, fundamentally one."[1] In Western, monotheistic traditions (i.e., Judaism, Christianity, and Islam) God is theistic, understood as a personal divine being separate from the created world though at times manifest within it. In Eastern traditions, God/Ultimate Reality is impersonal without form or substance but at times given form to serve as a window to the truth of the unity beyond everything. Western religions are dualistic—that is, there is God and humanity, spiritual and physical, good and evil.

---

[1] Ward J. Fellows, *Religions East and West* (New York: Harcourt Brace, 1998).

To try a map of Asia online, go to https://lizardpoint.com/geography/asia-quiz.php

MAP: ASIA (ACTIVITY – IDENTIFY COUNTRIES)

Rainier Lesniewski/Shutterstock.com

Another difference between Eastern and Western religions involves the way time is understood. In Judaism, Christianity and Islam time is viewed as linear with a single point of creation and a purposeful movement toward an often climactic end to history usually involving some final judgment. However, in Eastern religions time is understood as cyclical with multiple points of creation and destruction. In the religions of India, each world cycle is broken up into stages which grow progressively worse in terms of ethical and religious practice. At the end of the final stage, a new period of creation and a renewed sense of virtue begins.

The individual reigns supreme in the West. In fact, individual rights often take precedence over the common good. In the Jewish tradition, although the attainment of perfection is not likely, it is deemed possible. In all three monotheistic traditions, individuals have unique souls that live 1 Ward J. Fellows, Religions East and West (New York: Harcourt Brace, 1998). eternally. In Eastern philosophical traditions, greater emphasis is placed on social harmony than on individual perfection. In Confucianism, there are five basic human relationships and if there is harmony in those five relationships, then there is harmony in society. The Indian caste system and the emphasis on fulfilling one's social duty are intertwined with the cycle of birth, death, and rebirth.

Spiritual practices in the West are centered on prayer, often defined as communication between an individual or community and God. Prayer generally includes some supplication; that is, asking God to respond to a particular need. In Eastern traditions, meditation is emphasized more than prayer. Although devotion to a particular representation of Absolute Reality is a strong part of Hindu tradition, most Eastern traditions emphasize the quieting of the mind. A sense of oneness, peace, and enlightenment are the primary goals of meditation. When prayer is utilized in Eastern religions, it is predominantly seen as a focusing of energy rather than a petitioning of a deity.

Most Eastern religious traditions (with the exception of Japanese religion) value artistic representations of divinity in a variety of forms including murals, statues, and other images of gods, goddesses, and teachers. The images are honored as guests and believed to facilitate meditation and the ability to see and be seen by the deity. In the Western worldview, statues are often viewed negatively as idols. In the Roman Catholic tradition, it is acceptable to depict saints and biblical characters in art, but not to depict God. In the Islamic tradition, no images are acceptable at all whether they are of God or the prophets.

Common Threads

Despite the presence of a multitude of differences in varying degrees, there are also common threads we see weaving through most religious traditions. One of the most obvious is what is referred to as *karma* in many Eastern traditions; that is, moral cause and effect. We see this in Western traditions as well with the idea that "we reap what we sow." In addition, there is great similarity between the ethical principles and moral codes of all the great religious traditions. The five precepts of moral behavior and the Chinese principles of ren (compassion) and shu (reciprocity) have much in common with the ten Commandments and the Sermon on the Mount. Religious traditions from East to West emphasize selfless service and compassion.

As all people sin, according to the apostle Paul, each religion has its means of cleansing or ritual purification as well as means of purification and forgiveness. Cleansing rituals are prominent in every religious tradition:

◆ Bathing in the river Ganges for Hindus removes all negative karma;
◆ Misogi—a Shinto rite of purification under a waterfall;
◆ Mikvas—cleansing baths in Judaism restore ritual purity;

◆ Baptism—sprinkling or immersion to cleanse from sin in Christian traditions; and
◆ Ablutions—washing of the face, hands, and feet before Muslim prayers.

In addition, in many religious traditions there are means of forgiveness or grace either through an act of purification or through the deity bestowing forgiveness on the worshipper. In the Bhagavad Gita, Krishna says

> Letting go all dharma, take refuge in me alone;
> I shall deliver you from a00ll your sins; do not grieve

—(Bhagavad Gita 18:66)

In Eastern and Western religion, though there is much we can do in service, righteous living, devotion, or discipline, we are still in need of purification.

Most religious traditions also share a common practice of pilgrimage. Travelling to sacred sites and circling the site a specific number of times are part of Eastern and Western traditions. Communal worship is also a part of many religious traditions; however, in the East even worship in the temple is more fluid with people coming and going freely. The emphasis in Eastern traditions is on daily worship at home altars or shrines rather than weekly gatherings for study and prayer

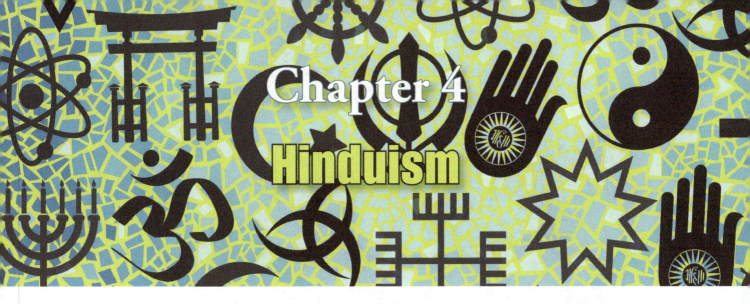

Chapter 4
Hinduism

Learning Outcomes

By the end of this lesson, students should be able to

☞ explain the development of Hinduism from the pre-Vedic practices through the Upanishads;

☞ identify the major Hindu deities and their roles;

☞ name the Hindu sacred texts and explain the philosophical concepts that derive from them.

☞ describe the four major yogic pathways; and

☞ characterize Hindu worship and explain what is meant by darsan.

Key Terms

Atman	Ganesh	Puja
Bhakti	Holi	Samsara
Brahma	Karma	Sanatana Dharma
Brahman	Kumbha Mela	Shiva
Brahmin	Lakshmi	Upanayana
Caste	Mandir	Vedas
Chakra	Mantra	Vishnu
Darsan	Moksha	Yoga
Dharma	Mudras	
Diwali	Navagraha	

INTRODUCTION

Vivid images, bright colors, and unbelievable diversity in practice and belief make Hinduism a fascinating and complex religion to study. Not only is there regional diversity between northern and southern India, but also diversity exists among various sects, communities, and ethnic groups. Although Indian in origin, Hinduism has spread throughout the world and with this spread, diversity in practice continues to increase.

Source: Stephanie Curran.

Figure 1   Sri Bhaktha Anjaneya Temple, Ijamsville, Maryland. This temple is devoted primarily to Hanuman, the loyal monkey deity who helped Lord Rama rescue Sita from the evil king, Ravanna in the Ramayana.

From the cornfields of Newburgh, Indiana, and the rolling countryside of Ijamsville, Maryland, to larger cities like Boston, Los Angeles, and Washington, DC, Hindu temples are integral to the cultural landscape of the United States (Figure 1). At least 40 states including Mississippi, Texas, and Wisconsin have Hindu temples; but what is Hinduism?

Hinduism is an umbrella term applied to the religions of the Indus Valley. The Indian term for the faith is **Sanatana Dharma**, meaning eternal order, and encompasses ancient practices that bring order and meaning to life. Historically, Hinduism is rooted in the indigenous religion of India blended with Indo-European (Aryan) religious practices. The primary, though not universal, theory for how this came about is that the nomadic Aryans migrated to India around 2,000 BCE from central Asia.

Hinduism encompasses a diverse set of practices and beliefs. As with all religions, not all Hindus believe and practice in the same ways. This reality was brought home to me in class one spring. Two Hindu friends were students in my class. One day, we watched a video about Hindu practice. In the video, the narrator described how Hindu children kiss their parents' feet first thing in the morning. After class, the girls approached me, and I asked what they thought of the video. One student remarked, "You know, that video is kind of outdated. No Hindu children kiss their parents' feet anymore." The other student looked a bit surprised and exclaimed, "I do." This example is just one of many that came up over the course of the semester and served as an important reminder that no religious tradition is homogenous. Each sect, and each follower within a sect, adds uniqueness and variety to a faith tradition.

SACRED TEXTS

Hinduism is the oldest of the global world religions. The earliest period in the development of Hinduism described by historians is the Vedic Period (1,750–500 BCE). However, some speak of an early Vedic period dating as far back as 10,000 BCE. It is during the later Vedic period that the earliest Hindu texts came into being. Hindu texts are divided into two types: Sruti ("that which is heard") and Smriti ("that which is remembered"). The Sruti are the primary sacred texts of Hinduism consisting of the Vedas and the Bhagavad Gita. The Smriti are additional sacred writings that seek to explain the Vedas. The Sruti are believed to have divine origins stemming from the rishi, or ancient sages. The Smriti include the epics (i.e., Mahabharata and Ramayana), the sutras (i.e., Yoga Sutra of Patanjali), the Puranas (folklore and narratives about the various deities, pilgrimage sites, etc.) and the Code of Manu (code of law guiding social interaction).

The Vedas

The word Veda derives from the Sanskrit root, *vid*, which means, "to know." The Vedas are the most ancient of Hindu texts and consist of four books. The four books are the ***Rig Veda***, the *Yajur Veda*, the *Sama Veda*, and the *Atharva Veda*. They are written in the ancient language of Sanskrit, which continues to be the language used by priests (brahmin) in worship (puja). English translations have been produced; however, the Sanskrit is central to Hindu faith and practice. Each book is also made up of four parts, the *Samhitas* (mantras), *Brahmanas* (ritual material), the *Aranyakas* (developed by hermits in the forest and more philosophical and meditative in nature), and the **Upanishads** (further philosophical material in the form of dialogue between guru and student).

The oldest of the Vedas is the *Rig Veda*, which is a collection of over 1,000 hymns and prayers to the ancient gods. Some of the deities referenced in the Vedas are no longer central to the daily worship life of modern Hindus, while others (such as Agni) continue to be influential. The Rig Veda describes the original order of creation and includes the earliest formulations of the caste system. It is also thought to be an early record of Aryan civilization.

☯ Look up a hymn from an English translation of the Rig Veda, such as the one found at http://www. hinduwebsite.com/sacredscripts/rigintro.asp. Write down key words and/or frequently appearing words and see if you can discern a theme. If you would like to experiment with word clouds, copy and paste a portion of a hymn into a word cloud generator, such as https://www.wordclouds.com. What key words were highlighted? Can you discern any themes based on those words?

_____

_____

_____

_____

The *Sama Veda* includes additional hymns often used in devotional singing. The Yajur Veda takes two forms: the White (Shukla) and the Black (Krishna); however, both forms address rituals including the offering of sacrifice. One of the primary deities of the Vedas is **Soma**. He is associated with the moon and said to be present in the soma plant whose juice was used for offerings and as a drink. As an intoxicating drink, it was thought to inspire creativity and bring healing as well as immortality to the gods. The Yajur Veda describes the soma offering.

The final Veda is the *Atharva Veda;* this text is believed to be the last of the Vedas written and only became part of the canon later in the Vedic period. Magical spells, prayers, and incantations to protect from disease and death, as well as to attract a lover, are popular elements of this Veda. In addition, prayers entreat the gods for healing, fertility, and health for cattle; not to mention warding off illnesses such as dysentery. Blessings for a new home, happy newlyweds, a speedy plow, and success in gambling also make this a popular text.

The Upanishads

The *Upanishads* are sometimes considered part of the Vedas and other times viewed as separate texts. They date from between 500 BCE and 500 CE and consist of a number of books, perhaps as many as 350.[1] Transcendentalists of the 19th century in the United States (i.e., Ralph Waldo Emerson, Henry David Thoreau, etc.), as well as German philosophers, like Schopenhauer and Kant, praised the Upanishads as a source of wisdom and insightful teaching about the nature of the self and the universe. As philosophical material, they introduce some of the central concepts of Hindu theology including Brahman, atman, karma, samsara, and moksha. These concepts are explored more fully later in the chapter.

The Epics and the Bhagavad Gita

The two major epics in Hinduism are the *Mahabharata* and the *Ramayana.* Both were composed around 300 BCE. The *Mahabharata* is a very long epic poem that tells of the battles between two clans, the Pandavas and the Kauravas, for kingship. The tale is 18 chapters and 100,000 verses in length. The war is a bloody and ruthless one that lasts for 18 days. Ultimately, the Pandavas prevail. The key chapter in the *Mahabharata* actually precedes the epic battle and is a discourse between Arjuna, a warrior of the Pandavas, and Krishna. This chapter, itself, became a much-loved sacred text in Hinduism, the *Bhagavad Gita.*

The Bhagavad Gita describes a conversation between Arjuna and Krishna, the eighth incarnation of the Hindu god, Vishnu. Arjuna sees family and friends on the other side of the battlefield and is reluctant to fight. Krishna explains that because Arjuna is a warrior, his sacred duty (dharma) is to fight. The *Gita* outlines the various spiritual pathways and serves as a model for the practice of devotion to God (bhakti).

The *Ramayana* is also a long epic poem consisting of seven books. The poet, Valmiki, is said to have composed it. Rama, an incarnation of the Hindu god Vishnu, is the main character of the story. The narrative begins with Rama's childhood. He is the son of a king and is destined to succeed his father. Before he can assume the throne, he and his wife, Sita, are exiled to the forest. A series of unfortunate events takes place there; and, the evil demon king, Ravanna, kidnaps Sita.

---

[1] For a listing of 180 of the Upanishads with links to some English translations, see http://www.hinduwebsite.com/upalist. asp.

Rama and his friends, including the monkey king, Hanuman, rescue Sita and Rama is restored to the throne. The story of the *Ramayana* is retold often as part of various Hindu festivals, including Diwali, the festival of light.

HINDU DEITIES

It is often said that, in Hinduism, there are 330 million gods. This is, of course, another way to say, "Everything is sacred." There is one divine essence that is everywhere, in everyone and everything. Does this remind you of a term we learned in Chapter 1?[2] (See footnote for the term.) Because of the many deities in Hinduism, many say that Hinduism is polytheistic; however, many Hindus would argue that Hinduism is monotheistic. The one sacred essence, Brahman, is essentially one and without gender or form. At the same time, this formless essence manifests itself in various deities that help individuals realize their connection to and oneness with Brahman.

The earliest Vedic deities primarily controlled nature and the elements. **Agni**, the god of fire, remains a central figure in daily worship. The lighting of the lamp honors Agni as he carries the prayers of the faithful. **Indra**, the god of thunder and the lord of heaven during the Vedic period, has many hymns and prayers devoted to him in the Vedas. However, with the rise of the Hindu **Trimurti** (the triad of Brahma, Vishnu, and Shiva), his influence waned. Although he is still a major part of Hindu mythology, he is not an important focus of worship for Hindus today. Other Vedic deities included Usha, the goddess of the dawn; Yama, the god of death; and, Soma, the god of speech and inspiration.

Around 500 BCE, the Trimurti of Brahma, Vishnu, and Shiva emerged as the three major faces of the one God. Brahma is the creator; Vishnu is the preserver; and, Shiva is the god of death, destruction, and reproduction. Each male deity has a female counterpart, or **Shakti** (the power of energy and creation). The divine feminine takes many forms including **Saraswati**, Lakshmi, and **Parvati**. A chart is provided on page 48 to help you keep these deities and their relationships straight. The Trimurti is often compared with the Trinity in Christianity. However, unlike the Trinity, some Hindus worship Vishnu or Shiva as the sole expression of Brahman.

Brahma is viewed as the creator, but he is not often worshipped as a stand-alone deity. In fact, there are few temples in India dedicated specifically to Brahma. He is believed to be the source for the Vedas and to have established the dharma. In one Hindu creation narrative, Brahma is born from a golden egg. Hindu cosmology asserts that there are multiple world cycles. Each world cycle is 4,320,000 years, which is believed to be a day in the life of Brahma. Each cycle is divided into four periods, or **yugas**. Each period becomes progressively more morally corrupt than the previous one. It is believed that we are in the fourth period, the Kali Yuga, which began on a Friday in 3,102 BCE.

---

[2] The term is pantheism, the view that the divine is everywhere and in everything.

Gwoeii/Shutterstock.com.

Figure 2 The Goddess Saraswati.

Figure 2 is an image of Saraswati, the goddess of art and learning in Hinduism. Take note of the symbols in her hands. She rides on a swan which is symbolic of spiritual perfection. Each deity holds symbols that point to their purpose and are depicted riding on a sacred "vehicle," such as a swan, tiger or rat.

Vishnu is the god of love and benevolence. Vishnu takes various forms (**avatars**). He has already appeared in nine forms and has yet to appear in the tenth form. He breaks into the world cycle to restore order and peace. Some of the forms Vishnu has taken include a fish and a turtle, but his most well-known incarnations are that of Lord Rama (the main character of the Ramayana) and **Krishna**. Krishna is the teacher of the Bhagavad Gita who demonstrates the importance of devotion to God and moral responsibility. Some lists include Buddha as an avatar, but that idea was a later development and is not accepted by all Hindus. Lakshmi, the goddess of wealth and good fortune, is Vishnu's consort. She is often depicted seated or standing on a lotus. Lakshmi is also known as Sri. Those who worship Vishnu form a sect of Hinduism, known as **Vaishnavism**.

The third aspect of the Trimurti is Shiva (sometimes spelled Siva). Shiva is the god of destruction as well as the god of reproduction. Devotees of Shiva form the Saivism sect of Hinduism. Depictions of Shiva vary. Some forms of Shiva show him dancing, sometimes atop a demon he has destroyed. Other images depict him sitting in the lotus position and holding a trident. One of the most ancient practices expressing worship of Shiva is the anointing of lingams (Figure 3). Lingams are cylindrical stones that represent energy and generative power. In worship, a lingam is anointed with water, milk, juice, or ghee. In addition, offerings are made and the "ohm namah shivaya" mantra is recited expressing devotion to Shiva. A mantra is a repetitive sound, word, or phrase used in meditation or worship. Shiva's primary consort is **Parvati**, the benevolent mother goddess. She is also the mother of Ganesh, the elephant-headed god who is understood to be the god of good fortune and the remover of obstacles.

steve Estvanik/Shutterstock.com.

Figure 3   Hindu priest anoints lingam with juice of an orange.

According to the Hindu mythology, Parvati was going to take a bath and she created a boy from the dirt of her body to guard the door while she bathed. Shiva came home while she was bathing and Ganesh would not let him into the room. Shiva was furious and chopped off the boy's head. Parvati came out of the bath and demanded that Shiva restore the boy to life. Having been brought back to life, Ganesh needed a new head. Shiva sent out his men to find another head for the boy and the head they brought back was that of an elephant. When beginning a new venture, puja is offered to Ganesh with hopes that all will go smoothly. In addition, Ganesh is often depicted riding on a rat, symbolic of greed, and ego.

In addition to the consorts of Brahma, Vishnu, and Shiva, the mother goddess (Mahadevi) takes additional forms, such as Durga and Kali. **Durga** is the protective mother goddess who looks after all her children and seeks to relieve their suffering. She rides on a white lion, symbolizing light and power. Like a lion, she is ferocious in destroying evil. **Kali** is the other destroyer goddess. In Hindu mythology, Kali is born from the forehead of Durga. If Durga is ferocious, Kali is downright scary. She is often depicted with blood dripping from her mouth and a garland of human skulls around her neck. She slays demons and presides over the cremation grounds. Although Kali is perceived as evil and scary in the West, she is not viewed as evil in Hinduism. In Hinduism, as in other Eastern religions, death and life are two aspects of the same reality. Opposites are not viewed as polarities, but held together in harmony. This bringing together of polarities into a sense of balance is also seen in the yin-yang symbol of Chinese religion.

Time and space are also deified in Hinduism. Hindu astrology determines the most auspicious times for the celebration of festivals, for the beginning of new ventures, and other major life events.

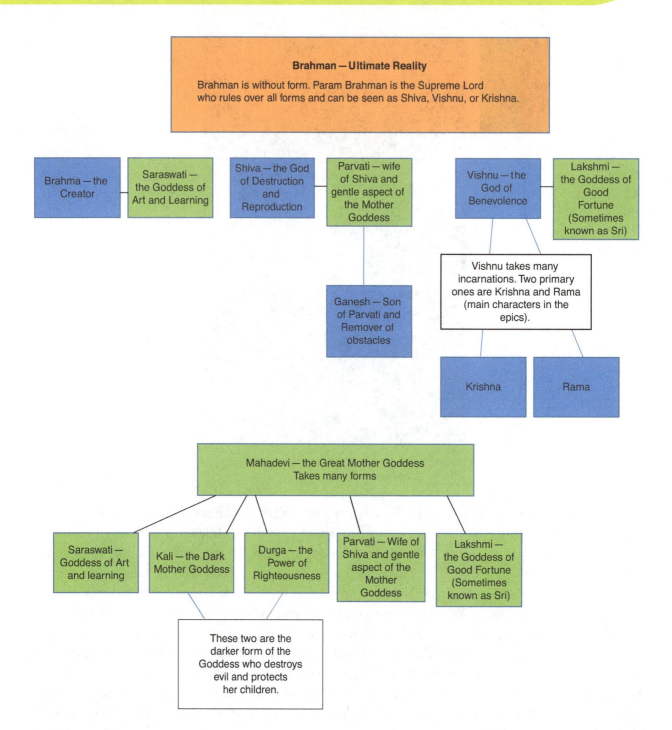

The **Navagraha**, or nine planetary deities, are found on altars in nearly every Hindu temple. Seven of the nine deities are associated with the sun, moon, and planets. These deities also have a specific day of the week. The sun is Lord Surya while the moon is Lord Chandra. The planets are Mars (Mangala), Mercury (Budha), Jupiter (Brihaspathi), Venus (Sukra), and Saturn (Sani). The other two deities, *Rahu* and *Ketu*, are designated as "shadow planets" and can either bring good or ill depending on their alignment with the other planets. Each of the nine deities has a gemstone, a mount they ride on, and special designations. For example, Lord Chandra is linked to the mind, beauty, and the feminine. One's astrological alignment is determined by the date, place, and time (down to the minute) you were born. Most Hindus give important consideration to the alignment of the planets in the planning of significant life events.

PHILOSOPHICAL CONCEPTS

As Hinduism developed, several philosophical concepts became central to its understanding of reality. The five major philosophical concepts include: Brahman, Atman, Karma, Samsara, and Moksha. In discussing the Hindu deities, the idea of Brahman was introduced. Brahman is Sacred Reality without gender, form, or attributes; it is a divine essence that permeates everything and an energy that pulses through the universe.

Living things have bodies and minds; however, most importantly they have **atman**, the True Self. Atman is spirit and the manifestation of Brahman in all humans, animals, and plants. Atman is not unique to the individual like the Western conception of soul. An important aspect of Hindu practice is developing one's realization of the divine in oneself and all other living beings. To understand the concept of atman and Brahman, imagine the great ocean as Brahman and atman as the individual drops of water in the ocean. The drop is not the ocean, but the drop contains the same elements as the entire ocean. One drop is not indistinguishable from the other. In fact, the illusion of separateness or duality is termed, **maya**. To see the world as it really is, one should not confuse that which is material with that which is eternal. In the words of Krishna:

> The impermanent has no reality; reality lies in the eternal. Those who have seen the boundary between these two have attained the end of all knowledge. Realize that which pervades the universe and is indestructible; no power can affect this unchanging, imperishable reality.
>
> —Bhagavad Gita, 2:16–18[3]

The practice of yoga enables human beings to see more clearly the distinction between the material and the eternal.

The remaining three concepts—karma, samsara, and moksha—are interrelated as well. **Karma** refers to actions and motivations as well as their consequences. The good a person does leads to good fruit and the harm one does leads to harmful fruit. Karma carries forward from one's previous life, influences one's current life, and has implications for one's future life. There is no divine judge meting out "karma"; rather, these are the natural consequences and energies that flow from the actions and intentions of the living. When the living die, they will be reborn based on the karma they have produced. The cycle of birth, death, and rebirth is known as **samsara** in Sanskrit. It is a concept that is present in Hinduism, Buddhism, Jainism, and Sikhism. The ultimate goal that human beings strive for is freedom from this cycle of birth, death, and

Figure 4 Aum is believed to be the very first sound of creation and connecting to its vibration brings harmony and healing.

Igor Shikov/Shutterstock.com.

---

[3] Bhagavad Gita translated by Eknath Easwaran (New York: Random House Vintage Spiritual Classics, 1985), 10.

rebirth. Freedom, or liberation, from samsara is **moksha**. Moksha is not heaven, but rather union with God. It has also been described as enlightenment or nirvana. In Hinduism, multiple paths to this goal are possible; there is not a single prescribed pathway. In the Yoga and Spiritual Pathways section of the chapter, we look at various yogic pathways, including bhakti, karma, jnana, and raja yoga.

SYMBOLS

One of the most important symbols as well as the most sacred sound is Aum (ohm) (Figure 4). It is a three-syllable elongated sound. When the sound is made audible, there is a feeling of energy or vibration to it. It is said to be the original sound of creation and has multiple meanings. Some say the three syllables (aum) represent three states of consciousness. Others link them to the Trimurti of Brahma, Vishnu, and Shiva together forming Ultimate Reality (Brahman). This symbol is present in Hinduism, Jainism, Buddhism, and Sikhism as well.

One of the most ancient symbols in Eastern religions is the swastika, which represents the sun. It is not uncommon to find an image of the swastika on the open palm of an image of a deity, such as Ganesh. We talk more about the swastika in Chapter 6 when we discuss the symbols of Jainism.

The cow is another symbol that is closely associated with Hinduism. The cow is respected for the fact that it provides all we need to survive: milk, leather for shelter and protection, dung to fertilize fields and to burn for heat. Like an ideal mother, the cow freely gives of herself to sustain life. The cow is also associated with Krishna who was said to have appeared as a cow herder and danced with milkmaids. Although not all Hindus are vegetarian, they generally do not eat beef.

The lotus flower is also a symbol in both Hinduism and Buddhism. It symbolizes transcendence. In **kundalini yoga**, a form of yoga that incorporates meditation, physical postures, and breathing exercises to open energy fields in the body, the lotus flower is a symbol of opening the crown chakra, the energy field at the top of the head. Many other symbols are present in Hinduism as well. The vehicle (yana) on which each of the deities rides is symbolic as are numbers, colors, and items held in the hands of the deities, such as the trident or conch shell.

☮ Choose a Hindu symbol you would like to know more about and research what it represents. Share your findings here.

_____

_____

_____

_____

WAY OF LIFE

Many followers of Hinduism describe it as a way of life as much as a spiritual practice. Like some other religious traditions (i.e., Judaism and Islam), Hinduism offers guidelines for all aspects of daily life. Historically, the caste system has divided Hindus into four main groups based on the work they contribute to society.

These four main castes (social groupings) dictated all aspects of life from how one made a living to who one could marry and with whom one could socialize. The groupings are priests (**brahmin**), warriors and nobility (**kshatriya**), merchants and farmers (**vaishya**), and laborers and artisans (**shudra**). A subcategory of the shudra caste is the **Dalit** (Untouchable). The word "dalit" literally means, "oppressed" or "broken"; it traditionally referred to those in Indian society who are at the bottom of the social order. They were given tasks that lead to ritual impurity (i.e., cleaning toilets, handling trash, carrying bodies to the cremation grounds, etc.), which kept them out of the temple. Gandhi worked to ban untouchability; and, the 1950 Indian Constitution banned the practice of untouchability. However, in much the same way as antidiscrimination laws in the United States do not eradicate racism or sexism, discrimination of dalits still exists today.

The epics speak of four stages in the life of a Hindu. Three are a normal part of the life cycle whereas the fourth represents renunciation of the material world. The first stage is that of a student. It encompasses the period of youth and education. The second stage is the householder. During this time in life, one marries and pursues a family and career. The third stage is that of retiree. In this phase of life, the children are grown and supporting themselves. This allows a person to spend more time devoted to spiritual pursuits. Greater amounts of time are spent during this stage in prayer, meditation, study, and service. The last stage is optional; it is the renunciate (**sannyasin**). One can become a renunciate at any of the three aforementioned phases of life by renouncing name, family, and possessions, and by devoting oneself entirely to spiritual pursuits. Some sannyasis live in a retreat community (**ashram**), whereas others are wandering ascetics travelling from place to place.

Hindu texts describe four aims (or goals) in life appropriate to various life stages. Three goals represent desires relating to the material world; these are dharma (right action), **artha** (security or wealth), and **kama** (pleasure or desire). Hinduism does not look negatively on the pursuit of security, wealth, or sexual pleasure with one's spouse. In fact, these are entirely appropriate goals during the householder phase of life; however, they do not offer release from the cycle of birth, death, and rebirth. Hindu literature, such as the *Arthashastra*, the *Kama Sutra*, and the *Dharmasastra*, outlines codes of conduct in fulfilling these aims. The fourth goal is that of moksha (liberation). In addition to freedom from attachment and desire, its focus is spiritual and represents freedom from the cycle of samsara.

YOGA AND THE SPIRITUAL PATHWAYS

The term "yoga" comes from a Sanskrit root word meaning "yoke" or "union." The goal of yoga, and the various spiritual pathways (**marga**), is to experience union with God and to uncover the true Self. The classic yogic text is the *Yoga Sutras of Patanjali*, which dates from 200 BCE to 200 CE depending on which scholars are followed. In it, Patanjali describes the purpose of yoga:

> Yoga is experienced in that mind which has ceased to identify itself with its vacillating waves of perception.
>
> When this happens, then the Seer is revealed, resting in its own essential nature, and one realizes the True Self.[4]

[4] YOGA SUTRAS OF PATANJALI © 2002 Mukunda Stiles used with permission from Red Wheel Weiser, LLC Newburyport, MA www.redwheelweiser.com

Four major yogic pathways (**margas**) are provided to reach the True Self and to connect with Ultimate Reality (Brahman). The paths are not mutually exclusive; one can practice multiple paths in varying degrees. How does a person choose a path? Generally, it is the role of the **guru**, spiritual teacher, to help individuals to discover the path that is best for them. In a sense, the path develops out of the experience of an individual's spiritual journey and may take different forms at various stages in life. The four major pathways are devotion (Bhakti yoga), service (Karma yoga), knowledge (Jnana yoga), and meditation (Raja yoga).

Bhakti Yoga, the Path of Devotion

Bhakti yoga, or the path of devotion, is a path that centers on love for God. Bhakti yoga is practiced through daily worship (**puja**), singing or playing devotional songs (**bhajans**), celebrating festivals honoring the various deities, pilgrimages, and expressions of love for God. Puja can be practiced at home or in the temple and involves ringing a bell, lighting an oil lamp, chanting prayers, and making offerings. The goals of worship are to express love for God and experience darsan. Darsan literally means, "seeing." Through worship, a devotee sees and is seen by the holy, and makes both a physical and spiritual connection with God.

Many from Western religious traditions are uncomfortable with the use of images in worship and see them as "idols." However, the images in Hinduism are tools for making the connection with God. Although the presence of the deity is not only in the image; through consecration, the presence of the deity is established within the image. When an image is created, the last things to be drawn on the statue are the eyes. Great power comes from the opening of the eyes.[5] One can see and be seen by the Sacred through worship, pilgrimages to sacred sites, and glimpses of gurus or other holy persons.

During puja, the image of the deity is treated like a holy guest. The deity may be bathed in offerings such as milk, water, ghee (clarified butter), yogurt and honey, and anointed with sandalwood oil. The image is also dressed in flower garlands and sometimes draped with fabric. Flowers are often placed around the feet of the deity. Food offerings (**prasad**) are made that often include fruit, sweets, herbs, and spices such as turmeric and saffron (Figure 5). The food given is blessed, offered to the deity and then may be eaten by the worshippers.

Utopia_88/Shutterstock.com.

Figure 5   Offering for hindu puja.

Markings on Hindu foreheads are common and often misunderstood. The **bindi** is a dot on the forehead often worn by women. Various colors of dots signify marital status, stage of life, and so forth. The dot is placed on the location of the "third eye," and it symbolizes the loss of one's ego. Many will apply a dot or other marking after worship to remind themselves throughout the day of their spiritual purpose. Different markings, or **tilak**, can signify devotion to certain deities. Sandalwood paste or ashes are often

---

[5] Diana Eck, *Darsan* (Chambersburg, PA: Anima Books, 1981), 7.

used to make the markings. They are believed to have a cooling effect on the body. A U-shaped marking or vertical lines represent devotion to Vishnu. Horizontal lines represent devotion to Shiva. A red dot can mean a woman is married or it can represent devotion to the Mother Goddess. Finally, the markings on the forehead of priests can signify a particular school of thought that the priest follows.

The practice of singing and playing devotional songs is also part of bhakti. **Bhajans**, or devotional songs, express honor and love for God. The songs often focus the mind and the heart on God.

☯ Listen to a few bhajans. You can find them on YouTube as well as other websites. A couple of links include: https://www.youtube.com/watch?v=QY_IH-pPYFU or https://www.youtube.com/watch?v=UrmrMcnI0eg. The first is a variety of morning bhajans and the second are bhajans devoted to Ganesh. After listening to a couple of different samples, describe your perceptions of the songs. Could you recognize any words? What themes or characteristics did you notice? How would you describe the music itself? Alternately, choose a Hindu instrument to describe. Explain two new things you learned about this instrument, such as how it is made or how it is used. A possible links to explore: http://www.metmuseum.org/toah/hd/indi/hd_indi.htm

_____

_____

_____

_____

Karma Yoga, the Path of Selfless Service

In Hinduism, as in many other religious traditions, the idea of compassion and selfless service are emphasized. One comes to the aid of others, not to be rewarded, but simply because it is the faithful thing to do. In this path, one achieves union with God through serving others and relinquishing the ego. One serves as an expression of love for God and for all life. In a sense, following the path of karma yoga involves offering your time, energy and effort to God; in that those served are manifestations of the sacred.

Jnana Yoga, the Path of Knowledge

Those who are very rational and intellectually curious are likely drawn to **jnana yoga**, the path of knowledge. Through this path, individuals study the sacred texts and seek to apply their understanding from the texts to their way of life. Jnana yoga is closely related to the **Advaita Vedanta** philosophy of nondualism. Advaita literally means "not twoness, embodying the monism that characterizes this philosophy."

The Hindu philosopher, **Shankara**, is viewed as the founder of Advaita Vedanta. The central tenet of this philosophy is monism. Monism is the belief that there is only one reality; the Self and Brahman are one. This view led Shankara to say that devotion to deities is unnecessary because devotion or worship implies that the object of our devotion is separate from us. Later Advaita Vedanta philosophers, such as Ramanuja, softened this view to allow for devotion as a means of recognizing the essential unity of all reality. Ramanuja himself was a devotee of Vishnu.

Raja Yoga, the Path of Meditation

Raja yoga is the path of meditation. This path is rooted in the Eight Limbs of Yoga outlined by Patanjali in the *Yoga Sutra*. The Eight Limbs include practices such as ethics, postures, breath control, concentration, meditation, and ultimately, the goal of union with God (**samadhi**).

The first two limbs deal with ethics expressed both through moral discipline and the cultivation of a pure heart. The ethics are outlined in what some call the "ten commandments" of Hinduism: the **yamas** and the **niyamas**. Many of these same virtues are emphasized in both Buddhism and Jainism as well. The yamas are nonviolence (**ahimsa**), honesty, not stealing, moderation, and nonattachment. The niyamas are contentment, purity, study, self-discipline, and surrender. An ethical lifestyle is the foundation of all yogic pathways.

Figure 6   Various yoga mudras.

Pikoso.kz/Shutterstock.com.

The third limb involves **asanas**, or bodily postures. The position of our bodies can inhibit or enhance the flow of energy. For meditation, the most common posture is the lotus posture with legs crossed. Savasana, or corpse pose, is another posture for relaxation and meditation. This pose involves lying on your back with your arms and legs relaxed. In addition to bodily postures, various hand gestures (**mudras**) are common in meditation. Each mudra has a distinct meaning and channels energy in a specific way. One of the most common hand gestures is the prayer position of the hands at the heart. It is used in prayer, as a greeting and as a way of showing respect. This mudra is referred to as Namaste and is a way to acknowledge the sacred in one's self and others (Figure 6).

Breath control (pranayama) is the fourth limb. This practice typically distinguishes Hindu meditation from Buddhist meditation. In Buddhist meditation, it is more common to observe the breath rather than to control it. Two common breathing techniques include matching the length of inhale and exhale breaths as well as alternate nostril breathing. If you are curious what alternate nostril breathing is about, there are some great technique videos on YouTube, such as https://www.youtube.com/watch?v=Xbbr6Udg1UA

Controlling the senses is the fifth limb and is closely related to the sixth, which is concentration. Both of these limbs serve the purpose of limiting distraction. Often, concentration on an object or the use of a mantra can help to control the senses. In meditation, it is easy to become distracted by sounds, movement, and smell. By focusing on an object (such as a lamp or statue of a deity), one's breath, or the repetition of a sound or phrase, distraction can be mitigated.

The final two limbs of yoga are the meditation (**dhyana**) itself and a sense of union with God (**samadhi**) achieved through the practice. Many think of meditation as emptying the mind and cannot imagine ever being able to do that. Just as important in meditation is the journey, which involves observation of thoughts and letting them go. In the process, the mind is stilled and one is able to see the inner nature of the self. Though thought is rarely completely absent, it can be slowed through practice. Another form of meditation, mentioned earlier, is kundalini yoga. In this method, one begins at the base of the spine and opens the energy fields one by one until reaching the opening of the crown chakra. Some systems recognize seven chakras, and others 12 or more. Chakras are both inside and outside the body and can include energy fields above the head (referred to as higher chakras). The physical postures, in and of themselves, can be a means of meditation and prayer. Seane Corn refers to this practice as "body prayer."

☯ As you think about the different yogic pathways, what questions do you have? Why do you think there are different pathways to God in Hinduism? What pathway appeals most to you? What draws you to this pathway?

_____

_____

_____

_____

HINDU RITUALS

A variety of rituals are celebrated in Hindu tradition including worship, rites of passage, festivals honoring deities or marking seasons, and pilgrimages. As discussed with bhakti yoga, puja (worship) takes place daily in many homes. In addition, priests preside over worship daily in the temple. Although many retirees may go daily, families generally go to the temple for special occasions. With the exception of festivals, worship is very individually focused. If you visit a Hindu temple, you will notice individuals and families coming and going throughout the day. With the help of a priest, they pray and make offerings at various shrines honoring specific deities.

Rites of Passage

Rituals mark life transitions in most religions. In Hinduism, many rituals mark occasions in the lives of young people such as conception, birth, naming, first feeding of solid food, puberty, and initiation rituals. In addition, there are rites of passage for marriage and death. The naming ceremony takes place for the infant usually in the first month of life; it can take place at home or in the temple and the father whispers the child's name in his/her ear.

The initiation ritual for boys who begin study of the *Vedas* is called the sacred thread, or upanayana. Traditionally, this rite of passage was performed only on boys from the upper three castes and took place at, or after, the age of eight. Over time, for many, this simply became a family tradition rather than an official start to a sacred journey of study. Some communities, especially in the West, are reassessing this practice and allow for any boy or girl who desires to study the sacred scriptures to have an upanayana ceremony.

Marriage is a sacred ceremony in Hinduism. Historically, marriages in Hinduism are facilitated or arranged and are considered a sacrament. However, in the United States, this practice of arranged marriages is becoming less frequent. Whether the marriage is facilitated or not, children seek the blessing

Figure 7 Hindu Wedding.

of their parents before marriage. Weddings are elaborate affairs and may take place over several days. Specific customs differ by region and caste but, generally, there is the exchange of flower garlands and the tying of a knot in addition to the exchange of vows (Figure 7).

Hindus approach death as a release for the soul. Generally, the soul is believed to be reborn rather quickly. To facilitate the release of the soul, it is typical for Hindus to practice cremation. Ideally, a person dies at home while reciting their favorite mantra. If they are not conscious, often someone will whisper the mantra in the person's ear. The family traditionally cleans and prepares the body. A special fire is lit and prayers and hymns are sung. The men in the family carry the body to the crematorium; typically, women do not go to the cremation grounds. After the ceremony, the family returns to clean the house and later collects the ashes and any bone fragments. In some traditions, the ashes are read (a form of divination) to determine the next life of the deceased. Special days of mourning are prescribed in Hindu tradition including the 1-year memorial of a person's passing.

Hindu Festivals

Hindu festivals are colorful gatherings with visits to the temple, music, food, dance, and drama. Across India, many different festivals are celebrated, each with regional variations. Nearly every month, a Hindu festival is celebrated. Hindus, like many other religious traditions, follow a lunar-based calendar rather than the Western solar-based Gregorian calendar. Therefore, the dates for Hindu festivals vary from year to year; however, they generally fall within a 4- to 6- week period. The three festivals we focus on are Holi, Navaratri/Durga Puja, and Diwali. One of the largest pilgrimages in the world is the **Kumbha Mela**. The festival rotates between four cities in Northern India. The frequency of the festival is dependent on astrological and religious factors; however, the Maha Kumbha Mela, the most massive of the gatherings, happens every 12 years.

Holi is a popular spring festival that is also known as the festival of colors because of the colorful powders and paints people throw on each other. The celebration of this festival served as inspiration for the Color Run in the United States. In Hindu mythology, the colors come from the tradition of Krishna playing with colors with Radha (his consort) and the milkmaids. Another tradition associated with Holi is the lighting of

Figure 8 Celebration of Holi in New Delhi. Take note of the many colors and the joy manifest in the celebration.

Figure 9   Diwali celebration in Trafalgar Square 2008.

a big bonfire the night before the more colorful festivities. This practice is also rooted in mythology. An evil king wanted everyone to worship him; however, his son refused. His son, Prahlad, was a devotee of Vishnu. The king kept trying to kill his son. His last attempt was to have his sister, Holika, who was immune to fire, hold him in the midst of a huge fire. Unbeknownst to Holika, her immunity only worked if she was alone in the fire. Prahlad was spared by Vishnu; thus, the festival also celebrates the victory of good over evil. This festival usually falls in March.

Navaratri is a nine-night festival honoring the goddess in her many forms. Durga Puja, the worship of the goddess Durga, is part of this festival. Typically, the festival occurs in late September to mid-October. Durga, Lakshmi, and Saraswati are the major expressions of the goddess worshipped during Navaratri. In the spring of 2015, I happened to be at the Sri Shiva Vishnu temple in Lanham, Maryland, during Navaratri for a class field trip. During our visit, a special puja for Lakshmi was taking place. She was bathed in gallons of milk as well as yogurt, honey and turmeric as the priest chanted from the *Vedas*.

One of the most widely celebrated festivals in India by Hindus, Buddhists, Jains, and Sikhs is the festival of lights, or **Diwali**. Diwali is a celebration of the New Year, and generally falls in late October or November. Houses are cleaned and many oil lamps (**dipas**) are lit. Another name for the festival is Deepawali for the row of lamps that are lit during the festivities. Like Holi, this holiday also celebrates the victory of good over evil. The story of the *Ramayana* and Lord Rama's victory over the evil king, Ravanna, are featured during this celebration. In addition to India, big Diwali celebrations are held from London and Leicester, United Kingdom to San Antonio, Texas (Figure 9).

☯ Explore some images of Hindu festivals on the Internet. What do you notice about the celebrations? Choose one festival and find out an interesting fact about that festival. What did you discover?

_____

_____

_____

_____

WOMEN IN HINDU TRADITION

The role of women in Hinduism is extremely complex. On the one hand, the idea of the divine feminine has always been deeply embedded in Hindu spirituality. Women cannot be priests; however, they have been and currently are sadhvi (holy women), saints and gurus? On the other hand, practices that violate women are an historical reality. One such historic practice is **sati**, a practice by which a widow commits suicide often by throwing herself on the cremation fire of her husband. Thankfully, this practice is outlawed today, but it does occasionally occur. The practice was viewed as a way to rid oneself of karma; and, women who chose this path were viewed as goddesses (sati devi). Another complex practice is the role of a young woman as a devadasi, a woman married to a goddess. It sounds like a positive role, like a nun married to Christ, until you discover that the devadasi is a temple prostitute who is often "married" off at the age of 8 or 10 by poor families who cannot otherwise provide for their daughters. This practice is also illegal across India as of 1988; however, many still suffer from this practice amidst poverty and disease.[6] To read more about the view of women in Hindu society in the 21st century, see the article presented by Dr. Shukla-Bhatt at Wellesley College found at http://www.iop.or.jp/Documents/0919/shukla-bhatt.pdf

HINDUISM IN THE UNITED STATES

Trade with India first introduced Americans to Hinduism in the 1780s. However, American's real fascination with Hinduism began with the World's Parliament of Religions in Chicago in 1893. In Chapter 2, we discussed this important interfaith gathering. Seven Hindus spoke at the event, but Swami Vivekananda was by far one of the most popular speakers. While touring the United States after the fair, he established the first Vedanta society in New York City. A few years later, he returned to the United States to establish a second Vedanta society in California. [7] Hindu temples now dot the religious landscape all over the United States, but the first temple was built in California in 1903. These temples, or **mandirs**, serve as a place of worship, community service, and fellowship.

Hinduism continues to grow in the United States through immigration and affiliation. Indian immigration has been steady, but, in addition to that, non-Indians are drawn to affiliate with Hinduism because of its tolerance, philosophy, and yogic pathways. Between 2007 and 2014, Hinduism has grown from 0.3% of the US population to 0.7%. In real numbers, there are around 2.3 million Hindus in the United States.[8] Interestingly, in 2014, Hinduism was the second largest religion practiced in Arizona.[9] This statistic was drawn from measurements of worship attendance at religious congregations in the state in 2010 rather than population; however, it speaks to the commitment and presence of Hindus in the United States.

☯ On a visit to a Hindu temple or in a conversation with a practitioner of Hinduism, what questions would you ask? What do you wish you knew about Hinduism?

_____

_____

_____

_____

[6] For more information see on devadasi in Hindu culture today, see http://www.thehindu.com/features/magazine/slaves-of-circumstance/article5028924.ece.

[7] http://www.pluralism.org/religion/hinduism/timeline/america.

[8] http://www.pewforum.org/2015/05/12/americas-changing-religious-landscape/.

[9] http://www.azcentral.com/story/news/local/phoenix/2014/07/17/temples-cultural-hubs-arizonas-hindu-worshipers/12769349/.

WEB RESOURCES FOR FURTHER STUDY

https://bhagavadgita.io/—This site includes various ways to read, view or listen to the Bhagavad Gita.

https://www.healthandyoga.com/html/meditation/mudras.aspx—A resource on the benefits of each mudra with a picture to illustrate the various hand gestures.

http://www.hinduismfacts.org/hindu-festivals/—A resource for information about the various Hindu festivals.

https://www.hinduwebsite.com/sacredscripts/sacredscripts.asp—An excellent source for translations of Hindu sacred texts.

https://www.huffpost.com/entry/the-future-of-hinduism-in-americas-changing-religious-landscape_b_7348140—An interesting article on the future of Hinduism in the United States.

http://kumbh.gov.in/en—A resource for learning more about the Kumbha Mela festival.

http://sacredmusicradio.org/hindu-sacred-music/—A great resource for information about Hindu sacred music, including information on scales, musical instruments, and devotional songs.

Comparison Chart of Key Concepts in Hinduism, Buddhism, and Jainism.

Hinduism	Buddhism	Jainism
Karma	Karma	Karma—physical "coat of clay"
Samsara	Samsara	Samsara
Moksha	Moksha	Moksha
Meditation	Meditation	Meditation
Dharma—truth, sacred duty	Dharma—teachings of the Buddha	Dharma—truth or teaching
Atman/theistic	Anatman (anatta)/nontheistic	Jiva/non-theistic
Caste	Rejected caste	Rejected caste
Priestly rituals	Rejected priestly rituals	Rejected priestly rituals

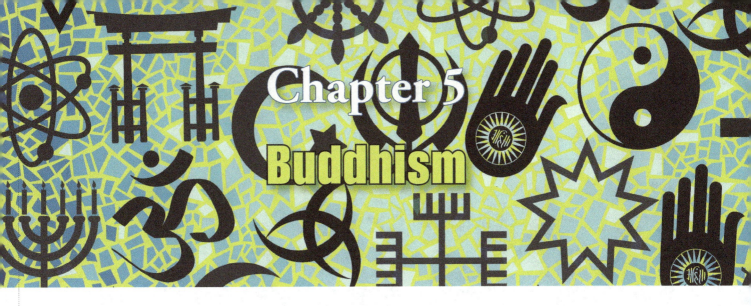

Chapter 5
Buddhism

Learning Outcomes

By the end of this lesson, students will be able to

- outline the key events in the life of Siddhartha Gautama, the Buddha.
- describe the Four Noble Truths and the Noble Eightfold Path.
- explain the key philosophical concepts in Buddhism including the views of nonself and impermanence.
- distinguish between the major branches of Buddhism; and
- convey the importance of practice in Buddhism.

Key Terms

Amida Buddha (Amitabha)	Karma	Pali Canon (Tipitaka)
Anatman (anatta)	Koan	Samsara
Bodhisattva	Lamas/tulkus	Sangha
Buddha	Mandala	Satori
Dhammapada	Mantra	Stupas
Dharma	Mara	Sutras
Dukkha	Moksha	Triple Gem
Impermanence (anicca)	Nirvana	Zazen

AXIAL AGE (ROUGHLY 600–300 BCE)

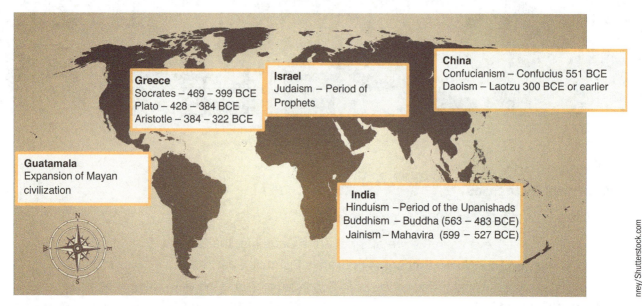

Greece
Socrates – 469 – 399 BCE
Plato – 428 – 384 BCE
Aristotle – 384 – 322 BCE

Israel
Judaism – Period of Prophets

China
Confucianism – Confucius 551 BCE
Daoism – Laotzu 300 BCE or earlier

Guatamala
Expansion of Mayan civilization

India
Hinduism – Period of the Upanishads
Buddhism – Buddha (563 – 483 BCE)
Jainism – Mahavira (599 – 527 BCE)

The Axial Age was a period of great activity philosophically, religiously, and culturally around the world, but particularly in Asia and the Middle East.

INTRODUCTION

Buddhism began in the sixth century BCE in India. This period is often referred to as the Axial Age, a period of intense philosophical and religious change and development around the world. Jainism also developed in India during this time along with the composition of the Upanishads. As noted in the chart at the end of chapter 4, Buddhism and Jainism share Hinduism's view of **samsara**, **moksha**, and **karma**. Buddhists and Jains also believe that human beings are tied by karma to a cycle of birth, death and rebirth from which they long to be liberated (moksha). While in some ways, Buddhism was a response to the ritual emphasis in Hinduism at the time, even more it emerged from one person's attempt to come to terms with life's suffering.

LIFE OF SIDDHARTHA

Siddhartha Gautama was born in the foothills of the Himalayas in what is now Nepal. His father was the king of the Shakya clan; and, Siddhartha spent his first thirty years sheltered in the palace in Kapilavastu. Legend has it that Siddhartha's mother, Queen Maya, had a dream in which a white elephant entered her side. Nine months later, in Lumbini, as Queen Maya traveled home, Siddhartha was born emerging from her side. Some speculate this might have been an early description of a caesarean section. However, whether it is purely mythic or a literary way of expressing a medical reality, the message this story conveys is that there was something special about this baby.

The king and queen gave their son the name, Siddhartha, which means, "wish fulfiller." The sages and fortune tellers, who came to visit the king and queen, predicted that their infant son would either grow up to be a powerful king or he would renounce his title and become a great spiritual teacher. Siddhartha's mother died a few days later. As you might imagine, his father wanted him to become a powerful king. Siddhartha grew up in the luxury of the palace sheltered from human suffering. At the age of 16, he married and seemed on track to follow in his father's footsteps.

When he was twenty-nine years old, his curiosity led him to travel outside the palace with his chariot driver to survey life outside the strict confines of his home. On the first trip, they encountered an old man struggling to walk down the road. He asked his chariot driver, what the meaning of this sight was, and the driver responded, "We all will grow old." On the second trip, they saw a sick man; and, on the third time out, they saw a corpse. Siddhartha's eyes were opened to the realities of change, suffering and death on these first three trips. Although this probably was not the first time he had seen such things, the scales fell from his eyes and the reality of suffering and mortality became real to him. He clearly understood the transitory, and sometimes painful, nature of life. Furthermore, he knew on a deeper level that he was not immune to them.

On the fourth journey with his driver, he saw a wandering ascetic sitting under a tree meditating and observed the look of calm the man seemed to possess. Not long after seeing the fourth sight, he left his wife and newborn son in the palace. He became a sannyasin, or renunciate, in the Hindu tradition in which he was raised. The journey toward enlightenment began when he joined up with five wandering ascetics and sought to learn from their practices. He met with various gurus, denied his body and practiced intense meditation.

One day, after a period of intense fasting, he collapsed while traveling with his companions. A young girl came out from the village and saw him lying there near death. She brought a bowl of rice pudding and fed him a few spoons. He sat up and took nourishment and was strengthened by the food and the young girl's kindness. His companions left him in disgust, telling Siddhartha that it was clear to them that he could not let go of his life of luxury. Siddhartha realized that all the intense fasting and self-denial did not give him the answers for which he so desperately searched. He decided to sit under a tree, the Bodhi tree, and meditate. Realizing the answers he sought were within himself, he vowed to stay in that place until he discovered the truths for which he longed (Figure 1).

As he neared an understanding of the true nature of things, he experienced great temptation. As Jesus experienced temptation many years later, Siddhartha was tested. The demon king, Mara, came to visit. He and his army hurled down weapons from the sky. However, as they neared Siddhartha, the army's arrows turned into flowers. He would not be overcome by fear. Next, Mara sent his beautiful daughters hoping to seduce Siddhartha. He watched them dance in front of him, but he was no longer driven by passion and desire. In the last temptation, Mara whispered words of doubt in Siddhartha's ear, "Who says you

Figure 1 Bodh Gaya, the place of Buddha's enlightenment is still visited today by faithful pilgrims.

are worthy of true understanding?" Siddhartha simply touched the ground. He would not be moved. It was at that moment that the ground shook, and he came to understand the true nature of reality. He had achieved enlightenment and become the Buddha. The title, Buddha, means, "awake." Unlike other titles given to religious founders, like Christ, anyone can become a Buddha. To distinguish the historical Buddha from other Buddhas, he is sometimes referred to as Shakyamuni Buddha, or the Sage of the Shakya clan.

After reaching enlightenment, the Buddha began to share his teachings. He preached his first sermon to the five wandering ascetics who had earlier abandoned him. The sermon is called The Deer Park sermon because it is said that he gave this teaching at a park outside of the holy city of Varanasi, India (Figure 2).

Only Fabrizio/Shutterstock.com.

Figure 2 Shakyamuni Buddha statue. Notice the hand touching the ground. This mudra represents the Buddha touching the earth as he reached enlightenment.

TEACHINGS OF THE BUDDHA

Four Noble Truths

The core of the Buddha's first sermon was about suffering and how to alleviate it. Central to this goal is what is referred to as The Four Noble Truths. These truths address the reality, the cause and the cure for suffering. The first Noble Truth is the reality of suffering. Not one of us is exempt from suffering. All of us will experience varying degrees of suffering throughout our life. Buddha was not saying that this is the way it should be, rather, he simply recognized that is the way things are.

The second Truth, according to the Buddha, is that our suffering is caused by desire or craving. We crave pleasure. We desire to avoid pain. We long for things to stay the same even in the face of the reality that nothing is permanent. Our desires naturally lead to suffering. The desire to be loved often leads to suffering; not necessarily because it turns out wrong, but because ultimately, separation through death will be the result. Perhaps you have lost a pet. Often, the first instinct when that happens is to say, "I'm never going to have a dog again." The thought of the losing another pet, at that moment, is not worth the joy of loving. The second Noble Truth addresses the root cause of our suffering. Fortunately, according to the Buddha, there is a relief from suffering. The promise that relief can be found is the Third Noble Truth.

In the Fourth Noble Truth, the Buddha addresses the path that leads to enlightenment and an equanimity that is not changed by joy or suffering. The Buddha taught that the way to achieve these goals is the Noble Eightfold Path. The elements of the Path are right understanding, right thought, right speech, right action, right livelihood, right effort, right mindfulness, and right meditation. These eight elements can be categorized into three areas: ethics, concentration, and wisdom. Ethics encompasses the way followers speak, act and earn their living.

Moral guidelines are outlined in the Five Precepts of Moral Behavior, which are closely related to the **yamas** in Hinduism and the Five Great Vows of Jainism. The first guide is nonviolence (**ahimsa**) or not causing harm to any sentient beings. Sentient beings are those creatures with the ability to see and sense; they are aware and can experience pain. All people and animals, including insects, are sentient beings. Though some Buddhists are vegetarian, not all are. The second precept is to abstain from taking anything that is not yours. It goes beyond stealing to include appropriating things for yourself that others need. Being responsible in sexual relations is the third precept. Sexuality is a gift not to be abused or treated lightly. Sometimes, this precept is described as responsibility in relationships. Training in this precept involves approaching all relationships with respect, love and trust. Honesty, closely connected to right speech, is the fourth precept. The training in honesty includes integrity and kindness in speech and action. The connection between the precepts is clear. In human relationships, do no harm. The final precept is mindful consumption. Part of this precept involves the avoidance of intoxicants, including drugs and alcohol. In addition, the precept encourages followers to practice mindfulness in where food comes from, how it is eaten, and what is taken in through the senses. Toxins are ingested not only through our mouths, but also through our eyes and ears. What is watched, listened to and read is also part of mindful consumption. What is taken in through the body nourishes seeds of health and wholeness or seeds of negativity, depending on what individuals choose to consume.[1] Right action is closely related to right livelihood, in that, the way we earn a living ideally is consistent with the ethical values espoused.

The paths of right effort, right mindfulness and right concentration or meditation are closely inter-related. Right effort ties ethics and meditation practice together. The investment of time and energy should reflect the goals of wisdom and compassion. Mindfulness involves being fully present in the moment. When eating, be fully aware of each bite and the subtle tastes of the food. When conversing with another, be fully present in the conversation rather than thinking what needs to be done later. Mindfulness comes from the practice of concentration or meditation. Meditation helps to slow the mind and teaches awareness. The practice makes one more aware of each breath, sound and thought. Meditation practices will be explored in greater detail later in the chapter.

The outgrowth of ethics and meditation is wisdom. Wisdom involves the insight to see the true nature of things. Right thought encompasses eliminating negative thinking and focusing one's intentions on compassion and loving-kindness. Right understanding refers to the experience of the reality of the Four Noble Truths. Buddhists are not taught to accept these principles on faith. Rather,

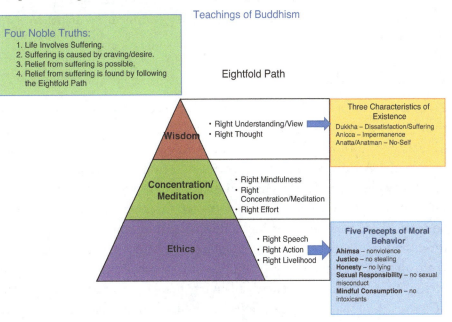

Teachings of Buddhism

Four Noble Truths:
1. Life Involves Suffering.
2. Suffering is caused by craving/desire.
3. Relief from suffering is possible.
4. Relief from suffering is found by following the Eightfold Path

Eightfold Path

Wisdom
• Right Understanding/View
• Right Thought

Three Characteristics of Existence
Dukkha – Dissatisfaction/Suffering
Anicca – Impermanence
Anatta/Anatman – No-Self

Concentration/ Meditation
• Right Mindfulness
• Right Concentration/Meditation
• Right Effort

Ethics
• Right Speech
• Right Action
• Right Livelihood

Five Precepts of Moral Behavior
Ahimsa – nonviolence
Justice – no stealing
Honesty – no lying
Sexual Responsibility – no sexual misconduct
Mindful Consumption – no intoxicants

[1] For a thorough look at the Five Precepts of Moral Behavior, see Thich Nhat Hahn, *Living Buddha, Living Christ* (New York: Riverhead Books, 1995), 90–110.

for Buddhists, these principles are only true if they prove true through experience. In addition to the Four Noble Truths, right understanding involves recognition and understanding of the three characteristics of existence.

Characteristics of Existence

The three characteristics of existence are **dukkha**, **anicca**, and **anatta**. Dukkha is suffering or dissatisfaction. Dissatisfaction is inevitable in life. No one escapes suffering. The recognition of this reality is not a giving in to it, but rather, a step toward diminishing it for one's self as well as for others. In Buddhism, the recognition of suffering is meant to lead to an elimination of the root causes of suffering, which are craving and desire.

Most human beings desire a sense of permanence. Often, dissatisfaction arises from change. The reality is that nothing stays the same. Anicca is the reality of **impermanence**. For example, a person may love their favorite t-shirt and wear it all the time. Eventually, the t-shirt is threadbare and holey. There comes a point when it cannot be worn anymore and must be discarded. Likewise, the human body does not stay the same. It is constantly changing. Over time, people's bodies wear out and eventually they become sick and die. Thoughts and tastes, likes and dislikes change over time, too. Maybe as a young person, the thought of broccoli caused you to feel sick. Now, you eat broccoli once a week and enjoy the taste and texture. Perhaps you once leaned toward one political perspective, and now you lean toward another. Relationships change over time. Parents must eventually let go of their children, spouses pass away, and friends sometimes lose touch with one another. Change is inevitable.

In a similar recognition of change and impermanence, in Buddhism, there is no permanent self (anatta). Human beings are aggregates of several things: matter, senses and feelings, perceptions or recognition, thoughts, consciousness, and awareness. These elements are constantly changing. Human beings are not their body; they are not their thoughts or feelings or perceptions. According to Buddhism, human beings are not even all these elements combined. Permanence is an illusion; and, ignorance to the reality of change causes suffering.

Dependent Origination

Permanence is an illusion, but interdependence is a reality. Nothing arises of itself, nor can anything exist alone. Living beings and inanimate objects all exist in the context of, and as a result of, other conditions. Cookies need ingredients, someone to stir the ingredients, and heat to come into being. A shirt requires the growth of cotton and the processing of it into fibers. Those fibers must be woven into fabric, cut into pieces and sewn together for the shirt to come into existence. Human beings are born when a sperm fertilizes an egg. They are dependent on the relationship between these two units for life to form. In the same way, to survive, humans are reliant on air, food, and water. Beyond the physical needs in life, human beings are dependent on relationships with one another for many of our emotional needs of love, belonging, and security. Awareness of the interconnection between all living beings can lead to compassion for others as well as for ourselves. Compassion and a desire to help all beings achieve enlightenment are at the heart of Buddhist practice.

Triple Gem

For Buddhists, the core of the practice is stated in the Triple Gem. When a person formally becomes a Buddhist, it is through recitation of the Triple Gem: "I take refuge in the Buddha, I take refuge in the Dharma, I take refuge in the Sangha." The Buddha is the one who shows the way or the path to enlightenment. By taking refuge in the Buddha, a person commits to stepping onto the path toward enlightenment. "Taking refuge in the Dharma" involves accepting the Four Noble Truths, the Eightfold Path and the characteristics of existence as being an accurate portrayal of the nature of reality. The Sangha originally referred to the community of monks and nuns, but in some sects of Buddhism it is understood to represent the entire Buddhist community.

Pali Canon

Faithful monks committed the Buddha's sermons to memory over the course of his 45-year ministry. These memorized sermons were passed from teacher to student. Ananda, one of the Buddha's closest associates, is said to have committed all of Siddhartha's sermons to memory. It is said that Ananda's memory of the sermons of the Buddha resulted in the eventual compilation of the *Pali Canon*, the authoritative text in Buddhism. The *Pali Canon* is named such because it consists of the teachings of the Buddha, written in the language of Pali (as distinguished from Hindu teachings which are written in Sanskrit). The collection is also sometimes referred to as the *Tipitaka* (the "three baskets of the law"). It is made up of three parts and is one of the largest sacred texts of the major world religions. In the picture to the right you can see a collection of the Pali Canon stored in a cabinet at the Wat Thai Buddhist temple in Silver Spring, Maryland (Figure 3).

The *Pali Canon* is the only authoritative text in Theravada Buddhism and is made up of three sections. The first section is the *Vinaya Pitaka*. This section is devoted to the guidelines that order the life of monks and nuns. The second section, *Suttanta Pitaka,* or Discourses, includes the sermons of the Buddha as well as some of the early Buddhist teachers. All of the major concepts of Buddhism are outlined in this section. The Dhammapada, a collection of the sayings of the Buddha, is a part of this collection of sermons. The third, and final section, is called the *Abhidhamma Pitaka*. The *Abhidhamma* consists of seven books that describe moral, physical, psychological, and philosophical aspects of human life.[2]

Figure 3 A picture of the cabinet in which the Pali Canon is stored at the Wat Thai Temple in Silver Springs, Maryland.

Source: Stephanie Curran.

---

[2] To read many of these writings translated to English, see www.palicanon.org.

☯ Read a passage from the Dhammapada available free online at https://www.accesstoinsight.org/tipitaka/kn/dhp/index.html, or another site such as http://www.buddhanet.net/pdf_file/scrnd-hamma.pdf. What passage did you read? What aspect of human experience was the passage seeking to convey? What did you sense was the tone of the passage?

_____

_____

_____

_____

_____

Nirvana

Though the goal of enlightenment may take many lifetimes, once one reaches it, craving and suffering end. One of the most common terms for enlightenment is nirvana. Nirvana literally means, "to blow out" or "extinguish." The idea is that the flame of desire and craving are no longer a driving force in life. The individual experiences a sense of peace and equanimity whether the sun is shining or the storms are raging. This goal is not reached through divine intervention or through mystical powers; rather, this goal is reached through practice.

Sometimes, there is a tendency to equate nirvana with the Christian heaven, but these are very different ideas. Nirvana can be experienced now; on the other hand, the Christian view of heaven is generally understood to be an afterlife experience. In addition, in heaven, the belief is that the individual soul lives forever. As stated earlier in the chapter, in Buddhism, there is no permanent soul to live eternally. In some branches of Buddhism (such as Mahayana), there are multiple heavens and hells. However, none of these heavens or hells is permanent; and, one does not achieve release from the cycle of birth, death and rebirth from these states. If a person is in heaven, he or she is there until the karma that lead to such a state is used up. Once that karma is used up, the person is reborn. It is only in human life on this earth that one can achieve enlightenment. Kusala Bhikshu in an article on www.urbandharma.org offers a helpful illustration of karma and rebirth. Imagine Jane's karma filling a suitcase and being set on a conveyer belt at the airport. The suitcase gets on the plane, but Jane does not. At the end of the flight, Jane's next incarnation picks up the suitcase and continues the journey.[3]

BRANCHES OF BUDDHISM

Interestingly, though Buddhism began in India, it grew and expanded primarily in other parts of Asia, particularly southeast Asia, Tibet, China, and Japan. In a sense, the various branches of Buddhism represent different ways to reach the goal of enlightenment. Nirvana is sometimes described as the "farther shore," the goal of Buddhist practice. Imagine standing on the bank of a wide river looking across to the other side (the goal). How will you reach the other side? The various branches of Buddhism can be compared to vehicles used to reach the same common goal.

---

[3] See http://www.urbandharma.org/udharma/heaven.html for a full explanation of Kusala's explanation of heaven and karma in Buddhism.

	Theravada (Hinayana)	Mahayana	Vajrayana
Definition	The Tradition of the Elders ("Lesser Vehicle")	"Greater Vehicle"	"Diamond Vehicle"
Enlightenment	Monastics	Anyone	Anyone in single lifetime
Primary Location	Southeast Asia	China and Japan	Tibet, Nepal, Bhutan, Mongolia
Sacred Texts	Pali Canon (Tipitaka)	Pali Canon plus Sutras	Pali Canon, Sutras, and Tantras
Buddha	Historical Buddha	Three Bodies of the Buddha	Three Bodies of the Buddha

Theravada

Continuing our illustration of standing on the shore of a wide river, the path of Theravada Buddhism is sometimes described as a "small raft," or Hinayana, which literally means "lesser vehicle." The designation is not meant as a diminishment of the tradition. Rather, it is meant to convey the difficulty of achieving enlightenment on this path; however, many Buddhists consider the term disrespectful. In Theravada Buddhism, an individual must become a monastic to achieve enlightenment; and, those who are successful are called **arhats**. An individual must become a monastic to achieve enlightenment. For the lay follower of Theravada Buddhism, the emphasis is on meditation, as well as on diminishing karma through practices, such as providing for monks and nuns and showing reverence for the Buddha and his teachings. Theravada Buddhism is the oldest form of Buddhism and is most prominent in Thailand, Myanmar, Cambodia, and Laos.

Mahayana

Mahayana Buddhism developed in the first and second century CE and is an umbrella term for many forms of Buddhism, particular those of China and Japan. The term literally means "greater vehicle" and refers to the idea that one does not have to be a monastic to reach enlightenment. In addition to the Pali Canon, Mahayana Buddhism also draws on various sutras, such as the Lotus Sutra, the Heart Sutra, and the Diamond Sutra. These texts further elaborate on the **dharma**, or the teachings of the Buddha.

Mahayana Buddhism teaches the concept of the Three Bodies of the Buddha, furthering the concept of Buddhanature beyond simply the historical Buddha. The first body is understood to be the historical Buddha, Siddhartha Gautama. The second body, or bliss body, refers to the bodhisattva and other enlightened beings, who have delayed entry into nirvana to help ease the suffering of others. The third body, or the truth body, is the eternal Buddha principle that has always existed, and will continue to exist, but is without form or substance. The truth body represents ultimate reality or the essence of enlightenment.

Source: Stephanie Curran, August 2019.

Figure 4 Kuan Yin is the Bodhisattva of compassion. A **Bodhisattva** is a person or being who delays nirvana out of desire to help relieve the suffering of others.

Two of the major sects of Mahayana Buddhism are Zen and Pure Land. Both developed in China and spread to Japan. In China, Chan (Zen in Japanese) Buddhism began in the fifth century CE. Zen emphasizes transcending reason and uncovering the pure mind, which reveals the true nature of reality, that is ultimately enlightenment. The primary means of revealing the pure mind is through sitting meditation, **zazen**. In Zen Buddhism, enlightenment comes in a flash (**satori**). Certain practices, such as koans, facilitate this flash of insight. **Koans** are riddles that help one transcend reason. The most common koan is "what is the sound of one hand clapping?"[4] Zen followers also use action to promote meditation. Some of the arts/actions that have been used to enhance mindfulness are calligraphy, the tea ceremony and the training of Bonsai plants. Zen has impacted popular culture in the West through writings such as Zen and the Art of Motorcycle Maintenance, The Dude and the Zen Master, and the poetry of Allen Ginsberg.[5]

Pure Land is another major sect of Mahayana Buddhism that is prominent in China and Japan. Pure Land Buddhism is said to date back to the earliest days of Buddhism and, in particular, draws from the Larger and Smaller Sutras on The Buddha of Infinite Light (also known as Amitāyus or **Amida Buddha**). In Pure Land, one can achieve enlightenment through meditation on, and faith in, the Amida Buddha. The Amida Buddha is the Buddha of Boundless Light and Eternal Life. The core tenets of Pure Land are described well by Suzuki. "Amida is Infinite Light, and, therefore, there is no corner of the human heart where its rays do not penetrate: he is Eternal Life, and, therefore, there is not a moment in our lives when he is not urging us to rise above ourselves."[6] Amida Buddha presides over a Pure Land of love, peace and bliss that human beings can inhabit through the unconscious mind. This unconscious mind can be tapped through meditation and can be more fully experienced after death. Dwelling in the Pure Land is living in a continual state of enlightenment filled with a love and compassion for all beings.

Vajrayana

The third major branch of Buddhism, Vajrayana, developed from the Mahayana tradition and shares many of the basic ideas and texts of Mahayana. Vajrayana allows for the ability to reach enlightenment in a single lifetime through a variety of special techniques and practices. These techniques are passed from teacher to student. In addition, some are outlined in texts known as **tantras**. The terms, Tantric or Esoteric Buddhism, have also been used to describe this path. The primary form of Vajrayana Buddhism familiar to the West is Tibetan Vajrayana.

Tibetan Vajrayana developed as Buddhism mingled with the indigenous religion of Tibet, called Bon, in the second and third centuries CE. Some imagery and practices of Tibetan Buddhism are rooted in this indigenous history, such as prayer flags, musical instruments, tulkus, and bardo. Prayer flags adorn the mountains and sacred sites of Tibetan Buddhism. These flags are white, red, yellow, blue, and green representing the five elements; in addition, each flag has a mantra or prayer written on it. As the wind blows the flags, the energy of the prayers is released.

---

[4] For more on Zen koans, see the article, "These Zen Koans Will Open Your Mind" at https://www.huffpost.com/entry/zen-buddhism-koan_n_563251dce4b0631799115f3c

[5] For more on Zen in Pop Culture, see http://zensanity.net/.

[6] Daisetsu Teitaro Suzuki, "The Shin Sect of Buddhism," *Muryoko: The Journal of Shin Buddhism*, https://www.nembutsu.info/suzuki1.htm.

Prayer wheels are also sacred objects in Tibetan Vajrayana (Figure 5). They can be small and handheld or large and fixed into the wall of a monastery. The wheels are metal canisters which also contain sacred mantras and prayers that are released as the canister is spun. The **mantra** contained in many prayer wheels is the compassion mantra: Om Mani Padme Hum.[7] Meditation centers and monasteries are also adorned with **thangkas**, or wall hangings, depicting various symbols, and mandalas. **Mandalas** are diagrams that can be drawn on thangkas or configured with sand (as in the following picture). The mandala is a geometric configuration representing the universe. Some mandalas include symbols that are readily recognizable, while others contain representations that must be explained by a teacher.[8] Some mandalas are found on thangkas; and, monks create others with sand. Mandalas are focal points for meditation, and creating them is an act of meditation in itself (Figure 6).

Teachers, or **lamas**, are extremely important in Tibetan Buddhism. Monasteries are generally aligned with a particular lineage of teachers. The honored teacher of a particular tradition is called, Rinpoche. This teacher often reincarnates, like a bodhisattva, to continue to pass on the teachings of compassion and enlightenment.

Figure 5   Prayer wheels at a monastery in Bhutan.

Figure 6   Image of Buddhist Monk creating a sand mandala in Ladakh, India in 2011. Additional mandalas can be seen painted behind him.

Reincarnated lamas are called **tulkus**. The Dalai Lama is an example of a tulku, but he is not the only one. The term, Dalai Lama, means "ocean of wisdom," and is reserved for the highest spiritual leader of Tibetan Buddhism. Historically, the Dalai Lama also served as the political leader of Tibet. However, in 2011, the Dalai Lama retired from political leadership, transferring all political authority to the democratic institutions of the Tibetan government in exile headquartered in Dharamsala, India.

The death practices of Tibetan Buddhism are also unique. The bardo is an in-between place after death and before rebirth. During the spirit's time in bardo, it is subject to various tests. By successfully completing the challenges, a spirit can escape the cycle of birth, death, and rebirth. If the spirit is not successful, it will be reborn to try again. The process of navigating death is described in *The Tibetan Book of the Dead*, which is often read aloud to those who are moving through the dying process. The book also explores the psychology of the human mind. Another widely known death practice of Tibetans is sky burial. Because the landscape is harsh and not conducive to burial and there are not enough trees for cremation, this ancient practice of dismembering the corpse and placing it in a secluded spot for the vultures to pick evokes the teaching of impermanence. The vultures are thought to be **dakini**, or "sky dancers" and are symbols of the feminine spiritual energy.

---

[7] To listen to the mantra, see https://www.youtube.com/watch?v=ZIVNY_JnuD0.
[8] https://aras.org/sites/default/files/docs/00030MandalaBrauen.pdf.

Tibetan practices have drawn a lot of attention from Western Buddhists because of Tibetan Buddhism's perceived magic and mystery. Explore one of the unique aspects of Tibetan Buddhism (i.e., thangkas, prayer wheels, mantras, music, death meditation, bardo, and tulkus). Some helpful sites include: https://library.brown.edu/cds/BuddhistTempleArt/buddhism2.html.

https://www.tibettravel.org/tibetan-buddhism/ritual-items-of-tibet-buddhism.html

https://info-buddhism.com/

http://www.lamayeshe.com/teachings;

Tibetan death meditation: https://www.youtube.com/watch?v=xRAfGkqw_cU

Tibetan Buddhist music (see pp. 17ff): https://digitalcollections.sit.edu/cgi/viewcontent.cgi?referer=https://www.google.com/&httpsredir=1&article=2077&context=isp_collection.

After researching a little about a practice, write a few sentences about what you learned.

_____

_____

_____

_____

Additional Sects

Many sects and sub-sects of Buddhism have developed throughout Asia and traveled to Australia, Europe, and North America. Some of these sects include Shingon and Nichiren.

Shingon Buddhism is a form of Vajrayana Buddhism. It originated in Japan with the teachings of a monk named, Kukai, in the ninth century BCE. Kukai was later given the title, Kobo Daishi. This form of Japanese Esoteric Buddhism emphasizes meditation on mandalas as a visual tool to enlightenment. Shingon Buddhists also focus on Dainichi Nyorai, the Cosmic Buddha, and view him as a deity. The mudra most associated with the Cosmic Buddhas is the "Mudra of the Six Elements," or "fist of wisdom," in which the left index finger is encircled by the five fingers of the right hand. A sacred pilgrimage to Mt. Koya is also practiced in this tradition (Figure 7).

Nichiren, and its sub-sect, Soka Gakkai, both began in Japan before crossing to the West. The monk, Nichiren, founded the movement in 1253 CE. In Nichiren and its branches, the focus is on the Lotus Sutra. A mantra, *nam myoho renge kyo*, is practiced to express devotion and to cultivate compassion for all living things. Nam myoho renge kyo can be roughly translated as "devotion to the Lotus Sutra." Through meditation using this mantra, it is believed that the Buddha Nature of all living things can be realized and all can become Buddhas in this present world.

Figure 7   Notice the hand position of the Buddha. This is the Mudra of the Six Elements characteristic of Shingon Buddhism.

Puripat/Shutterstock.com.

SOCIALLY ENGAGED BUDDHISM

Socially Engaged Buddhism is a more recent designation in Buddhism that is closely associated with Thich Nhat Hanh, the Vietnamese Buddhist monk, author, and retreat leader. This aspect of Buddhist practice is not limited to a particular branch or sect, but rather is a movement of Buddhists worldwide who seek to actively engage in the world around them to promote compassion and alleviate suffering. In the *Metta Sutta* of the Pali Canon, the Buddha says that loving-kindness can be described as embracing all living things in the same way that a mother cherishes her only child.[9] In addition, socially engaged Buddhism offers the ability to look at the root causes of suffering in an effort to alleviate it. For example, in looking at the problem of hunger worldwide, the socially engaged Buddhist might ask, "What is the root cause of hunger?" Determining the root causes of hunger on a personal, societal and global scale can then lead to not just individual change but systemic change.[10]

SACRED PRACTICES

Although the sacred practice most thought of in relation to Buddhism is meditation, there are a variety of other practices in which Buddhists engage, including honoring the Buddha and other teachers, providing for monks and nuns, and pilgrimages and festivals.

Tak Bat

In Thailand, Laos and other places across Southeast Asia, each morning the monks take to the streets to collect food for the day. Monks in Theravada Buddhism are not permitted to have money, and therefore, cannot buy and cook their own food. Faithful Buddhists line the street to fill the monks' bowls or baskets with food. Typically, Theravada monks eat two meals a day, breakfast and lunch. The food they receive in the morning is spread over the two meals. Food offerings to the monks, giving robes, and other gifts are part of the practice of **dana**, generosity (Figure 8).

Meditation

The primary sacred practice in Buddhism is meditation. Meditation is a practice in mindfulness. Although calming, the major purposes of meditation are to develop insight and compassion. Insight meditation, **vipassana**, involves observing the mind, diminishing negative thoughts and emotions, and gaining insight into the true nature of reality, including

Figure 8   Tak Bat food offering.

Zhang I'm Possible/Shutterstock.com.

---

[9] For the exact verse, see http://www.accesstoinsight.org/tipitaka/kn/snp/snp.1.08.amar.html.

[10] A great resource for information on socially engaged Buddhism is the "Field Guide to Socially Engaged Buddhism" produced by authors from Seattle University, accessed http://northwestdharma.org/wp-content/uploads/2012/06/Field-Guide-to-Socially-Engaged-Buddhsim.pdf.

the true nature of the self. Through vipassana meditation, a person can see the causes of suffering as well as the path to liberation.

Walking meditation and meditation in action are additional meditation practices employed in Buddhism. Many Buddhists will alternate between sitting and walking meditation. In sitting meditation, the focus is often on the breath, not to control it, but rather to observe it. In walking meditation, the focus is on the movement of the feet and the feel of them rising and falling with each step. Those who have trouble sitting still may find walking meditation a more conducive practice to stilling the mind and increasing mindfulness. Along this same line, Chögyam Trungpa, a Tibetan monk, who taught extensively in the West, wrote and spoke about "meditation in action." He recognized the Western preoccupation with busyness and emphasized meditation through movement. Dipa Ma, an Indian laywoman, also taught this practice. Anything a person does repeatedly can be an opportunity to practice mindfulness. Washing dishes, lifting weights, and peeling vegetables all provide an occasion to be present in the moment and aware of our movement. Through concentration on an action, an individual can observe and let go of thoughts, emotions, and preoccupations.

Metta, or loving-kindness meditation, is another practice within Buddhism. Through metta meditation, the practitioner directs loving-kindness toward the self, toward others the person cares for, and ultimately to those who have caused pain or suffering. The longer the meditation practice is sustained, the more the practitioner will discover he or she loves all beings, including oneself and one's worst enemy, equally. This love is not a blind love that is oblivious to faults and failings, but a sense of love and compassion in the face of flaws. The Buddha identified eleven benefits of metta meditation including better sleep, a clear mind, a radiant face, and the ability to die unconfused.[11]

Offerings and Prostration

Wandering around a meditation center, a person cannot help but notice small offerings in front of stupas and statues of the Buddha. A **stupa** is a monument that often contains relics of the Buddha or one of the arhats (saints). The stupa also stands as a symbol of enlightenment, which usually has a peak at the top to represent the attainment of wisdom. (Figure 9) Devotees will often bow in front of a stupa or statue as a sign of respect. They may also leave offerings of incense, rice, flowers, sweets, money, or other small objects. Some Buddhists will also prostrate themselves before a shrine as a sign of respect for the Triple Gem or as a way to encounter the ego and tame it.

Figure 9   Image of offerings at a stupa.

AtthameeNi/Shutterstock.com.

---

[11] For more on metta meditation, see Sharon Salzberg, "Facets of Metta," http://www.vipassana.com/meditation/facets_of_metta.php or her book, Loving Kindness: The Revolutionary Art of Happiness.

Relics

Relics of the Buddha, and other Buddhist teachers, have been part of Buddhist iconography from the earliest days of Buddhism. The legend is that when the Buddha died, in the cremation ashes, were the remnants of tooth and bone. These relics were divided into eight portions and spread throughout Southeast Asia. The relics of the Buddha and other teachers often appear like small pearls of various colors and are held in mini stupas. They absorb energy and can either multiply or decrease in amount based on the practice of the community (Figure 10).

Source: Stephanie Curran.

Figure 10   Image of relics in small stupas from Wat Thai in Silver Spring, Maryland.

Festivals

Although there are festivals specific to Buddhist countries such as celebrating the New Year or the Sri Lankan Festival of the Sacred Tooth,[12] the most widely celebrated Buddhist festival is **Vesak** (sometimes spelled Wesak). This festival celebrates the major events in the life of the Buddha, including his birth, enlightenment, and death. The date of this festival varies between late May and early June from year to year. As Buddhists generally follow a lunar-based calendar, the dates of this festival vary between late May and early June depending on the year.

In addition, the dates can vary by country as well. Celebrations typically include parades, music, lighting lanterns, eating vegetarian meals, visiting monasteries and temples, and practicing charity (dana) (Figure 11).

Calvin Chan/Shutterstock.com.

Figure 11   Vesak procession in Malaysia.

☯ Choose a Buddhist festival or sacred practice to look into a little deeper. What did you choose? Briefly describe two new things you learned about this festival or practice.

_____

_____

_____

_____

_____

---

[12] For more information about the Sacred Tooth Festival, see https://theculturetrip.com/asia/sri-lanka/articles/the-festival-of-the-tooth-a-unique-symbol-of-sri-lanka/

BUDDHISM IN THE UNITED STATES

Buddhism first came to the United States through Chinese immigrants in the 1840s. Buddhists, including a Zen master and a Theravadan monk, were also part of the World's Parliament of Religions in 1893. Furthermore, the Transcendentalists, like Thoreau and Emerson, and members of the Theosophical Society, such as Madame Helena Blavatsky and Henry Steele Olcott, were very interested in Buddhism. Olcott is sometimes described as the first American Buddhist.

The first Chinese temple was built in San Francisco in 1853. It combined Buddhist and Taoist practice. By the turn of the century, the West Coast was home to many Chinese temples. Americans of European descent founded a sangha based on Jodo Shinshu in 1900. One of the oldest Buddhist organizations in the United States is the federation of the Buddhist Churches of America, which grew out of the Jodo Shinshu mission and has over 60 temples across the country today.[13]

Source: Stephanie Curran.

Figure 12   Land Purification Ceremony for peace pagoda at Xa Loi Temple. The event included participation from a group of visiting Japanese monks as well as Native American dancers.

From early in its history in the United States, Buddhism has grown not only through immigration, but also through conversion. Many in this country are drawn to the philosophy and practices of Buddhism. Buddhist temples, monasteries, Sanghas, and meditation centers dot the landscape across the country. In Frederick, Maryland, two Buddhist centers are an integral part of the community. Chua Xa Loi Temple, a Vietnamese Buddhist Center, houses many relics of the Buddha and other spiritual masters. The center provides meditation classes and weekly services. They are also building a peace pagoda as a witness to peace and as a way to bring all people together. The other community is the Tibetan Meditation Center (TMC) located in Gambrill State Park. The TMC was founded in 1982. It has recently expanded its offerings to the community by opening a second meditation center in downtown Frederick as well. TMC offers meditation classes, courses on Buddhism, and weekly services. Both Xa Loi and TMC offer the community a quiet retreat to meditate and contemplate through beautiful grounds, stupas, and statues of the Buddha (Figure 12).

---

[13] For more detail on the timeline of Buddhism in America, see The Pluralism Project, http://pluralism.org/timelines/tradition/buddhism/

☯ What questions did you have as you read the chapter? What more would you like to know about the history or practice of this religious tradition?

_____

_____

_____

_____

_____

WEB RESOURCES FOR FURTHER STUDY

http://www.bdk.or.jp/document/dgtl-dl/dBET_ThreePureLandSutras_2003.pdf—This document is an English translation of the three major Pure Land Sutras done in 1995.

http://www.buddhanet.net/ebooks_ms.htm—This site offers various translations of the major Mahayana sutras.

https://digitalcollections.sit.edu/isp_collection/1065/—This link is to a great article on the role of music and ritual in Tibetan Buddhism.

http://www.nembutsu.info/—Online Journal of Shin Buddhism with some great articles describing Pure Land Buddhism.

http://northwestdharma.org/wp-content/uploads/2012/06/Field-Guide-to-Socially-Engaged-Buddhsim.pdf—This guide explores various aspects of socially engaged Buddhism from its definition to its application.

http://www.palicanon.org/—This website is a great resource on the history of the Pali Canon as well as a translation of some of the text.

http://www.vipassana.com/meditation/facets_of_metta.php—An article by Sharon Salzberg on metta, or loving kindness, meditation practice.

http://zensanity.net/—This blog explores the intersection between Zen and popular culture.

Chapter 6
Jainism

Key Terms

Ahimsa	Jiva	Nirvana
Ajiva	Kalachakra	Sallekhana
Anekantwad	Karma	Samsara
Aparigraha	Kevala	Svetambara
Digambara	Loka	Swastika
Diksha	Mahavira	Tirthankara
Jina	Moksha	Tonk

INTRODUCTION

Both Buddhism and Jainism deviated from the Vedic scriptures and the religious implications of the caste system. Jainism has never condoned war, the caste system or the killing of animals for any reason. Some consider Jainism an offshoot of Hinduism. However, Jain scholars believe it has ancient, non-Vedic, and indigenous origins. Jains have their own unique identity, scripture, and practice which is distinct from Hinduism. The essence of Jain dharma is the truth of nonviolence and asceticism as the way to achieve enlightenment and release from the cycle of birth, death, and rebirth. The quote regarding

> The essence of right conduct is not to injure anyone; one should know only this, that noninjury is religion.
> —Naladiyar 14, 15

nonviolence as religion comes from the Naladiyar, one of the most important Jain ethical writings originating in the Tamil region of India.

Jain Cosmology

As with Hinduism, Jains believe that time is cyclical and unending. The universe is driven by an eternal energy. Each world cycle is divided into two halves; each made up of six time periods. The total of 12 periods in the world cycle is demonstrated by a wheel with 12 spokes, called **Kalachakra**. During the first half of the world cycle, things get progressively worse; while, in the second half is one of ascending morality and happiness. During each world cycle, 24 **tirthankaras** are born to show the way to enlightenment. The Jain universe is referred to as **loka**, vast, finite, and eternal space. There is no beginning and no end; therefore, there is also no emphasis on a creator being.

Tirthankaras

Jain tradition states that there are 24 tirthankaras (ford-makers or crossing builders) born into the world during the third and fourth periods of each world cycle to steer people away from evil and toward the path to enlightenment. These spiritual teachers serve as bridges between this life and **Nirvana** and point the way to ethical living. Another term used for the Tirthankaras and others who are viewed as teachers is **jina**. A jina is one who has conquered passions and attachments and has achieved a state of equanimity and peace. It is from this title that Jainism gets its name. Jains do not hold the

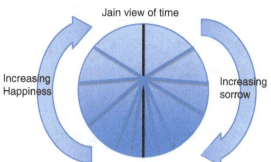

In Jainism, time is cyclical. When one cycle ends another begins. Each cycle is divided in halves. The first half is a period of increasing suffering and sorrow. The second half is one of decreasing sorrow and increasing happiness and peace. Each half is divided into six periods of differing lengths.
Source: Stephanie Curran

belief that these individuals can get you to Nirvana; rather, they believe that the teachings they offer and the practices they suggest, when applied to one's life, can help an individual achieve liberation (**moksha**).

Mahavira

Mahavira is the last of 24 tirthankaras. He was born around 599 BCE in the fourth period of this world cycle. The "wretched" fifth period, in which we now live, began 3 years after Mahavira died. He is another of the great religious leaders who came out of the Axial Age discussed in the chapter on Buddhism.

His birth name was Nataputta Vardhamana; and, he was born in Kundagrama, near Patna in Northeast India close to the sacred Ganges River. The term, Mahavira, is a title, meaning "great hero," rather than a proper name. Like Siddhartha Gautama, the founder of Buddhism,

Figure 1   Mahavira meditating.

he was a prince of the Kshatriya caste who renounced his position at the age of 30 to wander as a spiritual seeker. He practiced extreme asceticism, or denial of the body, and is said to have endured the cruelty of villagers. After 12 years of meditation, fasting, and silence, Mahavira achieved liberation and perfection.

The two major branches of Jainism, the Digambaras ("sky clad") and Svetambaras ("white clad") differ in their understandings of how Mahavira spent his time after enlightenment. Mahavira died and was released from the cycle of rebirth at the age of 72. The monastic life is considered the ideal in Jainism and from the earliest days the community of Jains consisted of monks and nuns. Interestingly, the number of nuns in the early days outnumbered the number of monks. However, nuns never had the status afforded to monks.

☯ What do you think may have attracted people to this movement? Read the brief article at http://www.jainpedia.org/themes/people/women-in-the-jain-tradition.html. In a sentence or two, summarize the view of women in Jainism.

_____

_____

_____

_____

MAJOR BRANCHES OF JAINISM

As mentioned earlier, there are two major branches, or sects, of Jainism: the Digambaras and Svetambaras. Each branch also has one or two subsects. The stricter, more orthodox sect is the Digambaras. The word, Digambara, is translated as "sky clad." The term derives from the fact that monks in this tradition do not wear clothing. Nuns, however, wear a simple white robe. Digambaras believe that only men can achieve liberation; women must be reborn as a male to be released from the cycle of birth, death, and rebirth.

The Svetambaras, or "white clad," differ from the Digambaras on several points. First, Svetambharas monks do not practice nudity; both monks and nuns wear white robes. Second, Svetambharas believe that women can achieve liberation and assert that the 19th tirthankara was a woman. An additional difference is related to the two sect's views of the sacred texts.

SACRED TEXTS

The reciting of sacred texts is one aspect of Jain rituals; however, the various branches of Jainism have differing beliefs about which texts are canonical, or authoritative. Many of the early texts have been lost. The scriptures can basically be divided into two types: the Agam Sutras and Non-Agam writings. The 12 original Ang Agam sutras were collections of the sermons of Mahavira. The Digambara sect believes that all of these originals were lost; however, the Svetambhara sect asserts that 11 of the originals and between 21 and 34 additional Agam Sutras survive and form the basis of the Jain canon today. These sutras outline the doctrines and traditions of Jainism. There are two ancient texts written by Jain scholars that are recognized as sacred by the Digambara sect: the Satkhandagama (Scripture in Six Parts) and the Kashay Pahud (Treatise on the Attachments to this World). The texts for both sects were passed on orally from teacher to students before being written down. Jains continue to practice this tradition by studying the scriptures with a teacher.

The Non-Agam writings are commentaries and explanations of the earlier teachings of the Agam sutras as well as other scholarly works. An important example of the non-Agam sutras is the Kalpa Sutra, which contains stories about all of the Jain tirthankaras.[1]

MAJOR BELIEFS

Jainism holds several beliefs in common with Hinduism and Buddhism. They share the views of samsara, moksha, and nirvana. Jains, like Hindus and Buddhists, also believe in karma; however, in Jain understanding, karma takes on a physical reality as minute particles. As clay clings to one's hands, so karma clings to one's body and literally holds people to the cycle of birth, death, and rebirth. Like Theravada Buddhism, Jainism is also nontheistic. An individual's life is a direct result of his or her own actions; and it is only through effort and practice on the part of the individual that liberation from the continual cycle of birth, death and rebirth can be achieved. Spiritual beings exist, but they are subject to the same limitations as human beings. One can only achieve liberation from a human state. Jainism has also been called, transtheistic. Transtheism refers to a belief in a Truth or Reality greater than gods or gods.

Jainism is dualistic in understanding. That is to say, there are two separate realities—jiva (the soul or spirit) and ajiva (matter or the physical realm). Jiva is similar to the concept of atman in Hinduism. All living things have jiva and are capable of suffering. This belief leads Jains to seek to cause as little harm as possible in the world. It is said that nonviolence (ahimsa) is the essence of Jain religion. Although it is impossible to avoid all harm, the goal is to do the least amount of harm possible.

Jains are strict vegetarians eating no meat, fish, or eggs. Many also do not eat root vegetables, such as potatoes, carrots, and onions because they are uprooted from the earth killing the plant and potentially harming living organisms in the soil. Dairy products are acceptable, but cheese and yogurt must be made and consumed the same day. Yeast and fermented foods, such as vinegar and alcohol are also discouraged. Strict Jains also avoid eating after dark. Some Jains wear a cloth mask over their mouths in order to prevent breathing in tiny organisms.

Nonattachment (aparigraha) is also central to Jain understanding. You may remember that aparigraha is also one of the five yamas (ethical principles) in Hinduism. Like karma, attachments can also weigh us down to the cycle of birth, death, and rebirth. Jains live simply and avoid the accumulation of wealth by practicing charity. Though monks and nuns avoid attachment to human relationships, they strive to cultivate compassion toward all people. Meditation and fasting are practices that help foster nonattachment.

A third important belief for Jains is the affirmation that our own understanding is limited (anekantwad). Our view of truth is only partial, and our perception is limited. It might help to think of anekantwad as nonattachment to ideas or thoughts. Knowledge and reason are prized, as is scientific discovery, but they are necessarily incomplete. The story of the blind men touching the elephant is a

---

[1] To learn more about the Jain sacred texts, see http://www.sacred-texts.com/jai/.

great example of this principle. The one who holds the tail describes what an elephant looks like much differently than the one who is touching the side of the elephant. Like Buddhists, Jains recognize that things are constantly changing and the way something appears next week is different from the way it appears now. This principle also fosters tolerance of other's viewpoints.

JAIN SYMBOL

The Jain symbol pictured at right combines key aspects of Jain thought. The semicircle at the top points to the dwelling place of those who have achieved liberation from the cycle of birth, death, and rebirth. The three dots represent the essence of Jain practice: (1) right faith, (2) right knowledge, and (3) right conduct. The swastika itself represents well-being, while the four spokes represent the ever turning cycle of reincarnation. The raised hand reminds one to stop and think before engaging in any activity. The wheel, like the spokes of the swastika, is symbolic of the cycle of samsara. Inside the wheel are 24 radiating lines signifying the 24 tirthankaras. The word inside the wheel is "ahimsa," the central tenet of Jainism. The outline encompassing the dots, swastika and hand represent loka, or the finite space in which all beings live.[2]

Infinite Graphics/ Shutterstock.com.

Figure 2

SPIRITUAL PRACTICES

In both branches of Jainism, the monastic lifestyle is the ideal, and the only way, one can achieve liberation and enlightenment. In Jainism, the state of enlightenment is known as kevala. It is a state of omniscience in which one can see everything as it is, including one's own past life as well as the past lives of others.

One becomes a monk or nun by going through an initiation ritual (diksha). During this initiation, one's hair is removed and the initiate receives the traditional whisk or broom that is one of the few possessions of a monk or a nun. The whisk is used to brush off chairs before one sits or to brush the path on which one is walking in order to avoid harming insects or other tiny living organisms. Depending on the sect, one also receives a water bowl and an alms bowl used to receive food from lay followers. Only one meal a day is consumed as part of the monastic lifestyle of abstinence and restraint.

Monks and nuns take five great vows including nonviolence, honesty, not taking anything that has not been freely given, celibacy, and

Daniel J. Rao/Shutterstock.com.

Figure 3

---

[2] For more information on the Jain symbol, see https://jainworld.com/education/jain-education-material/jain-symbol/.

the avoidance of attachments. Monks and nuns spend their time in meditation and in the teaching of lay followers. They walk barefoot wherever they need to go; however, they avoid going out during the 4-month rainy season to prevent harm to living things they cannot see in the puddles. Lay followers of Jainism also strive to live by many of these virtues to the extent possible.

Sallekhana

One of the most controversial practices of some Jain monks and nuns is that of fasting until death (sallekhana). It should be stated that not all monks and nuns engage in this practice; and, it is only undertaken after careful discernment and in the context of community. According to Justice Tukol in his book, Sallekhana is not suicide; sallekhana and its parameters can be defined as follows:

> *Sallekhana is facing death (by an ascetic or householder) voluntarily when he is nearing his end and when normal life according to religion is not possible due to old-age, incurable disease, severe famine, etc. after subjugation of all passions and abandonment of all worldly attachments, by observance of austerities gradually abstaining from food and water, and by simultaneous meditation on the real nature of the Self until the soul parts from the body. (Tukol, 7)*[3]

The practice involves embracing death on one's own terms with a sense of serenity and complete nonattachment. The process of engaging in this form of death takes a month or more; and, the community gathers around the individual to meditate, sing sacred songs and chant mantras.

Sallekhana raises issues of the human relationship to decisions of life and death. It encourages us to explore questions of who controls life and death as well as the myriad of ways individual decisions contribute to one's death. Sean Hillman, a PhD candidate at the University of Toronto, wrote a fascinating article several years ago about the lessons of sallekhana in relationship to end of life care.[4] He suggests that the Jain practice of withdrawing life sustaining treatment (whether food, liquid, or medical interventions) while simultaneously tending to emotional and spiritual preparations for one's passing can be useful in palliative care for non-Jains.

☯ Think of end of life decisions as a continuum of involvement in one's own passing with "natural" death at one end of the spectrum and what we typically think of as suicide on the other.

⟵――――――――――――――――――――――⟶

Natural death   Suicide

Where would you put the following forms of death on the continuum? Refusing medical treatment? Abstaining from food after the loss of a life partner of many years? Bad health habits, such as smoking or

---

[3] Justice Tukol, *Sallekhana is Not Suicide* (Ahmedabad: LD Institute of Indology, 1976).
[4] "Sallekhana and End-of-life Care: Jain Voluntary and Controlled Death in Equanimity through Fasting and Reduction of Activity as a Model for Secular Health Care." International Summer School for Jain Studies research conference; New Delhi, India (2010).

overeating? Drinking and driving? Martyrdom? Sallekhana? What are your thoughts on the end of life decision-making? Do you think sallekhana is suicide? Why or why not? _____

_____

_____

_____

_____

_____

Meditation

As it is in Hinduism and Buddhism, meditation is a central spiritual practice in Jainism. Meditation is also known as the practice of equanimity. Observant Jains practice daily meditation as well as the chanting of mantras and prayers.

The story of Bahubali, a Jain saint, illustrates the importance of meditation. Bahubali was the son of the first tirthankara. He refused to submit to the authority of his brother. There are various accounts of the struggle between the two brothers, but ultimately Bahubali chose to renounce attachments to the world. From that point, he stood on the very spot he fought with his brother and meditated. It is said that he meditated so long that vines began to creep up his body. A 57-foot statue of Bahubali meditating was built in Karnataka, India, to commemorate his perseverance. Standing meditation is very common among Jain monks and nuns.

Figure 4

Confession

Confession, repentance, and making amends for one's transgressions are important practices for Jains. Twice a day, Jain monks and nuns reflect on their thoughts and actions, confess their wrongdoing and seek forgiveness. Lay followers of Jainism also practice confession and repentance regularly every few weeks or months as well as during festivals.

Puja and Veneration of the Tirthankaras

Puja, including veneration of tirthankaras and teachers, is an important part of spiritual practice for many Jains. Puja can be performed at home at a household shrine, or more elaborately at the temple. Bowing, waving a lamp, lighting incense, and offering rice, flowers, or fruit are common aspects of puja. Puja may also involve bathing a statue of the tirthankaras with milk or water. The liquid used is often collected and used to anoint the worshipper's forehead. As in many religious traditions, bathing before worship is crucial in Jain tradition. Often, lay followers will have a special set of clothes that they only wear to the temple.

Universal Forgiveness Prayer

खामेमि सव्वजीवे, सव्वे जीवा खमंतु मे।
मित्ती मे सव्व भूएसु, वेरम् वेरं मज्झं न केणइ॥

Khāmemi Savva Jive, Savve Jivā Khamantu Me,
Mitti Me Savva Bhuesu, Veram Majjham Na Kenai.

I forgive all living beings,
May all living beings grant me forgiveness.
My friendship is with all living beings,
I have no enmity with anyone.

"Universal Forgiveness Prayer" translated by Pravin Shah. Translation copyright © 2015 by Pravin Shah. Reprinted by permission.

Prayers for peace and the giving of thanks for the teaching of the tirthankaras are another aspect of veneration. The goal of prayer is not to seek blessings, but to express gratitude and a desire to cultivate the virtues taught by the great teachers within one self.[5]

Festivals and Pilgrimages

Rather than celebrations with dancing and feasting, Jain festivals are times of fasting, abstinence, confession, and recitation of sacred hymns. Diwali is commemorated in Jainism, but not in the same way as in Hinduism. In Jainism, Diwali marks Mahavira's attainment of moksha, liberation from the cycle of birth, death, and rebirth. One of the most important pilgrimage sites is the temple at Patna in Bihar, in eastern India. It is believed that Mahavira gave his last sermon here. Some make this pilgrimage on Diwali as it is also the place where he experienced moksha.

Other pilgrimages sites for Jains include various temples as well as the sacred Mount Parsvanatha, in the state of Jharkand. Jains believe 20 of the 24 tirthankaras achieved moksha on this sacred mountain. The walk to the shrine honoring the 23rd tirthankara is nearly 18 miles long up and back.[6] Every 12 years, pilgrims travel to Karnataka for the anointing of the statue of Bahubali. Other sacred temples are located in Rajasthan and Gujarat.

JAINISM IN NORTH AMERICA

Jainism was introduced in the United States at the World's Parliament of Religions in 1893 when V.R. Gandhi addressed the gathering. Today there are between 100,000 and 150,000 Jains in the United States as well as many Jain temples in states from Missouri, Ohio, and Pennsylvania to New Jersey, New York, California, Oregon, and Texas. Most of the Jain population came to the United States after the

---

[5] Universal Forgiveness Prayer from http://www.jainelibrary.org/$Jain_Catholic_Diagogue/Jain-Catholic_Dialogue_on_Compassion.pdf.
[6] http://www.vam.ac.uk/content/articles/j/jain-pilgrimage/.

Immigration Act of 1965. The Federation of Jain Associations in North America formed in 1980 and is an active voice for Jainism today.

A Jain monastery, and the first Jain pilgrimage site outside of India, is located in the Pocono Mountains. Siddhachalam was founded in 1983 and has 31 tonks, places of meditation marking sites of enlightenment. A dedication ceremony for the last one was held November 15, 2015.[7]

Young Jains have also organized in the United States to promote their faith. Their organization is the Young Jains of America (www.yja.org). They hold regular regional and national gatherings for Jain youth between the ages of 14 and 29.[8] The organization is engaged in community service, fellowship and education and helps connect Jain youth across the country as well as promote Jain values of nonviolence and simplicity.

☯ Explore the website for the Young Jains of America (www.yja.org). Describe at least one interesting piece of information you found as well as one insight or connection you were able to make to the information in this chapter.

_____

_____

_____

_____

_____

_____

WEB RESOURCES FOR FURTHER STUDY

https://www.jaina.org/?ReligiousArticles—This link provides information about the basic thoughts or ideas that are central to Jain philosophy.

https://www.jainuniversity.org—A wealth of information about the history, beliefs, and practices of Jainism.

---

[7] http://www.siddhachalam.org/.
[8] http://yja.org/yja-convention/.

https://jainworld.com/philosophy/prayer-prarthana/ —The article at this link discusses the Jain view of prayer given that Jains believe that salvation is purely through one's own efforts. The homepage of this website (www.jainworld.com) offers a variety of resources and information about Jainism.

https://www.nytimes.com/2010/07/18/books/review/excerpt-nine-lives.html —An abbreviated version of a chapter from William Dalrymple's book, *Nine Lives*. This article offers a nun's reflection on the practice of Jainism and more specifically sallekhana.

https://yja.org/ —This is the homepage for Young Jains of America. Resources include educational tools, recipes, and information about prayer and meditation.

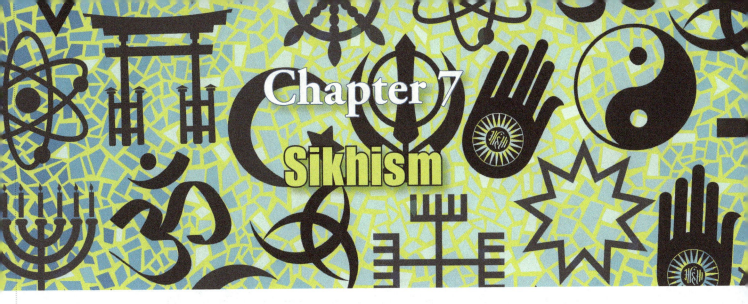

Chapter 7
Sikhism

Learning Outcomes

By the end of the chapter, students will be able to

- ☞ describe the origins and development of Sikhism;
- ☞ identify the founder, sacred texts, and central beliefs of Sikhism;
- ☞ discuss the view of guruship related to God, teachers, scripture, and the community;
- ☞ trace the historical development of the ten gurus; and
- ☞ explain the sacred practices of Sikhism.

Key Terms

Adi Granth (Guru Granth Sahib)	Kachera	Langar
Amrit	Kangha	Mool Mantra
Amrit Sanchar	Karah Prasad	Nam
Amritsar	Kesh	Nam Simaran
Gurdwara	Khalsa	Ramananda
Guru Gobind Singh	Khanda	Sants
Guru Nanak	Kirpan	Sat
Japji	Kirtan	Sikh

INTRODUCTION TO SIKHISM

The final religious tradition that we will explore which arises out of India is Sikhism. Having been founded in the late fifteenth and early sixteenth centuries, it is one of the newest major religions. Although Sikhism shares some characteristics with Hinduism and Islam, it arises from a totally new revelation. Some of the similarities result from Sikhism's origins in the Punjab region of India where Hindus and Muslims lived together. At times, the relationship between the two religions was tense, but some Hindu and Muslim mystics sought to build bridges between the two religions by gathering to pray, sing, and worship. Three examples of these early efforts with mystical union include:

♦ The work of the Hindu saint, Ramananda, who engaged in theological debates with representatives of both religions seeking to find and highlight the common ground between the two.
♦ Second, a group of sants (think of saints without the "I") gathered together to worship and encourage devotion to God. They transcended religious divisions and sought to break down barriers between people. They were part of a bhakti movement in Northern India.
♦ Third, the Muslim weaver **Kabir** (1400–1518) became the student of the Hindu saint, Ramananda. Kabir wrote songs expressing devotion to God and asserted that differences between Hinduism and Islam could be overcome through mystical experience. He believed that different religions offered paths to communion with the same God.

Guru Nanak, founder of the Sikh tradition, shared these views and sought to bridge the gap among religions through an emphasis on devotion.

LIFE OF GURU NANAK

Guru Nanak was born to a Hindu family in the Punjab region of India in 1469. As a child, he seemed to be in another world most of the time. When he reached adulthood, he married and had two children. Although Nanak worked for a while as a bookkeeper, he did not enjoy this job. Nanak and his childhood friend, Mardana, began to meet early in the morning and in the evenings to sing hymns and discuss religious truth. Mardana, a Muslim, was a poet and musician. In the tradition of the sant, others began to join them.

At the age of thirty, Nanak had a profound religious experience of immersion in the river and communion with God. Nanak and Mardana went to the river Bain to bathe. After going under the water, Guru Nanak did not resurface. Everyone thought he had drowned. However, he emerged three days later in the same spot and spoke the first words of the Japji, that form the beginning of the Sikh scripture and the start of morning prayers. During this mystical experience, God gave Nanak a drink from the cup of immortality. The nectar in the cup is referred to as amrit, a mixture of ground sugar and water.

From the moment of his immersion and experience with God, Nanak felt called to teach people to live compassionate and holy lives. Nanak traveled with Mardana throughout India, Afghanistan, Iraq, and Syria to preach and sing about devotion to God and living lives of compassion and justice. Tradition holds that they traveled over 30,000 miles primarily on foot.

Nanak claimed to be neither Muslim nor Hindu. He blended the clothing style of both groups. He drew followers from both religious traditions and continued to teach and preach until his death in 1539. A similar story is told of both Kabir and Nanak that illustrates the unwillingness of either sant to be known as exclusively Hindu or Muslim. Before his death, his followers debated over how his body should be handled when he died. Muslims do not cremate, whereas, Hindus do.

To settle the dispute Nanak told his Muslim followers to put flowers on one side of his body and his Hindu followers to put flowers on the other side. He declared that the side whose flowers remained the freshest the next morning would decide the way in which his body would be handled. The flowers and the body were covered with a sheet. The next day, when his followers raised the sheet, they found no body, only the flowers which were still fresh and fragrant (Figure 1).

Figure 1 Procession in New Dehli celebrating the birthday of Guru Nanak.

THE SUCCESSION OF GURUS

In the formative years of Sikhism, a series of ten gurus guided and furthered its development. Before his death, Nanak appointed a disciple, Angad Dev, as his successor. Angad Dev continued the Sikh tradition in the common language of the people (in contrast to Hinduism which was taught in the orthodox language of Sanskrit). He also collected the traditional stories about Nanak, which are referred to as *Janam–sakhi*, stories of the gurus. Amar Das furthered the message of equality and particularly championed equality for women, opposing the Indian practice of **sati**, the tradition of a wife committing suicide by throwing herself on the funeral pyre of her husband. Ram Das, the fourth guru, emphasized the practice of **kirtan**, hymn singing; and, as with other gurus, wrote many hymns that would become part of the Adi Granth. One of his hymns is the foundation of the Sikh wedding service.

Arjan Dev, the fifth guru, built the Golden Temple and collected the 3,000 hymns together to create the Adi Granth, the sacred scripture of Sikhism (Figure 2). He is also said to have created

Ten Gurus of Sikhism		
1.	Nanak	1469–1539
2.	Angad Dev	1539–1552
3.	Amar Das	1552–1574
4.	Ram Das	1574–1581
5.	Arjan Dev	1581–1606
6.	Har Gobind	1606–1644
7.	Har Rai	1644–1661
8.	Har Krishnan	1661–1664
9.	Teg Bahadar	1664–1675
10.	Gobind Singh	1675–1708

a system of charitable giving similar to the Islamic pillar of zakat. Arjan died of torture because he refused to adopt full Islamic practice. Arjan's death by torture led to a more military tradition, as a means of defense. Har Gobind, Arjan's successor, employed martial arts and the carrying of weapons. This began a long tradition within Sikhism of performing martial arts, showcased each year in the celebration of Holla Mohalla, a festival instituted by Gobind Singh, the tenth guru.

Figure 2   Golden Temple at Amritsar.

Har Rai and his son, Har Krishnan were the seventh and eighth gurus. They continued the military tradition started by Har Gobind, Har Rai's father. Before Har Rai passed away, he named his younger son, Har Krishnan as his successor. Har Krishnan was only five years old, but was known to heal many during a smallpox epidemic in Delhi. Unfortunately, he succumbed to the disease when he was eight years old.

Many of the gurus were known for standing up for religious freedom and opposing the Moghul practice of forced conversions. The ninth guru, Teg Bahadar continued the fight to oppose involuntary conversions. In addition, he built the Sikh city of Anandpur Sahib, which continues to be a holy site for Sikhs today. He was martyred for refusing to convert to Islam.

The tenth and final human guru, **Gobind Singh** (Gobind the Lion) established the **Khalsa**, the community of baptized Sikhs. The Khalsa will be described in more detail in the section on sacred practices. The Moghuls martyred four of Gobind Singh's sons. Perhaps anticipating his own assassination, Gobind Singh transferred authority to the Adi Granth (the sacred text) declaring that the living presence of the Gurus was embodied in the sacred scriptures. The Adi Granth became known as the Guru Granth Sahib, the eternal guru.

SACRED TEXTS

The **Adi Granth, or Guru Granth Sahib** is the central scripture of Sikhism. It is made up of 5,867 hymns and is divided into three sections:

◆ The first section includes the morning prayer, *Japji*; the evening prayer; *Rahiras*; and the *Kirtan Sohila*, a series of hymns recited before bed. The Japji is a fairly long poem by Nanak that summarizes the religion and is recited as part of morning prayers.

◆ The second part is a collection of thirty nine tunes (or **ragas**) by Nanak and later Gurus. There are ragas associated with certain times of days as well as seasons of the year.[1]

◆ The third part, the post raga section, is a collection of additional poems and hymns that end with a verse affirming that nothing can be added to the sacred text.

---

[1] Simren Kaur, Sri Guru Granth Sahib: Its Structure, Sikh Institute, http://sikhinstitute.org/july_2012/6-simran.pdf.

In addition to the Adi Granth, the **Dasam Granth,** containing additional poems, prayers, and hymns compiled by Gobind Singh is the second most important text. The scriptures are treated with reverence, read daily, and consulted for solutions to everyday problems.

The Guru Granth Sahib is kept in every gurdwara (place of worship) as well as prayer rooms in people's homes. It is read devotionally and treated reverently. The text is elevated above the floor and holds pride of place in the room. One's shoes should be removed when entering the room and the text covered when not in use. When it is read, a whisk, or **chaur**, is waved over the text as a sign of respect. This practice represents Indian culture rather than holding a specific religious meaning.

CENTRAL BELIEFS OF SIKHISM

The followers of Guru Nanak were referred to as Sikhs, which means "disciples, students or seekers of the truth."[2]. The first central belief in Sikhism is the tenet that there is one God, The True Name. God has many names or characteristics but these names represent the same power. Some "names" for God in Sikhism include Sat (Truth), **Ik Onkar** (the One Supreme Being), and Vaheguru (Wonderful Lord). Recitation of the names of God (nam simaran) is an important devotional practice in Sikhism. Nanak believed that God could be contacted through the human heart. The use of images of the gurus is expressly forbidden in Sikhism as it can lead to idolatry. In April 2015, a controversy arose over the depiction of Nanak in an Indian movie about the founder, *Nanak Shah Fakir*. Eventually the producer withdrew the film at the direction of Sikh leaders. Although the film did not show the "face" of the guru, some Sikhs felt even the depiction of the life of the prophet in a movie violated Sikh precepts.

Nanak accepted the Hindu doctrines of reincarnation and karma and taught that we can escape rebirth by achieving mystical union with God through the practice of meditation. Devotional singing, kirtan, is often part of meditative practice. The sacred sounds of God's name can bring you closer to that sense of oneness with God. The Mool Mantra[3], is repeated at least three times a day as part of prayer. This passage is at the beginning of each of the three sections of the sacred text.

In Sikhism, there is a strong sense of social equality and responsibility. God's light is spread throughout the world through hard work, worship, charity, love, and justice. Sikhism opposed the caste system and continues to teach that all people should be treated equally. A couple of Sikh practices directly contrast with the caste system in India. First, the communal meal, langar, is served daily at many **gurdwaras**. Everyone eats together, a practice that was forbidden by the caste system (those of lower caste could not eat with those of higher caste). The meal is typically vegetarian so that no one is excluded. A second practice that emphasizes equality is that baptized Sikh men have the last name Singh (which means "lion"). Baptized women have the last name Kaur (which means "prince" or "princess"). Guru Gobind Singh instituted this practice of same last names because in India one's last name generally denoted caste. In addition, men and women are treated equally in Sikhism. Religiously and socially, women are viewed equally and can both perform religious ceremonies and tasks.

---

[2] Mary Pat Fisher, *Living Religions* (Prentice Hall, 2012), 275.

[3] To read the text of the Mool Mantra see: http://www.bradfordgurdwara.com/intro-to-sikhism/mool-mantar/; to listen to the prayer, visit https://www.youtube.com/watch?v=eZxzuwQVk2M

SACRED PRACTICES OF SIKHISM

The devout Sikh prays five times a day. As with other traditions (including Hinduism and Islam), purification is essential before beginning prayers. One aspect of prayer practice that is central to Sikhism is the idea of subduing the ego. Our human tendency is to see ourselves as the center of the universe. Through prayer and meditation, human beings can change this view to see God as the center of the universe. Repetition of the name of God (**nam simaran**) is also an important part of daily meditation. In reciting the name of God, one experiences union with God. The **nam**, or name of God, is seen as the essence of divine presence. In the practice of meditation, Sikhs meditate on the names and the characteristics of the sacred.

Sikhs hold worship services in **gurdwaras** ("gates to the gurus") or temples. The most sacred site for Sikhs is the Golden Temple at Amritsar. It is often a place of pilgrimage. However, the sacred text, the Guru Granth Sahib, warns that pilgrimages and fasts are useless if they are only done to elevate the self.

Many gurdwaras hold services twice daily (morning and evening). However, in the United States, the largest services are typically on Sundays. All are welcome at the gurdwara. When entering the prayer room, people remove their shoes, and men and women cover their heads. Everyone sits on the floor and one's feet should not face the sacred text. The service is led by a **granthi**, anyone who reads from the sacred text. Any baptized Sikh can lead prayers and readings. Those who serve as granthi for a congregation are not seen as superior to or separate from other Sikhs; rather, they have taken on the responsibility to read, study, and serve as caretaker for the sacred text. Often, they are responsible for scheduling services and leading kirtan. Congregational worship includes prayers, hymns, a sermon, and the offering of **karah prashad**. Karah prashad is a sweet pudding made of equal parts of flour, butter, and sugar; it is representative

> Even if one takes cleansing baths at the sixty-eight shrines of pilgrimage, and wanders over the whole planet, and performs all the rituals of purification day and night, still, without the true guru, there is only darkness.
>
> — Guru Granth Sahib 495

of the sweet grace offered by God to all. While making the pudding, the sacred scriptures are recited. After the service, a communal meal, **langar**, is served at which all are welcome (Figure 3). As mentioned earlier in the chapter, this meal was a direct challenge to the caste system. The meal combines elements of hospitality, justice, and community.

Kirtan, or devotional singing, is another important practice in Sikhism. Kirtan is part of festivals, personal devotion, and services at the gurdwara. For many religious traditions, the singing of hymns as a form of devotion is an essential sacred practice.

Saikat Paul/Shutterstock.com.

Figure 3 Community Langar in Calcutta. The langar is a meal shared by the whole community and is prepared daily in many gurdwaras.

Listen to a kirtan from http://www.sikhnet.com/gurbani/album/shabad-kirtan, You Tube or other music source. What did you notice about the music? List at least three words that describe the music and your experience of it. As an alternative, explore things to know when visiting a gurdwara. Share two new insights you learned. Some links to explore include: http://wanderlustandlipstick.com/blogs/travelpurpose/2012/02/29/visiting-a-sikh-temple-how-to-step-inside-respectfully/ or http://www.sikhiwiki.org/index.php/Visiting_a_Gurdwara.

_____

_____

_____

_____

_____

Another important aspect of Sikh practice is the giving of offerings to those in need. In Sikhism, like Islam, a portion of one's income is to go to those who are suffering. Ten percent of one's income is given directly to charity in service to others. The giving of gifts to God, **dana**, is found in all Indian religions. Giving is an act of humility and another way to tame the ego.

The Khalsa

The Khalsa is the community of baptized Sikhs begun by the tenth guru, Gobind Singh. Although not all Sikhs choose to be baptized into the Khalsa, both men and women of orthodox practice undergo the ceremony to be part of this sacred group. The ritual baptism into the khalsa is called **Amrit Sanchar**. One joins the Khalsa by undergoing a ritual baptism. In this ritual, five baptized Sikhs stir a bowl of sweetened water (amrit) with a **kirpan** (sacred sword or dagger); and, the water is sprinkled on the initiate as he or she is instructed in the truths of the faith. There is no specific age for baptism in Sikhism; it is performed whenever a person is ready to take on the sacred practices.

Symbolic of these practices are five characteristic elements of the Khalsa dress code. The first is **kesh** (uncut hair) worn in a turban. Men are required to wear the turban while for women it is optional. No hair on the body is cut. This practice is important to keep in mind if you are a health care professional ministering to a Sikh patient. Hair is held in place by a **kangha** (comb). The kangha keeps hair out of the face and is a symbol of cleanliness. The kirpan, or ceremonial sword, is symbolic of a Sikh's commitment to justice and the responsibility to protect the weak. In many Western countries, the legality of the kirpan has been challenged particularly in heightened security areas such as schools and airports. The Sikh Coalition has provided a brochure regarding the legality and regulations associated with carrying a kirpan (http://www.sikhcoalition.org/advisories/2013/new-federal-kirpan-policy-what-you-need-to-know). **Kachera** (special shorts worn as undergarments) are symbolic of chastity and purity. They are tied at the waist and worn at all times. In case you are wondering, they have more than one pair and launder them. Finally, the **kara**, or bracelet, symbolizes strength. As a circle, it points to God unending love. Traditionally, men wear the kara on the right wrist while women wear it on the left. However, some Sikhs wear one on each arm or only one on their dominant side.

☯ Many religious traditions have dress codes. What are your thoughts about the Sikh dress code as it relates to schools, businesses and other institutions in society? What are specific issues related to the Sikh articles of faith? One site to check out is https://www.learnreligions.com/tsa-turban-regulations -2992999

_____

_____

_____

_____

_____

RITUALS AND FESTIVALS

As in all faiths, ceremonies mark rites of passage related to birth, puberty, marriage, and death. One such rite of passage, **Naam Karan**, uses the scriptures in the naming of children. When a new baby is born and welcomed into the community, the baby's parents take him or her to the gurdwara. The sacred text is opened to a random page. The child's first name begins with the first letter of the hymn on that page. The family serves everyone gathered karah prashad, the sweet pudding. The mother and baby are also given **amrit**, the sweet nectar.

Baptism takes place whenever a person feels they are mature and ready to take on the commitment of following the faith. In addition, to the five K's, additional expectations are described to the initiate by the five baptized Sikhs conducting the ceremony. For example, baptized Sikhs are to worship only God; they are to abstain from alcohol and tobacco; they will not believe in castes, magic, or practice fasting. The code of conduct for baptized Sikhs is aimed at keeping the faith, honoring the body, and practicing compassion and justice.

Marriage in Sikh tradition is sometimes facilitated by families but always with consent of both parties. In addition, marriage is viewed as an equal partnership between husband and wife. There is no dowry or giving away of the bride or groom. The ceremony may take place in the gurdwara or at home and includes readings from the Guru Granth Sahib as well as hymns and prayers. Following the religious ceremony, a banquet with singing and dancing is often held.

Sikhs view death as a natural process and simply a part of the life cycle. Family members bathe and dress the body of their loved one who has passed away. Cremation is the usual practice but there is nothing that forbids burial. Any gravestones are forbidden. Ashes are typically submerged in a river after cremation. The ceremony marking death includes the continuous reading of the scriptures for ten days either at home or in the gurdwara by members of the family. When the reading concludes the time of mourning has ended.

In addition to rites of passage, the Sikhs also celebrate annual festivals. Perhaps the most important of these festivals is **Vaisakhi**, which commemorates the founding of the Khalsa. It is a spring festival marked by street fairs and parades, singing of the sacred scriptures, a community meal, and martial arts displays. Baptism of new Sikhs and the changing of the Sikh flag on the gurdwara are also part of the celebrations. Another spring festival, **Hola Mohalla**, occurs around the same time as the Hindu celebration of Holi (Figure 4). This festival, like Vaisakhi, was started by the tenth guru. The day is marked by mock battles, martial arts displays, horse riding competitions, and poetry readings.

Figure 4   Sikhs celebrating Hola Mohalla in Anandpur Sahib, India March 2014.

In addition to seasonal festivals, the Sikhs also celebrate the birthdays of the gurus, the martyrdom of saints, and the start of each new month.

❧ Choose a Sikh ritual or festival to look into further and share two new things you learned about it.

_____

_____

_____

_____

SIKH SYMBOLS

The principal symbol of Sikhism is the Khanda. It is made up of three parts. The center of the image is a double-edged sword symbolic of truth freedom and justice. The circle points to the oneness of God. The two kirpan on either side represent political and religious power. A second important symbol is the title of God, **Ek Onkar**, the One Supreme Being. The symbol begins the sacred text and represents the emphasis in Sikhism on the oneness of God (Figure 5).

Figure 5   The Sikh symbols of Khanda and Ek Onkar.

SIKHISM IN THE UNITED STATES

The first Sikh immigrants arrived in the United States in the early 1900s to work building railroads and as migrant farmers in California. Several thousand Sikhs immigrated by 1917. However, in 1917, Congress passed an anti-immigration act that banned people from certain geographic regions of the world. India was part of the banned area. A Sikh immigrant fought in the U.S. Army during World War I, but was later denied citizenship because of the 1917 law. Many Sikhs have served with distinction in the U.S. Armed Forces (Figure 6). In recent years, a few exemptions have been made for facial hair and turbans. The first Sikh in Congress was Dalip Singh Saund who served two terms in the 1950s, representing California.[4]

The first gurdwara built in the United States was in Stockton, California, in 1912. A second gurdwara was built in 1948 in California. In the 1960s, however, immigration from India increased and more gurdwaras began to spring up across the United States. Today, somewhere between 250,000 and 500,000 Sikhs call the United States home.

© Associated Press. Photo by Darren Abate.

Figure 6 Sikhs have served proudly in the US military for many years. Recently, provisions have been made to regulations to allow Sikhs to wear the turban and not cut their hair.

WEB RESOURCES FOR FURTHER STUDY

http://www.khalsakids.org/—A website designed for Sikh kids to help them deal with the prejudice they often experience in school because of being different from the majority.

http://law.bepress.com/expresso/eps/902/—Great paper on the issues surrounding the free exercise of religion in the United States and the wearing of the kirpan.

http://www.sacred-texts.com/skh/index.htm—Link to translations of the sacred texts of Sikhism.

http://www.sikhnet.com/news/meaning-khalsa-colours—Good link about the meaning of the colors of the Khalsa and turbans worn.

http://www.sikhs.org/—The official Sikh homepage. Click on the icon to open up the main page, which gives information about all aspects of Sikh history, worship, and sacred practices.

http://www.youtube.com/watch?v=qYayqWne3Mg—The reciting of the morning prayer, the Japji Sahib.

https://www.youtube.com/watch?v=k-Znk9L38qA—Link to a video from the Sikh Coalition. The focus of the video is a congressional briefing on Sikhs in the military. Recent accommodations have been made for the turban and facial hair.

---

[4] http://www.pluralism.org/religion/sikhism/timeline/america

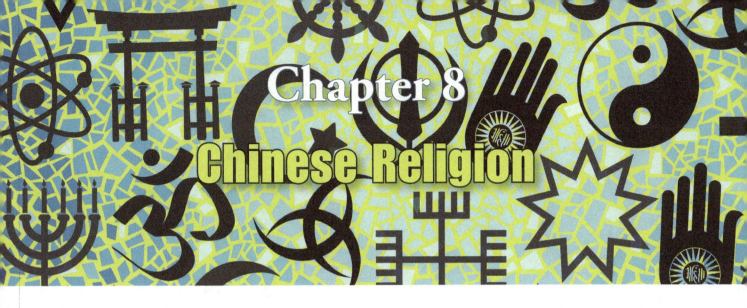

Chapter 8
Chinese Religion

Learning Outcomes

By the end of the lesson, students will be able to

☛ describe the syncretistic nature of Chinese religion.

☛ identify the elements of early Chinese religion.

☛ distinguish between Taoism and Confucianism and describe the basic beliefs of each; and

☛ explain the Confucian virtues and compare them to ethical frameworks in the other religious traditions with which students are familiar.

Key Terms

Analects	Hsun-tzu	Shangdi
Confucius	I Ching	Shu
Dao	Lao-tzu	T'ai chi ch'uan (Taiji quan)
Daodejing	Li	Tian
De	Mencius	Wu Wei
Divination	Qi (Ch'i)	Yin and Yang
Filial Piety (xiao)	Ren (Jen)	Zhuangzi (Chang-tzu)

A WORD ABOUT LANGUAGE

One of the challenges of learning religious and philosophical terms in this chapter is that there has been a change in the way that Chinese terms are translated into English. The earlier translation method is Wade–Giles; however, the more commonplace form today is Pinyin. Following is a chart demonstrating the difference between some common words in this chapter between the two translation styles.

Wade-Giles	Pin-Yin
Tao	Dao
Jen	Ren
Lao-tzu	Laozi
Ch'i	Qi
T'ien	Tian
Hsun-tzu	Xunzi

Pinyin is the format used by the Chinese government today and is the more intuitive in terms of pronunciation. Because of this, most words in the chapter follow the pinyin style.[1]

INTRODUCTION

In the United States, it is highly unlikely that someone would say, "I am a Lutheran and a Hindu." Or, "I am a Muslim and a Catholic." However, Chinese religion is highly syncretistic. In other words, the idea of practicing multiple faiths at the same time is commonplace. Chinese practice is typically a blend of folk religion, Daoism, Confucianism, and Buddhism. Despite religion being suppressed for many years after the rise of Communism in China, religious practices have not disappeared and, in fact, continue to flourish. Christianity has experienced some growth in China since the 1980s, but historically has not had a large impact on Chinese culture. According to the Pew Forum, in 2010, an estimated 5% of the Chinese population self-identified as Christian.

Islam is present in China as well, but is only about 2% of the population.[2] China legally recognizes five religions: Buddhism, Catholicism, Daoism, Islam, and Protestantism. Despite the legal standing of these traditions, religious persecution is still present in China; and, many religious traditions are practiced secretly or underground. Beginning with early Chinese religion, we will explore each of the major religious traditions rooted in China before looking at how Chinese religions has become part of the fabric of culture in the United States. (Figure 1).

© Francine Orr/ Contributor/ Getty Images

Figure 1   Lunar New Year celebration at Thien Hau temple in Los Angeles, February 2015.

---

[1] For more information on the language issues, see http://www.pinyin.info/romanization/wadegiles/.

[2] Pew Forum Study on the Global Religious Landscape 2012, p. 45ff. https://www.pewforum.org/2017/04/05/the-changing-global-religious-landscape/.

EARLY CHINESE RELIGION

Ancient Chinese religion has much in common with other indigenous religions discussed in Chapter 3. A reverence for ancestors, harmony with nature and spirits, and divination are just a few examples. One of the earliest characters in Chinese writing is **Tian**, sky or heaven (Figure 2). The character resembles a person and may point to the understanding of the Lord of Heaven (**Shangdi**), the transcendent aspect of the sacred in Chinese religion. At some points in Chinese history the two terms (Tian and Shangdi) were used interchangeably.

Figure 2 Chinese character T'ien meaning heaven.

The concepts of heaven and hell have been present in Chinese thought from the earliest known periods. In Chinese thought the soul divides at death: one part remains in the ground, another travels to heaven and hell, and the third remains with loved ones. The part of the soul that passes to the afterlife begins in the underworld where it faces various judgments for deeds committed in life. Hell is not permanent but a period one passes through to be punished for misdeeds. Eventually, the soul passes to heaven.

Heaven in Chinese thought was influenced by Buddhism's entry into China, particularly with the development of Pure Land Buddhism (see Chapter 5 for a refresher on Pure Land). Two bridges are thought to lead out of the underworld for those who led a model life; the Golden Bridge and the Silver Bridge. The Golden Bridge leads to the Pure Land of the Amida Buddha, whereas the Silver Bridge leads to heaven ruled by the gods and the Jade Emperor. The Jade Emperor is the ruler of a heavenly bureaucracy that mirrors the levels of government on earth.

Ancestor Reverence

Ancestor reverence plays a critical role in Chinese practice. Proper burials are extremely important. The belief is that if ancestors are treated reverently and respectfully and provided with what they need in the afterlife, then they will bless their descendants. If they

Figure 3 Ancestral Tablets at home altar.

are not, misfortune can result for the living. Ancestor reverence takes many forms. For example, in most Chinese homes, there is a family altar where the ancestors are remembered. Above the altar, pictures of the deceased are hung along with a plaque identifying them. Historically, the altar may also include an ancestral tablet made of wood on which the names of the various ancestors were etched (Figure 3). The names of deities were sometimes present as well. Daily offerings are also on the altar including wine, fruit, and sometimes food. The food is often a favorite dish of the deceased although meat offerings are typically avoided. Sticks of lighted incense are also placed on the altar each day. The incense carries thoughts and prayers and provides a link between the living and the dead. Offerings are also made on the anniversary of a loved one's death (Figure 4).

Festivals offer another opportunity to remember the ancestors. Qing Ming is the annual sweeping of the graves festival held each spring. During this festival, families gather at the cemetery to clean the graves, make offerings, and remember loved ones. In the fall, the Ghost Festival is also a time to offer food to the ancestors, report to them one's activities, and leave food out for hungry ghosts who wander during the Hungry Ghost month. Hungry ghosts are wandering spirits who have had a violent death or were not properly respected by their ancestors and cannot find rest.

Contributed by Vincent Nguyen. Copyright © Kendall Hunt Publishing Company.

Figure 4   Photo of family altar taken by student, Vincent Nguyen.

Local Gods and Spirits

In addition to the role of ancestors, deities and spirits populate Chinese folk religion. There are three realms of existence in popular Chinese thought: the heavens, the earth, and the underworld. Gods, goddesses, and spirits are active in each realm of existence. Each family was thought to have a **Kitchen God**, or guardian deity who protected the family. The Kitchen God, along with his wife, is pictured above the stove in many Chinese homes.

An Earth God (or Tudi Gong) also guarded villages and neighborhoods protecting them from evil spirits and a City God served as the divine administrator of a major city. The City God may even change periodically in the same way that a local human magistrate leaves office and another one takes his place. The City God was also thought to accompany a dead person's spirit to the underworld to face judgment. Festivals often marked the City God's birthday.

Yin and Yang

The idea of two opposing and complementary forces has an ancient history in Chinese philosophy and religion. Energy (**qi**) flows through the universe and is manifest in two forms. Yin represents darkness and earth. Yang represents light and heaven. In popular Western understanding, the yin–yang symbol is sometimes characterized falsely as good and evil. **Yin and Yang** are not good and evil, but the idea of a

Yin	Yang
Earth	Sky/heaven
Dark	Light
Female	Male
Winter	Summer
Water	Fire
Peace	War
Daoism	Confucianism

balance and harmony in life and in one's relationships. When looking at the image, one of the striking features is that there is always a little of one in the other and that they fit together in a cohesive whole. Following are some examples of yin and yang.

Much of Chinese culture including medicine, art, design, and the practice of divination relies on discernment of imbalance in yin and yang.

Divination

Divination is the art of discerning the proper course of action. Divination is deeply rooted in Chinese practice from the earliest recorded history. An early form of divination involved the use of oracle bones. A bone fragment of an ox or a part of a turtle shell was etched with a question and two possible answers. Then, a small hole was drilled in the bone. A hot spike was then inserted into the hole causing the bone to crack. The cracks were read to determine the answer to the question. The answer may also be inscribed on the bone (Figure 5).

Another divination practice common even today in Chinese temples is the casting of fortune sticks and moon blocks. The numbered sticks are in a canister. After posing a question and offering incense, the person seeking direction shakes the canister and draws a stick. The number on the stick corresponds to a passage that an interpreter at the temple will look up and read. To confirm the stick is the right one before consulting the interpreter, the questioner will throw moon blocks. Moon blocks come in pairs representing yin and yang. They are often painted red

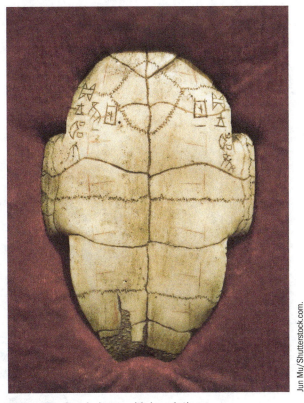

Jun Mu/Shutterstock.com.

Figure 5 Oracle bone with inscription.

and have a flat side (yang) and a curved side (yin). If one block lands flat and the other curved, it is a sign the right stick was selected and the spirits are pleased with the decision (Figure 6).

The *I Ching (Yijing)*, or Book of Changes, is the classic text on divination and is another means of determining the proper course of action. The system of trigrams (three line units) is attributed to the legendary emperor, Fu Hsi, who is said to have ruled China between 2852 and 2737 BCE. By the first century BCE, the text had become one of the Five Classics in the Confucian **canon**. The text describes and interprets the hexagrams created by arranging pairs of these trigrams. By casting coins and sticks, a pattern is created and the person seeking answers to a question is directed to multiple passages from the text. By reading the passages, a person discerns through intuition the message the texts are conveying. A variety of online *I Ching* resources, will allow you to test this method for yourself (Figure 7).[3]

---

[3] If you would like to experiment with the *I Ching*, some online sites include: http://www.ichingonline.net/; http://access-chinese.com/iching/iching_yijing.html.

Nunbhakdi/Shutterstock.com.

Figure 6   Fortune sticks in canisters with moon blocks.

Peter Hermes Furian/Shutterstock.com.

Figure 7   Eight trigrams of the I Ching with the yin and yang in the center.

Eating in a Chinese restaurant, perhaps you have looked down at the placemat and seen the Chinese zodiac. Astrology has long played a role in Chinese culture. Twelve animals, including the horse, boar, tiger, and snake, form a twelve-year cycle. In addition, there are elements and animals assigned not only to the year, but also to the month, day, and hour of one's birth.

DAOISM AND CONFUCIANISM

Daoism and Confucianism both developed in the Axial Age, that period of intense philosophical and religious inspiration. In essence, they are the yin and yang of Chinese religion. Daoism focuses on balance and harmony within oneself as well as between oneself and the energy flowing through the universe; it is the quiet, receptive yin. Confucianism focuses on harmony and balance within society and the relationships that hold society together; it is the social, assertive yang.

Daoism

The origins of Daoism are traced back to the legendary figure of Laozi around the sixth century BCE. Little factual information exists regarding his life and biography. The classical view is that he was a state archivist from southern China and an older contemporary of Confucius. The story is that he lived during the Zhou dynasty and grew tired of watching its decline. He decided to leave. When he neared the western border of China, a border crossing guard recognized Laozi as a man of wisdom and asked him to write down his philosophy before leaving.

The narrative follows that the words he wrote down form the **Daodejing** *(Tao te Ching)*, the oldest text of Daoism and one of the most translated sacred texts in the world. The title *Daodejing* is often translated as "the Classic of the Way and Its Power." It is a collection of eighty-one poems that, though brief, are filled with depth and wisdom. The written form is said to date to around 500 BCE. The second most important text in Daoism is the **Zhuangzi** (Chang-tzu) written a couple of centuries later. The title of the text is the name of its legendary author. Unlike the *Daodejing*, the *Zhuangzi* takes narrative form rather than poetic.

Daoist Principles

Balance and harmony are central to Daoist philosophy. The principle of the **Dao** translates as *"The Way" or "The Path."* It is an impersonal Truth and can even be used as a verb in terms of guidance or direction. In a sense, it is the Source that is never used up; "Invisible yet ever-present, you can use it forever without using it up *(Daodejing 6)*."[4] Moreover, it is sometimes compared with water. "The highest good is like water which benefits all things and contends with none. It flows in low places that others disdain and thus is close to the Tao *(Daodejing 8)*."[5]

Closely related to the concept of Dao is **de**, virtue or power. De is Dao in action; it is applying Dao to life and work. Although de implies action, it is held in tension with **wu wei**, "actionless action" or "purposeful inaction." Wu wei is very difficult to translate from the Chinese to the English. It refers to following intuition or discerning the subtle natural course to follow. Essential to the idea of wu wei is quiet contemplation and relying on the Dao to guide. Negatively stated it means "do not act in ways contrary to the Dao."

Daoism also emphasis a reverence for and harmony with nature. Simplicity and gentleness are valued as well. Although not a pacifist religion, Daoism does avoid unnecessary violence and seeks to promote peace. Simplicity coincides with the Buddhist ideal of not craving. It involves freedom from desire as well as a sense of purity that cuts through names "to the subtle heart of things."[6]

---

[4] Laozi, *The Tao Te Ching of Lao Tzu*, trans. Brian Browne Walker (New York: St. Martin's Press, 1995).
[5] Ibid.
[6] Ibid, 1.

☯ Select and read a passage from the *Daodejing*. Online versions can be found at https://www.yellow-bridge.com/onlinelit/daodejing.php or https://taoism.net/tao/tao-te-ching-online-translation/ Which passage did you choose? What drew you to it? What does it say to you?

_____

_____

_____

_____

_____

Daoist Religious Leadership and Sacred Practices

By the Han dynasty (200 BCE–200 CE), if not sooner, the Daoist philosophy became an organized religious practice with lineages of priests and a pantheon of deities, including a deified form of Laozi. Practices to promote longevity and immortality are central to religious Daoism. Daoist priests chant sacred texts, perform memorial and other ceremonial services, and cultivate the inner self.

From ancient times to the present, Daoist hermits have taken up residence in caves in the mountains practicing meditation and various forms of inner alchemy. People travel up the mountains to see the hermits and draw from their wisdom.

Alchemy in Daoism has both inner and outer forms. The word, alchemy, conjures of images of wizards trying to turn various substances to gold. However, Daoist alchemy is more about cultivating inner virtues, health, and longevity, and ultimately achieving transcendence and immortality. Outer alchemy involves studying with a Daoist master, carrying out various rituals of purification and prayers to the gods, mixing key ingredients, and ultimately drinking the Golden Elixir which enabled the seeker to achieve immortality.

Inner alchemy involves balances the flow of energy in the body and the breath. Meditation is central to inner alchemy, as is qigong exercises. Qigong is an inner martial arts practice that involves the breath, movement, and balance. The most well-known form of qigong exercises is T'ai chi ch'uan (Figure 8).

Traditional Chinese Medicine (TCM) is deeply rooted in the understanding of qi, life energy present in everything and everyone. This energy travels through the body along paths, known as meridians. The use of herbs, the consumption or abstention from certain foods, meditation, exercise, and acupuncture are all forms of balancing and unblocking the qi in the body. Those who practice TCM discern whether there is an excess of yin, a deficit of yin, an excess of yang, or a deficit of yang. Treatment is then determined to balance the yin and yang in the body. Long-life and immortality are important Daoist ideals; and, the practices of inner and outer alchemy are designed to facilitate the well-being of the mind and body.

Confucianism

Confucianism developed concurrently with Daoism and centers around the teachings of Confucius (Master K'ung). Unlike the legends around Laozi, the biography of Confucius is known in much greater detail. Confucius was born in the Chinese state of Lu in northeastern China in 551 BCE. His family was from the aristocracy, but the chaos of the times caused frequent wars and financial struggle. After the death of his father when Confucius was a young boy, his mother worked hard to provide him with an education. He became a teacher, married and had children. Confucius valued virtue over power and wealth. His teachings about virtue and education were not highly valued in his lifetime; but, within a couple of centuries of his death in 479 BCE served as the foundation of Chinese government and society.

Figure 8   T'ai chi exercise in park.

Confucian Texts

The Confucian canon is the Five Books and Four Classics. The Five Books includes the ancient texts of the *Book of Documents*, the *Book of Poems*, the *Book of Rites, Book of Changes* (*I Ching*), and the *Spring and Autumn Annals*. The Book of Documents consists of stories from ancient China. The Book of Poems has poetry, hymns, and folk songs from between the eleventh and seventh centuries BCE. Sacred rituals are key to the Confucian concept of **li** (proper action and respect) and to promoting harmony and piety; the Book of Rites is a collection of some of these ritual practices. The Book of Changes is the **I Ching**, discussed earlier in the chapter in the section on divination. The philosophical elements of this work have also had a lasting impact on Chinese culture. The Annals are historical records from the Chinese state of Lu compiled over a period of time.

The Four Books were the basis of the civil service exam in China for many centuries and included: the *Doctrine of Mean*, the *Great Learning*, *Mencius*, and the *Analects*. Moreover, Zhu Xi, a Neo-Confucian philosopher from the Song Dynasty, recommended reading the Four Books before the Five Classics, beginning with the *Great Learning*.[7] The *Great Learning* highlights the importance of education as a tool for cultivating morality. Next, he recommended reading the **Analects**, or the sayings of **Confucius**. The *Analects* emphasize the cultivation of wisdom as well as the value of education, etiquette, and ritual guidelines.

The third in the order recommended by Zhu Xi is *Mencius*, a document written from the perspective of a specific Confucian scholar. **Mencius** was a follower of Confucian thought who believed that human beings are born with the seeds of goodness. Education helps nurture that goodness and cause it to grow. Another Confucian thinker from around the same period (third to fourth century CE) is Xunzi (**Hsun-tzu**).[8] Xunzi shared Mencius' commitment to education but differed from him on the view of human nature. Xunzi said that people were essentially self-serving and prone to be immoral. Education was necessary to reform a corrupt human nature. Interestingly, though Confucius did not weigh in on the question of human nature, the book of *Mencius* is written as if it were a dialogue between Confucius and Mencius.

---

[7] Wilson and Wong, "The Confucian Canon," *The Cult of Confucius and the Temple of Culture*, 2010, https://academics.hamilton.edu/asian_studies/home/culttemp/sitePages/fiveclassics.html.

[8] This is not the same as Sun Tzu, the author of the Art of War. For more information on a a well done translation of this text see https://www.sonshi.com/original-the-art-of-war-translation-not-giles.html.

Finally, Zhu Zi suggested reading the *Doctrine of the Mean*, also sometimes translated as *Maintaining Perfect Balance*. This text is thought to have been written by Confucius' grandson and emphasizes following the Way in order to achieve harmony and balance in life. It also speaks of the importance of a government which follows the Way in setting an example for its citizens.[9]

Five Basic Relationships

Social relationships are key to harmony within society. Confucius taught that harmony in five basic relationships will lead to harmony within society. The five relationships are:

◆ parent–child (originally father–son);
◆ elder brother–younger brother;
◆ husband–wife;
◆ elder friend–younger friend (or mentor-student); and
◆ ruler–subject.

In the understanding of the time period, the relationships were viewed as hierarchical with the first person in the relationship having at least some measure of authority over the second. However, they were also reciprocal because each person in the relationships was responsible for the well-being of the other. Harmony in these social relations was achieved by cultivating and practicing the Confucian virtues.

Confucian Virtues

In Confucian understanding, ethics and morality in family and society are essential for social harmony. Ren, meaning "human-heartedness" or "benevolence" is the central Confucian virtue from which all other virtues originate. Ren is represented by two Chinese characters: person and the number 2. Because of this Peter Boodberg translates "*ren*" as "co-humanity."[10] Ren is how people should treat one another; in Confucius' eyes, it is what it means to be a human being. Closely related to ren is the virtue of shu. Shu is often translated as "reciprocity" or "self-reflection" and is encapsulated in the Silver Rule, "Do not do to others what you would not wish done to yourself." The resemblance to the Golden Rule is obvious. Interestingly, nearly every religious tradition from the most ancient to the present has a version of this ethical principle.[11] Xiao, filial piety, relates specifically to how members of the family treat one another. Filial piety refers to devotion to the welfare of the family which involves taking care of one another, helping each other out in a crisis, respecting one another, and participating in rituals and festivals that honor ancestors and family deities. An extension of filial piety to other important people in the community is **zhong** or loyalty. This virtue is also sometimes translated as "other-regard."[12] On the one hand, zhong promotes loyalty to others; on the other, it also preserves the status quo which may or may not be in the best interest of the greatest number of people. The virtue of **li** is often translated as

---

[9] See the aforementioned source to read English translations of each of the four books.

[10] Peter Boodberg's translation of the term, ren, as mentioned in the article on Confucianism from http://www.iep.utm. edu/confuciu/#H4. Peter Boodberg is a scholar of Chinese culture and language who taught at the University of California, Berkley for many years.

[11] For a list of passages from various religions, see http://www.religioustolerance.org/reciproc2.htm or http:// kidworldcitizen.org/2014/05/20/world-religions-golden-rule-across-cultures/.

[12] Jeff Richey, "Confucius." *Internet Encyclopedia of Philosophy: A Peer Reviewed Academic Resource*, http://www.iep.utm.edu/ confuciu/#H4.

"propriety"; it denotes doing the right thing in any given situation. Li involves rituals honoring ancestors and deities, showing respect to the emperor, conducting rituals of the court, and demonstrating proper etiquette in social situations. Confucian ethics emphasize doing what is right (**yi**) at all times.

Confucian Rituals

Confucianism is often described as a philosophy more than a religion. After all, there are no priests, ministers or specifically Confucian "churches" in China. Confucian temples are educational and cultural gathering places (Figure 9). However, having said that, one of the most continuous

Figure 9 Statue of Confucius at the Confucian Temple in Henan, China.

aspects of Confucianism is its rituals. Confucian rituals take two forms: divination and sacrifice. Divination is closely connected to consultation with the ancestors and deities to determine the proper course of action. Sacrificial rituals are offerings made to rulers, ancestors, and deities. Many of these rituals take place at home with the families offering food, rice, wine, and incense to ancestors and local deities. In addition, there are special celebrations honoring Confucius' birthday and pilgrimages to the Confucian temple at Qufu, marking the place of his birth. Music, dance, and the arts are also part of Confucian traditions.

☻ Listen to music from Confucian rituals on iTunes, youtube (i.e., https://www.youtube.com/watch?v=ym-iJo_CPwA) or Spotify (i.e. https://open.spotify.com/playlist/4dFLgf21lURfGli8LanrNw?replay=1. What instruments do you hear? Write down the instruments you hear as well as two to three words describing the sound. Alternately, check out a website on Chinese instruments. Describe the instrument and one new thing you learned about it. Examples of sites to check out include: http://www.topchinatravel.com/china-guide/traditional-musical-instrument/ or http://www.philmultic.com/home/instruments/

_____

_____

_____

_____

_____

FALUN GONG/FALUN DAFA

Falun Gong, also known as Falun Dafa, began in China in the early 1990s. A mixture of Buddhism and Daoism, it was founded by Li Hongzhi, a musician from northeast China. His system of thought is dualistic in that good action and suffering produce gong energy (positive energy) and bad deeds produce karma (negative energy). During the 1980s and 1990s, *qigong* movements experienced a boom. Many different movements and individuals claimed to have knowledge of special *qigong* practices that would promote healing, self-transformation, and material success. In this context, Li Hongzhi began to teach his own system while also claiming to be an incarnation of the Buddha. Falun Gong is based on three virtues: truthfulness, compassion, and forbearance. Li Hongzhi has claimed to heal many through his teachings and practices. He teaches that all have the Gong force which needs to be cultivated through training the mind and the body. Rather than a religious movement, he describes the system as a method of scientific self-cultivation practiced through five exercises which are easy to learn.[13] Like many new religious movements, it blends ancient teachings with modern ones and has appealed to a large number of people in China and around the world.

In 1999, the movement staged a demonstration that was aimed at clearing up untruths about the movement. Whether it succeeded in this effort or not, the protest definitely drew the attention of the Chinese government. The movement is banned in China and many followers have been arrested, tortured, or put to death. Li Hongzhi along with his family came to live in the United States in 1999; and, he has continued to draw followers.

A major difference from other new religious movements is that there is no hierarchy, many of the followers only know of Li through his teachings, and there are no church buildings or communal centers. The essence of the practice seems to be on mental and physical exercises tied to rigorous moral practice. If you would like to read more about the movement, check out the movement's home page www.falundafa.org as well as the writings and lectures of David Ownby or Harold White Fellow who both offer a relatively objective portrayal of the group.

Figure 10   Followers of Falun Dafa meditate on the lawn outside Independence Hall in Philadelphia.

Source: Stephanie Curran

FESTIVALS

Festivals are celebrated across China at various times of the year to promote good fortune and honor ancestors and deities. The festivals most celebrated include Chinese New Year, the Lantern Festival, Qing Ming, the Mid-Autumn Festival, and the Dragon Boat Festival. Not only are these festivals celebrated in China, but also you can find celebrations of these festivals around the world. Even Owensboro, KY,

---

[13] FalunDafa.org, p. 1. http://en.falundafa.org/introduction.html.

has a Dragon Boat Festival.[14] The Chinese calendar is a lunar calendar so the dates of festivals vary from year to year in China.

Chinese New Year

Chinese New Year usually falls in late January or February. The holiday traditionally lasted for fifteen days. It is celebrated with cleaning the house, family gatherings, fireworks, hanging or lighting red lanterns, and giving red envelopes filled with money to the children. Red is a lucky color and is thought to ward off evil. New Year's Eve is celebrated by generations of family coming together to share a special meal. At midnight, fireworks fill the night sky (Figure 11).

Figure 11   Red lanterns celebrating Chinese New Year.

The Lantern Festival

The Lantern Festival is held the last day (fifteenth day) of Chinese New Year. Traditions associated with the festival include lighting red lanterns and eating rice balls filled with various fillings such as sugar, red bean paste, or sesame. The lion dance and walking on stilts are also part of the festivities (Figure 12).

Figure 12   Walking on stilts performance for the Lunar New Year.

Qing Ming

Qing Ming is a spring festival that celebrates the ancestors. Families visit the cemetery to sweep and weed the graves, burn paper money and offer incense, food, and rice wine to the ancestors. Families travel from far away to join together to participate in these sacred rituals. Kite flying is also a tradition during this festival. It is interesting to note how many different religions and cultures include kite flying in their sacred festivals. For example, Gujurat, India, as well as Afghanistan, both have kite flying festivals.[15]

Dragon Boat Festival

This festival is also known as the double fifth festival because it occurs on the fifth day of the fifth lunar month. The festival honors Qu Yuan, a Chinese poet and statesman from the Warring States Period. He

---

[14] For more information on the Owensboro festival, see https://visitowensboro.com/event/owensboro-dragon-boat-festival-2/

[15] For more information on kites in various cultures, see https://drachen.org/10-best-kite-festivals/

lived from 340–278 BCE in the Chinese state of Chu. The legend is that he would rather die than see his state overrun by the state of Qin. He wrote one last poem and threw himself into the river. He was much beloved and the fishermen tried to save him, but were unsuccessful. To keep the fish from eating Qu Yuan's body, the people threw zongzi, sticky rice balls into the water.

The festivities celebrated during the Dragon Boat festival are the racing of long boats with dragons adorning the front. Teams race for good luck and fortune in the coming year. Celebrants also eat zongzi, beat drums, and hang herbs like mugwort around the home to ward off the diseases prevalent at the beginning of summer.

Mid-Autumn Festival

The Mid-Autumn Festival is also known as the Moon Festival. Families gather, eat moon cakes, and lay outside and gaze at the moon. The full moon during the festival signifies peace and prosperity. The celebration of this festival dates back over 3,000 years to the Shang dynasty. It is thought to have originated as a harvest festival and an honoring of the moon goddess, Chang-e (or Chang-o) (Figure 13).

© Jiangdi/Shutterstock.com.

Figure 13   Mooncakes are traditionally eaten during the midautumn festival. They are filled with a variety of fillings from chocolate to sweetened bean paste, peanut butter, and many more.

☯ Choose a Chinese festival (one listed or another such as the Hungry Ghost Festival or the Double Nines festival) to look into a little more. Write down which festival you chose and one new fact you learned about that festival.

_____

_____

_____

_____

_____

CHINESE RELIGION IN THE UNITED STATES

Chinese immigrants came to the United States in the 1850s to participate in the Gold Rush and to work on the railroad. The first two Chinese temples in the United States were built in California. However, the Chinese Exclusion Act of 1882 put an end to new immigrants coming to the United States. Those already here continued to worship and build Chinatowns in major cities, but a new influx of Chinese immigrants did not arrive in the United States until the Immigration Act of 1965 reopened the doors to more people. Many of the temples that were built between the 1850s and 1880s, were combined Daoist and Buddhist temples.

In the 1970s, Daoist centers began to pop up across the country. The largest organization of Daoist centers in the United States is a network of Healing Tao Centers. Some of these centers, such as the Center of Tao in Massachusetts, have non-Chinese Americans as their primary clientele as well as the majority of teachers at the Center. Westerners are drawn to the many longevity practices from Daoism, especially Tai Chi, meditation, and breathing techniques.[16]

Confucianism's presence has also been felt in the United States. Over sixty Confucian Institutes are in partnership with universities in thirty-seven states including Western Kentucky University, University of Maryland, the Community College of Denver, and the University of Montana. These centers were established in partnership with the Office of Chinese Language Promotion to encourage the study of Chinese language and culture. In addition, a Confucian Church in Stockton, CA, serves the Chinese–American community and promotes awareness of Chinese culture and application of Confucian ethics.[17]

☯ The Confucian Institutes are somewhat controversial as they are sponsored in part by the Chinese government. Read the article below on the Future of Confucian Institutes, then answer the following questions: What is the essence of the controversy over the Confucian Institutes? Do the benefits outweigh the drawbacks? Why or why not?

_____

_____

_____

_____

_____

THE FUTURE OF CONFUCIUS INSTITUTES IN THE UNITED STATES*

BY BECCA THORPE

Honor Leahy stood in front of the lecture hall, looking at her audience and taking a deep breath to calm her nerves as she waited for silence. Leahy was about to compete in the 2014 Chinese Language Competition at the College of William & Mary in Virginia.

The Tennessee native was only a freshman at the time and was still in her first year of learning Chinese. She had spent the last few weeks preparing a short phone conversation for the April competition. She was ready, but still nervous.

---

[16] "Folk Daoism Comes to the West," *Pluralism Project*. http://pluralism.org/religions/daoism/the-daoist-tradition/folk-daoism-comes-to-the-west/.

[17] For more information on the Confucian Institutes and the Confucian Church of Stockton, see https://stocktoncba.org/.

"It was like baking a cake for someone else using their own recipe," Leahy said. "You're giving something to them that's already theirs, so you hope it's good enough and you hope it's authentic."

The event was sponsored by the William & Mary Confucius Institute (WMCI), an educational organization that provides Chinese language and culture classes to the university students and surrounding community. The WMCI hosts cultural events throughout the year, from holiday celebrations to musical performances. It also partially funds several language instructors within William & Mary's Chinese Language and Literature department.

Before coming to William & Mary, Leahy had limited exposure to China—she says her only experience with Chinese culture was "Chinese food, and it was crappy Chinese food." Now she describes learning the language as one of her passions. In addition to potentially minoring in Chinese, Leahy also hopes to spend a semester in China. And she credits the WMCI will significantly strengthening her experience.

The Confucius Institute is not unique to William & Mary. In the United States alone, there are over 450 Confucius Institutes on university campuses and in K-12 schools, with many located around the world. For schools like William & Mary, relations between the university and the Confucius Institute have been quite harmonious. The two groups frequently work together to bring speakers and cultural programs to students as a way of augmenting the College's Asian Studies program.

Yet some schools, including the University of Chicago, do not have a harmonious relationship with their Confucius Institutes. For these schools, the tension does not come from the language and culture programs the Institutes provide, but rather the structure of the Institutes. The Institutes are run by highly trained staff and teachers, but their funding comes from the Chinese Ministry of Education.

The Confucius Institutes, which are run by a larger Chinese educational organization called Hanban, have been on American university campuses for over ten years, but only in the past few years has serious conflict erupted. In October 2013, Marshall Sahlins, professor Emeritus of Anthropology at the University of Chicago, published an article that decried the Confucius Institutes' practices on topics including censorship, secrecy, and discriminatory hiring practices. By June 2014, the American Association of University Professors (AAUP) had published a report calling on all American universities with Confucius Institutes to review their relationships with the Institutes and consider cutting ties. Just a few months later, in September, the University of Chicago decided not to renew its contract with its Confucius Institute. The following month, Pennsylvania State University did the same.

In Sahlins' opinion, the University of Chicago Confucius Institute infringed on the University's academic freedom. When he learned that the University of Chicago had signed a contract with Hanban for a Confucius Institute, Sahlins said, "it struck me as a scandal." He believed teachers from the Confucius Institute presented a one-sided view of China because Hanban hired and trained them. By utilizing these teachers and the Institute, Sahlins argued that the University was failing to uphold its tenants of academic integrity and, by extension, freedom of speech. As he saw it, "The gross idea of subcontracting teaching to a foreign government was of course contrary to the principles of academic freedom upon which the university was founded."

Academics such as Sahlins do not claim that Confucius Institutes enforce hard censorship, which would be an explicit ban on the discussion or research of certain topics. Instead, Sahlins argues these organizations implicitly encourage self-censorship. Individuals avoid talking about topics such as Tibet, Taiwan, or the Tiananmen Square massacre out of fear of offending the Chinese faculty that work with the schools' Confucius Institutes. Because such issues are not discussed, students do not get a well-rounded education on China, and faculty research is truncated. As Sahlins says, "All those things are politically off the agenda of the Confucius Institutes, deliberately so—which gives a very distorted view of what China is."

After Sahlins' article was published, there was an uproar in the media. Sahlins' article brought new attention to the conflict. In June 2014, the AAUP published a report calling on all American universities to sever ties with Confucius Institutes unless the university could establish unilateral control over the Confucius Institute. It also encouraged universities to ensure all Confucius Institute teaching staff the same academic freedom as its faculty, and that the university contract with the Confucius Institute is made public.

Joerg Tiede, an Illinois Wesleyan University professor who was on the AAUP subcommittee that authored this report, noted in a phone interview that the report was "not an attack on [Confucius Institutes and the Chinese government], so much as a response to the media." The AAUP subcommittee conducted no independent research on the topic according to Tiede, and the report itself only cites Sahlins' article. The subcommittee's responsibility, which mainly involves monitoring academic freedom at universities around the United States, was much too large for it to conduct its own research on specific topics like the Confucius Institutes. If there were specific cases of violation of academic freedom within the United States, the committee was obligated to conduct its own investigation. But for this case, he said media reports were sufficient evidence to write the AAUP report.

One professor at George Washington University disagreed with the AAUP.

"I think it's posed as a debate over academic freedom," Edward McCord, the director of the Sigur Center for Asian Studies said in a phone interview. "Somehow Confucius Institutes [are believed to] restrict academic freedom at some universities and frankly I just find that bogus and simply not true."

McCord believes that Confucius Institutes were specifically designed to avoid sensitive political issues. Their focus is on improving the understanding of Chinese language and culture, and not become a staging ground for political battles.

According to their constitution, Confucius Institutes are intended to "promote educational and cultural exchange" so as to combat misperceptions of China around the world.

As McCord says, the Chinese government "thinks China is not seen correctly in the West . . . and they think that if we understand Chinese language and culture, we'll have a better understanding of China."

Thus, Confucius Institutes only focus on language and culture instruction, much to the chagrin of Sahlins and others.

However, there is more to this debate than just teaching American students how to write Chinese characters or how to make dumplings. Confucius Institutes are seen as part of a wider Chinese soft power push around the world.

According to James Reardon-Anderson, a professor who specializes in China at Georgetown University's School of Foreign Service, the Confucius Institutes are a form of "soft diplomacy similar to U.S. initiatives since World War II."

Others, such as Nathan Beauchamp-Mustafaga, share this view. According to Beauchamp-Mustafaga, the Jamestown Foundation's China Brief editor, Confucius Institutes are a "part of a broader government initiative [to] push Chinese power abroad."

Reardon-Anderson believes that the Confucius Institutes are a "perfectly legitimate activity." He argues that their purpose is comparable to the United States' goal in establishing the Peace Corps. Soft power activities counterbalance hard power activities, such as military intervention or economic sanctions. However, Sahlins and others are strongly opposed to this kind of activity.

"It is a larger political problem of the outreach of the Chinese party state into the cultural life [in] various countries around the world," says Sahlins, "so obviously it's a global problem."

When put in context of current United States–China relations, Sahlins' reaction seems to be well founded. "As Chinese power has grown in other ways, people are seeing Chinese rise in hard ways," says Lauren Dickey, a research associate at the Council on Foreign Relations.

As China has risen in recent years, the American public has become more aware of China's presence in the United States. The Confucius Institute debate has arisen as America's relationship China has become more contentious.

"Progress has been tough or difficult. There have been a lot of areas we disagree with Beijing," says Dickey. At the top levels of government policy-making, "we've been recalibrating, but it has been a bumpy few years," she continues. Citing issues that span from territorial disputes to the treatment of ethnic minorities to US military action in the Pacific, Dickey notes, "often times we're talking past one another and not talking to one another." Both sides keep revisiting areas of tension, but so far solutions have been rare.

Dickey's analysis of the relationship between the two governments also sheds some light on the declining American public opinion of China. According to the Pew Research Center, 51% of Americans felt favorably towards China in 2011. However, by 2014, only 35% felt favorably towards China. Although Americans do not typically see China as a partner, they also don't see China as an enemy, according to 2013 Pew survey results. Public opinion of China seems to mirror government relations. As Tun-jen Cheng, a William & Mary professor who specializes in United States–China relations, said in an interview, "It's not quite equanimous relationships. definitely more adversarial than cooperative recently." While recently, the United States and China have had areas of great cooperation, tension still remains.

McCord believes there is a flaw in the way the American public views China. "They assume that there must be some kind of insidious Chinese plot under there that's going to undermine American freedom," McCord argues. "It's almost like an assumption: if it's Chinese, they must be doing this." According to McCord, this belief that there must be ulterior motives has driven the debate to where it is today. Even though Confucius Institutes were designed to combat misunderstanding, McCord believes that the debate arose because the Institutes themselves were misunderstood.

One of the main areas of misunderstanding is the actual purpose of the Confucius Institutes. Both an Economist article and Sahlins cite a Chinese government official, Li Changchu, saying that Confucius Institutes are "an important part of China's overseas propaganda set-up."

But McCord argues that the word "propaganda" (which is "xuanchuan" in Chinese) has a neutral connotation in Chinese, unlike the extremely negative connotation in English. The word originally meant to present the view of your organization, but now, "It's so tainted in English you can't even say it without raising eyebrows," McCord says. Making reference to the Catholic Church's use of the word he notes, "For the Church, propaganda was like 'we want to get the word out.'"

Each Confucius Institute is different in its affiliation to its host school and its relationship with the students. At the University of Maryland, the site of the first Confucius Institute, the organization only teaches non-credit-bearing classes and provides a teacher training program for the Chinese teachers brought in through the Institute. At William & Mary, however, the Institute teaches Chinese language classes through the Department of Modern Languages and actively supports the on-campus Chinese House, a dorm specifically dedicated to learning Chinese. Thus, misunderstanding also arises in these areas of difference between the Institutes.

Amid the confusion and misunderstanding, there are also undertones of fear. "There is a misunderstanding of what the Confucius Institutes are meant to do," says Dickey, "but there is [also] still a fear."

McCord also believes fear plays a role in the debate. "I think there is no academic freedom issue involved with this at all," he says, "[instead it may be] a fear that people have of China." The American perception of China is shaped by current events and government relationships with China. As government relationships have become bumpy and public opinion declined, a fear of China has been growing. Jennifer Lee, an assistant professor of Chinese Studies at William & Mary, notes: "We originally held an unquestioned position in the world, but now China is questioning that." She believes that American fear of China shows a lack of American confidence, but that "there is no need to be afraid of China."

A good number of China-related current events center around politically sensitive issues, like the treatment of ethnic minorities or territorial claims. Part of Marshall Sahlins' argument was that sensitive political issues were not part of the university dialogue with the Confucius Institute, even though in his opinion they should be. Just as at the government level, "We don't want them to be talking at us," Dickey says, "we want to be in a dialogue with them." Universities and local citizens want to be part of the dialogue with the Confucius Institutes. Both sides have their own opinions, but the challenge is articulating them in a way that engages the other side in the discussion.

Even though political dialogues are not part of the Confucius Institute agenda, this restriction does not mean that dialogues cannot happen elsewhere on campus. Stephan Hanson, the director of William & Mary's Reves Center for International Studies, points out, "Very few donors give you completely unrestricted money that you can do anything with." Donors can control what happens with their money, but they cannot feasibly control what else happens on a university campus. Hanson says, "If we were to actually not be doing any other activity at all, that would be completely unacceptable, but we don't allow those restrictions." William & Mary hosts numerous events through various academic departments on China-related topics, in addition to Confucius Institute–sponsored events.

Even though it can be challenging for universities and their Confucius Institutes to talk to and not past each other, Hanson believes it can be done. He states, "There are some ways in which you manage those relationships [between the school and the Institute] so that people are both understood and feel respected, but there is also diversity of opinion expressed freely on campus in general." He believes the WMCI has benefited William & Mary students. From language instruction to cultural activities to outside speakers, the WMCI contributions to the university "have ramped up our China program in a pretty significant way," says Hanson.

Leahy is one of many students who have benefited from the Confucius Institutes. She won the 2014 Chinese Language Competition in the beginners bracket and plans to compete again in the 2015 competition. For Leahy, language learning is less about government relations or current events—instead it is about interpersonal relationships. She has several good friends who are international students from China and loves practicing with them. "Although a lot of them do learn English, I feel like it is fair to meet them in the middle. You don't want to expect everybody to know what you know," she says.

WEB RESOURCES FOR FURTHER STUDY

https://academics.hamilton.edu/asian_studies/home/culttemp/sitePages/fiveclassics.html—Excellent introduction to Confucius, the Confucian canon, his teachings, the temple and ritual tradition.

http://afe.easia.columbia.edu/cosmos/main/t_index.htm—Great resource for articles and other information on Chinese religion produced by Columbia University.

https://tao.org/—This site has links to a wide variety of articles on Daoism and Daoist alchemy.

http://www.goldenelixir.com/index.html—Extensive resource for articles on Daoism and Daoist Alchemy.

http://www.iep.utm.edu/gender-c/—Excellent link on gender in Chinese culture and religion.

https://www.nla.gov.au/benjamin-perry/the-past-present-and-future-of-falun-gong—An interesting article written by Harold White Fellow on the past, present, and future of the Falun Gong movement in China.

https://socrates.arts.ubc.ca/resources/chinese-philosophy-resources/—Excellent link for information about Chinese philosophies and philosophers.

http://viewofchina.com/modern-chinese-hermits/—This site offers a visual travelogue of some of the features of Chinese culture; and specifically speaks of Chinese hermits past and present.

Chapter 9
Japanese Religion

Learning Outcomes

By the end of the chapter, students will be able to

☞ discuss the Buddhist and Confucian influences on Shinto;

☞ describe the mythology of Shinto and the role of the kami in Japanese religion;

☞ analyze the role of purification and purification rituals in Shinto; and

☞ identify the influence of Shinto on anime and manga.

Key Terms

Amaterasu	Kami	Misogi
Ema	Kami-no-michi	Musubi
Harae	Kannagara	Torii
Haraigushi	Kojiki and Nihon Shoki	Tsumi
Izanagi and Izanami	Matsuri	

INTRODUCTION

Shinto is the loosely organized, animistic religion of Japan. Like Hinduism, it has no founder and is an ancient practice that has stood the test of time. In addition, Shinto has no official canon of scripture. The collections of Japanese mythology, the *Kojiki* and *Nihon Shoki*, are the primary texts; however, unlike sacred texts of other faiths, they provide no organized doctrines or ethical guidelines. The name, Shinto, and its preferred Japanese counterpart, **Kami-no-michi**, mean "the way of the sacred." Shinto covers a wide variety of practices centered mainly on harmony with the natural world and ritual purification.

Japanese religion, like Chinese religion, is syncretistic. Shinto has blended with practices from Buddhism, Taoism, and Confucianism over the years. Shinto rituals primarily focus on life (birth, marriage, blessings for various seasons and ages), while Buddhist rituals help people cope with suffering and death. In fact, the term Shinto was not applied to Japanese religion until after Buddhism's arrival in Japan in the sixth century CE. The naming of Shinto was a way to distinguish it from Buddhism and identify the essence of Japanese faith, harmony with the spirits (Figure 1).

FORMS OF SHINTO

Historically, Shinto has taken three main forms: folk Shinto, state Shinto, and shrine Shinto. Folk Shinto is the term for the form of Shinto practiced by individuals and represents the intersection of spiritual practices often drawn from both Buddhism and Shinto. It is not based on

Figure 1   Torii Gate at a Buddhist Shrine in Japan.

doctrine, and it has no formal code of ethics. It is simply individuals seeking to connect with the sacred.

State Shinto began during the Meiji Dynasty in the late 1860s. In an effort to promote nationalism and patriotism, the Emperor made Shinto the state religion and persecuted other religious traditions (including Christianity and Buddhism). State Shinto continued in Japan until World War II. At the end of the war, State Shinto was disbanded; and, Shinto was no longer promoted through government institutions and schools.

Shrine Shinto is the primary form explored in this chapter. It is the type of Shinto represented at the many shrines throughout Japan and around the world. Shrine Shinto is rooted in the mythology of Japan and emphasizes purification, harmony with nature, and blessings for health and good fortune.

CENTRAL CONCEPTS

The term, **kami**, can be singular or plural and refers to the essence of the sacred. Kami can include deities, ancestors, creative forces, and natural formations (mountains, rivers, rocks, etc.). The major deities of Japan are the subjects of the mythology in the **Kojiki and Nihon Shoki** (Nihongi). **Izanagi and Izanami** are the divine pair responsible for creating the Japanese islands. In addition to deities, kami is present in all living things and sometimes in inanimate objects. Kami can also refer to abstract qualities, such as creativity or wisdom. At the same time, it should be noted that a kami might be good or bad. Kami are not perfect, nor are they all-powerful. They do not reside in some far off galaxy or supernatural space; rather, they live in the same world that human beings inhabit.

The natural world is alive with the sacred. Rocks, forests, mountains, waterfalls, ocean, and other natural phenomenon are all kami. Therefore, they are to be revered. Buildings are placed in such a way that harmony with nature (**kannagara**) is maintained. Because all life is descended from kami, human beings have a familial relationship with nature. Shinto festivals follow the agricultural cycle, particularly the cultivation of rice. Rice is seen as a sacred food and is often part of offerings placed at shrines. The life force or power of creation, **musubi**, originates from kami and can be seen everywhere in the natural world. This life force is revered as the essence of the sacred.

Thousands of shrines are located throughout Japan. From a small shrine on a busy city street to the elaborate complex of the Grand Shrine at Ise which honors the sun goddess, **Amaterasu**, shrines come in diverse sizes and can be found in a wide range of locations (Figure 2). The Japanese visit shrines for special occasions, significant birthdays, religious festivals, as well as to pray and pay respect to the kami. The entrance to shrines is marked by a torii (sacred gate). The arches of the torii are one of the distinguishing features of Japanese architecture. Another symbol frequently seen on shrines is the **shimenawa**, a straw rope that is often hung over shrines, homes, and other sacred spaces. The shimenawa marks sacred space and sometimes prayers on strips of white paper are tied to them (Figure 3). Visitors may also find symbolic representations of rice balls attached to them as an expression of hope for a good harvest.

Portable shrines, **mikoshi**, are used during Japanese festivals to parade various deities through the streets (Figure 4). Within the most sacred part of the shrine, a mirror or stone is used to represent the kami. Mythically, the mirror is believed to reflect the soul rather than one's physical appearance. Sometimes this sacred space is completely empty. Traditionally, it is believed that images of deities can stand in the way of worship. This iconoclastic emphasis is the exact opposite of the Hindu practice of darsan (discussed in Chapter 4). In Hinduism, images are believed to enhance one's ability to connect with the sacred.

Purity and the continual need for purification are central to Shinto. Ritual impurity, tsumi, is not the same as moral guilt. In addition to moral transgressions, ritual impurity may be caused by natural disasters, contact with the dead, childbirth and

Figure 2   Small Shrine in Kyoto.

Figure 3   Shimenawa.

Figure 4   Men carry a portable shrine in a Festival in Osaka in 2011.

menstruation, negative energy, or day-to-day contact with others. To remove ritual impurity and restore harmony, a number of methods are available. A simple way to restore purity is to be attentive to problems as they arise. This approach encourages individuals to seek forgiveness and reconciliation in their daily lives. This method, of course, applies primarily to moral transgressions involving interpersonal relationships or harm to the environment. The second way to remove impurity is for the kami to absorb or blow away impurity. A third way is to engage in purification rituals, such as harae or misogi.

SACRED RITUALS

Shinto is a way of life rather than a system of belief. Major practices include purification rituals, rituals honoring ancestors and kami, rites of passage, and the celebration of festivals.

Purification Rituals

In many religions, water is believed to be a great purifier. In Shinto, purification with water is essential when entering sacred space. Before entering a shrine, worshipers cleanse their hands and mouths with water. A ladle is dipped in the water, filled, and emptied into the left hand. After rinsing the left hand, water is placed in the right hand to rinse. The ladle is dipped back in the water and a small amount of water is placed in the hand and brought to the mouth. The mouth is rinsed, and then the water is spit out on the ground. The ladle is rinsed and replaced, and then the worshiper is ready to enter the shrine (Figure 5).

In another ritual of purification, a priest sweeps the air in front of a person or object with a branch from a sacred tree, or a wooden stick tied with strips of white paper or hemp (haraigushi) to remove impurity (Figure 6). If the strips of paper are tied to an evergreen branch, the sacred object is referred to as an **onusa**. Misogi is a ritual that often takes place under a waterfall, but can be in any running water. Following deep breathing exercises and preliminary purification rites (i.e., rinsing one's mouth out with

Key01/Shutterstock.com.

Figure 5 Purification fountain at a Shinto Shrine

Toshifumi Kitamura/Staff/Getty Images

Figure 6 Shinto priest waves a haraigushi.

rice wine or sake), the worshiper stands beneath a waterfall.[1] Following cleansing, individuals enter into a time of self-reflection through meditation and prayer. In addition to water and sake, salt is also seen as a purifying element.

Honoring Kami and Ancestors

In addition to purification rituals, there are also rituals to honor the kami. Many Japanese homes have a **kamidana**, a household shrine or altar. The kamidana usually faces east (toward the sunrise) or south (toward Mt. Fuji) and is placed in a quiet part of the home. A shrine replica is often placed on the altar along with vases for evergreen leaves and small, white dishes for offerings of rice, salt, water, and sake are common. Some will also place a mirror in front of the shrine and hang strips of white paper above it. Enshrined on the altar is usually an amulet (**ofuda**) that is believed to absorb evil spirits. Each year, a new ofuda is placed in the shrine to replace the old one with a new, pure one. When praying at the kamidana, wash hands and mouth (or take a shower), worshipers bow twice in gratitude, clap hands twice to get the attention of the kami and to show respect and joy, then bow once. Prayers are said and offerings are made to the kami. Often, Japanese families also have a **butsudan**. A butsudan is a Buddhist household altar where offerings are made to one's ancestors. The doors to the butsudan are often opened in the morning and food offerings are made to the ancestors along with requests for protection and blessings. Sometimes, requests are also made to the Buddha for peace in the afterlife.[2]

Rites of Passage

Shinto rites of passage focus on age-related ceremonies and weddings. The first important event is the baby's first visit to the local shrine where the infant is blessed and introduced to the kami. The next celebration of life is the Shichi-Go-San blessing. When boys are five and girls are three and seven, they dress up and go to the shrine for blessings of good health and protection. In Shinto, the coming of age ceremony occurs when the young person turns twenty. In the January that follows their twentieth birthday, young people celebrate **Seijin-no-hi**, or coming-of-age day. Special clothes are rented, or purchased, for this day. Young women dress in traditional clothing including kimono and sandals. Some young men wear traditional clothing, while others wear a suit and tie. The festival includes blessings at the shrine, a speech by local officials, and parties. Other significant milestone ages in Shinto are a person's fortieth and seventieth birthdays. These special days are also celebrated, in part, by visiting a shrine.

In Japan, couples are legally married at a local government office and no ceremony is technically necessary. However, most couples also choose to have a ceremony either at a shrine or a local hotel banquet hall that is setup with a Shinto altar. During this ceremony, the priest purifies and blesses the couple (Figure 7). One of the most important parts of the ceremony is the San San Kudo (literally translated "three three nine times") ritual. In this part of the ceremony, three different-sized cups of sake are placed before the bride and groom. The couple takes three sips from each cup.

---

[1] To listen to a priest chant the prayer before a misogi, go to http://tsubakishrine.org/misogishuho/misogiwithwater.MP3.
[2] Fabio Rambelli, "Home Buddhas: Historical Processes and Modes of Representation of the Sacred in the Japanese Buddhist Altar." Japanese Religions, no. 35(1 &2): 63–86.

As with all religions and rituals, there are variations in practice. For example, some couples have their parents participate in sipping from the cups as well. The symbolism of sharing the cups of sake demonstrates the unity of the couple and the unity of the families.

Funerals are typically officiated over by a Buddhist monk. The body of the deceased is cremated. The ashes are placed in an urn and kept on the family altar for thirty-five days. During that time, family and friends stop by to pay respects and incense sticks are kept continually lit for purification. After this time, the urn is buried in a Buddhist cemetery.

Figure 7   Shinto Wedding.

Festivals

An important part of Shinto practice is the celebration of seasonal festivals (**matsuri**). Beginning with the New Year, festivals mark various times and seasons as well as honor ancestors and kami. Some festivals are primarily Shinto, others Buddhist and still others have no specific religious connotations (i.e., the Sapporo Snow Festival). A Shinto festival generally has three components: welcoming the kami, a parade or procession with a portable shrine for the kami, and returning the kami to their heavenly home.[3]

To welcome in the New Year, people clean their homes, gather with family and friends, eat special foods, and visit the local Shinto shrine or Buddhist temple. The first shrine visit of the New Year (**hatsumode**) may take place just after midnight or anytime in the first three days of the year. At the shrine, the community gathers to offer prayers and special coins. They also write wishes on wooden plaques, called **ema**. People may also draw a slip of paper that forecasts their fortune for the coming year. Around January 15, the New Year's decorations and amulets are gathered at the shrine and burned as people pray for blessings of health and good fortune for the coming year.

An important Buddhist festival for the dead, Obon, is held in August each year. Obon has many parallels with the Ghost Festival in Chinese tradition. Graves are tended, the spirits of ancestors ceremonially return to visit, and then they are ritually sent back by lighting paper lanterns and floating them down a river.

One of the most important festivals is Niiname, an autumn festival in honor of the rice harvest. During this festival, rice, sake, and knot-shaped cookies are offered to the kami. It can be said that this festival is a Japanese Thanksgiving Day. The emperor instituted this festival of thanksgiving sometime between 600 BCE and 400 BCE to give thanks for the first taste of the new rice. The festival is held each November 23 and is celebrated at shrines throughout Japan with offerings, processions, and special dances.

---

[3] http://www.onmarkproductions.com/html/shinto-festivals.html#daijosai2.

☯ Explore information on Japanese festivals. Choose one festival and write down three facts that you learned about the festival. Be sure to include the source of your information.

_____

_____

_____

_____

_____

THE KOJIKI AND NIHON SHOKI

The *Kojiki* and the *Nihon Shoki* are collections of Japanese mythology and history. The Kojiki, or Records of Ancient Matters, includes the creation narratives of the Japanese islands as well as the origins of the various kami (spirits). The narratives were in oral form until around 712 CE when they were finally written down. The Nihon Shoki (or Nihongi) is the Chronicles of Japan. This text describes the origins and history of the imperial family and was committed to print in 720 CE. Similarity exists between the two, in part, because each seeks to explain the origin of the imperial family and promote the sacred narratives of Japan. While the Nihon Shoki is more of a historical narrative, the Kojiki reads more like a religious text.[4] The Kojiki is still a source of knowledge for Shinto priests. To advance in the priestly hierarchy, priests are tested on their knowledge and interpretation of this sacred text.[5]

According to the Kojiki, the divine couple, **Izanagi** (He-who-invites) and **Izanami** (She-who-invites), created the Japanese islands as well as many kami. While birthing the kami of fire, Izanami was badly burned. As a result, she died and descended to the underworld. Izanagi missed her so much that he followed her to the underworld in search of her. When he found her, he begged her to return with him. But, she told him that she needed to get permission from the gods of the underworld to fulfill his request. She promised to return shortly, but told him that under no circumstances should he try to follow her. After waiting patiently for some time, Izanagi could not resist searching for her. Once again he found her, only to discover she had become a rotting corpse. He was horrified at the sight of her and ran away. When he returned to the land of the living, he immediately purified himself in the first misogi ritual. As Izanagi washed his left eye, Amaterasu, the sun goddess emerged from his left eye socket. Tsukuyomi, the moon god, then emerged from his right eye. Izanagi cleansed his nose and gave birth to Susanoo, the storm god.

Amaterasu first sent her son to rule the Japanese islands; however, he told her it was too chaotic down there and returned to the heavens. Later, Amaterasu sent her grandson to rule the islands. It is believed that he was the first emperor of Japan. All the emperors of Japan trace their ancestry to Amaterasu.

---

[4] Brown, Delmer, "Japanese Historical Text Initiative." University of California at Berkley. August 22, 2006, https://jhti.berkeley.edu/search%20gateway.html

[5] Heather H. Kobayashi, "The Miko and the Itako: The Role of Women in Contemporary Shinto Ritual" (2013). Senior Capstone Projects. Paper 160 http://digitalwindow.vassar.edu/cgi/viewcontent.cgi?article=1159&context=senior_capstone.

Today, the role of emperor is mostly ceremonial. Three symbols of the imperial family are a jewel, a mirror, and a sword. These symbols derive from the mythology surrounding Amaterasu and her family.

☯ Explore   http://www.greenshinto.com/wp/2011/07/09/the-three-imperial-regalia/, http://www. greenshinto.com/wp/2014/03/26/imperial-regalia-mystery/, http://afe.easia.columbia.edu/special/ japan_1000bce_originmyths.htm. Describe the origin of the mirror, jewels and sword as symbols of the Emperor and what each signifies.

_____

_____

_____

_____

_____

RELIGIOUS LEADERSHIP

Priests offer primary leadership in the shrines. The majority of priests are male, but female priests have been present in Shinto for centuries. Despite this fact, the number of female priests is relatively small. In 2000, about 13 percent of priests were women.[6] The primary element that has challenged women's ability to exert leadership in shrines is connected to the idea of "blood impurity," which afflicts many women monthly. Historically, the role of women in Shinto has been to act as mediums and healers.

Priests can marry and have families. In addition, they do not wear their ceremonial dress outside of the shrine, which allows them some measure of anonymity outside the shrine. Before the Meiji era, priestly lineage was primarily hereditary. However, since World War II, a person must pass a series of exams given by the Association of Shinto Shrines to serve as a priest. Additional courses and tests are required for the priest to move up in the hierarchy.

Female attendants (miko) serve at shrines as assistants and dancers. They prepare offerings, sell amulets, and provide information to visitors about scheduling rituals (Figure 8). The young women wear white kimonos and capes, sometimes embroidered with the shrine crest. The skirts or trousers are vermillion as are many of the torii. The bright red color is believed to ward off evil and disease.

Figure 8   A Miko Overseeing Good Luck Charms at Shrine in Nara, Japan.

Cowardlion/Shutterstock.com.

---

[6] Ibid.

In northeast Japan, women with visual impairments serve as shaman (**itako**). The role itself blends folk tradition, Shinto and Buddhism. Only women can serve in this capacity. The role primarily involves contact with the spirits of the deceased to bring closure to a grieving family. To become an itako, a young woman must be either blind or visually impaired. It is thought that the lack of sight gives the women a special ability to hear the voices of the dead. Before puberty, a young girl is apprenticed to an itako. The apprentice embarks on a four- to five-year period of intense training that involves memorization of Buddhist sutras and extended periods of prayer and fasting. An initiation ceremony is held in which a male spirit, who will continue to be her contact with the spirit world, possesses the young apprentice. Following the possession, a ritual "wedding" is performed uniting the young woman with the kami.

CONTEMPORARY SHINTO

Although many Japanese identify themselves as nonreligious, the ancient rituals of Shinto continue to provide order and meaning in modern Japan. For instance, it is common for people to take their new car to the shrine to be blessed. Many participate in local festivals and honor ancestors and spirits at home shrines. Although many do not attend shrines frequently, they often visit a shrine during the celebration of the New Year in hopes of happiness and good fortune for the coming year. They purchase amulets and have their fortunes told. Such practices, however, are thought to be part of cultural life, as opposed to being representative of any religion affiliation. Even so, these ritual practices provide a framework that structures life and offers a sense of balance and harmony.

SHINTO AND POPULAR CULTURE

Shinto has also found modern expression in the art and drama of anime and manga. Shinto shrines and sacred spaces provide settings in various scenes in books, television shows, movies and games. It is not uncommon for monks, kami, and miko to appear in the cast of characters of anime, manga, and video games. Characters may be purified under waterfalls or offer prayers of protection at a shrine. Anime figures even appear on ema (wooden plaques with prayers written on them) for sale at local shrines (Figure 9).

Figure 9 Ema with Anime Drawing by Local Art Students.

Solkanar/Shutterstock.com.

☯ If you are not familiar with anime or manga, browse some videos and comics on YouTube, then share some of the features of Shinto you observed. If you are familiar with anime, manga, and references to Shinto in video games, share some examples that come to mind.

_____

_____

_____

SHINTO IN THE UNITED STATES

In the United States, Shinto shrines are more prevalent in Hawaii, but there is one shrine on the mainland. In Granite Falls, Washington, the Tsubaki Grand Shrine meets the needs of those in search of participation in Shinto rituals, spiritual practices and festivals. Although Japanese immigrants have been coming to the United States for well over one hundred years, Shinto does not travel well. As an animist religion, with deep roots in the local places and spirits of Japan, it is difficult to export. Japanese Buddhist temples have more readily made the transition to the West. However, themes of harmony with nature and purity can resonate with many here in the States.

The first Shinto shrines in the United States were in Hawaii. However, in 1987, the Grand Tsubaki Shrine was founded in Stockton, California. It was officiated over by Rev. Yamamoto, a high priest in the Shinto tradition. As early as 1969, Rev. Yamamoto offered a prayer at the United Nations gathering in New York City to bless the Apollo 11 mission. In the 1990s, Lawrence Barrish travelled to Japan and had a profound experience at the Tsubaki Shrine there. He desired to become a priest but was told that was not possible. So, he came home to Granite Falls, built a shrine and studied under Rev. Yamamoto. In the early 2000s, Barrish was ordained by Rev. Yamamoto and was the first non-Japanese Shinto priest in the United States. During this period, the shrine in Stockton and Barrish's shrine in Granite Falls merged into the Grand Tsubaki Shrine in Granite Falls, Washington. The shrine's website provides many valuable resources for studying Shinto and is listed in the links below.

WEB RESOURCES FOR FURTHER STUDY

http://www.greenshinto.com/wp/—This blog started by John Dougill in an effort to communicate an international and environmental form of Shinto.

https://www.jinjahoncho.or.jp/en/—The Shinto Online Network Association is a voluntary organization formed in 1946 led by Shinto priests to share information about Shinto with the larger world. There are a variety of good resources on this page about Shinto.

http://www.tsubakishrine.org/index.html—The website to the Tsubaki Grand Shrine in Washington state offers a wide variety of resources to better understand Shinto.

Part 3a: Zoroastrianism and Other Minority Middle Eastern Religions

Learning Outcomes

By the end of the chapter, students will be able to

- describe the development of Zoroastrianism.
- discuss the central beliefs and practices of Zoroastrianism
- explain how Zoroastrianism has influenced the development of other monotheistic religions.
- communicate the challenges currently faced by Zoroastrians.

Key Terms

Ahura Mazda	Nawruz (Nowruz, Naurooz)
Angra Mainyu	Spenta Mainyu
Avesta	Sudre
Gathas	Yasna
Koeshti	Zarathustra

INTRODUCTION

Zoroastrianism is an ancient Persian religion believed to have influenced the development of the Abrahamic faiths. Although it is one of the lesser known religions of the world, it is a vital faith that continues to sustain its often-persecuted followers. Today, communities of Zoroastrians can be found throughout the world, but particularly in India, Iran, Canada, and the United States. The key motto of their faith is "good thoughts, good words, and good deeds."

LIFE OF ZARATHUSTRA

Zarathustra (Greek: Zoroaster) is often described as the founder of Zoroastrianism. His life is cloaked in legend with people dating his birth anywhere from 2,000 BCE to 100 CE. Most Zoroastrians believe that he was born around 1,500 BCE or a little earlier. The dates are based on archaeological evidence and language similarities with the text of the Hindu Rig Veda which also dates to around that same period. Zarathustra is thought to have been born in Iran in a territory that is, today, part of Russia or Afghanistan. He is believed to have married and had children.

The region was polytheistic, but Zarathustra had a vision that there is only one God. For the first few years, no one paid attention to his teachings; however, when King Vishtasp learned of him, Zarathustra was brought into the royal court. The king became a follower of his teachings, and Zoroastrianism began to grow in popularity. This newfound enthusiasm for the prophet's message led to persecution and imprisonment, but he continued to preach until his assassination while praying at the age of 77. Zoroastrianism was the principal religion of the Persian Empire from sometime in the seventh century BCE to the sixth century CE.

CENTRAL BELIEFS

Zoroastrianism is thought to be one of the earliest monotheistic faiths and an influence on the prophet Abraham. While Zoroastrians believe in one God, they view the world as a place of struggle between the forces of good and the forces of evil. These two forces are manifest in human beings and the society they create as Spenta Mainyu (the good) and Angra Mainyu (the evil). Human beings, through their thoughts and actions, either strengthen the good or the evil. Though monotheistic, Zoroastrians have sometimes been erroneously viewed as dualists because of their view of these two competing forces. As a result of this emphasis on strengthening the good, ethical living is central to the practice of the faith.

Ahura Mazda created the world including the skies, seas, land, plants, animals, humans, and fire. Animals and plants have a special place in the created order with the dog being the most sacred animal. One of the primary tasks of human beings is to care for the earth and its creatures. A Persian proverb speaks to the sacred nature of establishing gardens: "Whoever creates a garden becomes an ally of Light; no garden having ever emerged from the shadows."[1]

The concept of heaven and hell is also evident in Zoroastrianism but with an interesting caveat. These eternal "destinations" are viewed less as places and more as "states of mind." Moreover, hell is not permanent in Zoroastrianism, and is also characterized by justice, a key virtue in the faith. Four days after death, the human soul is judged based on his/her deeds. When evil is finally defeated, all souls in hell will be purified and returned to God.

---

[1] Proverb from https://docplayer.net/104277943-C-o-n-t-e-n-t-s-hamazor-issue.html, p. 24.

SACRED TEXTS

The Avesta is the sacred text of Zoroastrianism and is a collection of writings from Zarathustra as well as other prophets after him. Arguably the most important part of the sacred text is a collection of hymns and prayers known as the Gathas.[2] The Gathas are part of the oldest Zoroastrian writings (the Yasna) and thought to have been composed by Zarathustra himself. Yasna 12 is the central creed, or statement of faith.[3] The memorization and recitation of the sacred texts is an integral part of worship at home and in the temple.

> "I shall lead my soul towards heaven by pure thought, and being well aware of the blessings which the Almighty, Ahura, shall pour down upon good deeds, I shall teach the people to strive for truth and follow righteousness."
>
> —Yasna 28, verse 4

RITUALS AND FESTIVALS

Asha is extremely important in Zoroastrianism and influences ethics and ritual. Asha is difficult to translate, but it is commonly rendered as purity, eternal law, or truth. Keeping the earth pure is one reason for the burial practice of placing the body of the deceased on a tower for the vultures to pick the bones clean.[4] Tibetans, Mayans, and Zoroastrians, among others, have all practiced this form of "burial." One of the most well-known structures connected to Zoroastrianism is the Tower of Silence, the term for the platforms built for sky burials.

Fire is a very important symbol of **asha** in Zoroastrianism. It is believed to represent the purity and goodness of God. Although Zoroastrian priests tend fires in temples around the world, they do not worship fire. Rather, both fire and water are viewed as pure and representative of the purity and goodness of God. Many Zoroastrians keep an oil lamp burning in their home as a symbol of light banishing darkness.

The hymns and prayers recorded in the sacred texts inform the worship life of priests and laity. Like their Jewish and Muslim cousins, Zoroastrian worship largely focuses on the recitation of sacred texts and prayers that are memorized. Accurate recitation is essential as mistakes impact the cosmic order.[5]

Figure 1   A Zoroastrian fire temple in Azerbaijan (September 19, 2016).

---

[2] To read the Gathas in English, see https://www.zarathushtra.com/z/gatha/az/The%20Gathas%20-%20FAZ.pdf
[3] To hear the creed recited, visit https://www.youtube.com/watch?v=Yh4KF0xUgGg
[4] For more information on vulture symbolism in various cultures, see http://www.campearth.org/vulture_medicine.htm
[5] http://www.iranicaonline.org/articles/zoroastrian-rituals

Traditionally upon initiation into the faith, both males and females wear a sacred white cotton shirt (sudre) and belt (koeshti) under their clothing. The shirt is similar to a t-shirt but has a small pocket at the base of the V-neck where good deeds are symbolically placed. The belt is symbolic of the need to "gird" oneself for the struggle to do good in the world. A special prayer is recited when tying and untying the koeshti.

While Zoroastrians celebrate six seasonal festivals, the most important is the Persian New Year, Nawruz (you will also find it spelled "Nowruz" or "Naurooz"), which coincides with the spring equinox. A special table is set with symbolic foods and images. Some of the items on the table include a mirror, flowers, nuts, fruits, wine, honey, and candles. A white table cloth is sometimes used to symbolize purity. Singing, dancing, gift giving, picnics, and visiting family and friends are all part of the celebrations. Traditionally, the festival lasts for nearly two weeks.

Figure 2   Nowruz table.

☯ Choose a Zoroastrian ritual, festival, or practice to explore further. Share what you looked into and two things you learned about it.

_____

_____

_____

_____

ZOROASTRIANISM IN THE UNITED STATES

Fleeing persecution, Zoroastrians have spread throughout the world. Approximately 11,000 Zoroastrians make their home in the United States.[7] In the last few years, a Zoroastrian temple has opened in New York.[8] In addition, a strong Zoroastrian community has been active in the Washington, DC, area for decades; but, in recent years, has built a community center and worship space in Boyds, MD. These examples are representative of Zoroastrian communities in at least twenty different states around the country.

---

[6] For a fuller discussion of the sacred clothing, see https://authenticgathazoroastrianism.org/2010/12/07/sudre-koeshti-the-sacred-shirt-and-belt-of-the-zoroastrians/

[7] http://www.heritageinstitute.com/zoroastrianism/demographics/#us

[8] https://www.usatoday.com/story/news/nation-now/2016/04/03/zoroastrian-temple-erected-new-york/82588552/

OTHER LESSER KNOWN MIDDLE EASTERN FAITHS

Zoroastrians are not the only minority religion that originated and is still practiced in the Middle East today. Other movements include Alawites, Druze, Mandaeans, Samaritans, and Yazidi. While there is no time to go into the background and practice of each of these groups, they are important for understanding the complex religious makeup of the Middle East and the geopolitical realities these groups face.

☯ Choose one of the abovementioned groups to explore a little further. Write down three facts you learned about the movement.

_____

_____

_____

_____

WEB RESOURCES FOR FURTHER STUDY

http://www.avesta.org/afrin/20100321_Naurooz_Prayer_Book_all_52_Pages_Landscape_Final.pdf. Prayer book in English and Farsi for the celebration of Nawruz, the Persian New Year.

https://fezana.org/. The website for the Federation of Zoroastrian Associations in North America offers many resources for exploring the beliefs, practices, and historic leaders of the faith.

http://www.huffingtonpost.com/entry/a-rare-glimpse-inside-a-zoroastrian-temple-in-new-york_us_570563d6e4b0537661888a74. Article about the Zoroastrian temple opened in New York to serve Zoroastrians in the area.

http://www.iranicaonline.org/articles/zoroastrian-rituals. Great resource on Zoroastrian rituals and how they have adapted in modern times.

https://zoroastrians.net/2014/12/03/zoroastrian-daily-prayers/. A sound recording of twenty-four Zoroastrian prayers.

https://www.nationalgeographic.com/news/2014/10/141026-yazidis-middle-east-iraq-islamic-state-religion-world-ngbooktalk/—A brief history of the Yazidi and their faith.

https://www.thoughtco.com/the-difference-between-alawites-and-sunnis-in-syria-2353572—A brief but thoughtful article about the relationship of Alawites to other Muslim groups.

http://www.pewresearch.org/fact-tank/2016/03/21/5-facts-about-israeli-druze-a-unique-religious-and-ethnic-group/—A link to the Pew Forum's five important facts about the Druze.

https://www.pri.org/stories/2016-10-06/these-iraqi-immigrants-worship-john-baptist-theyre-not-christians—This news story explores the Mandaeans, followers of John the Baptist.

http://www.mandaeanunion.com/history-english/item/170-brief-history-on-the-mandaeans—An excellent site exploring the Mandaeans, ancient followers of John the Baptist.

https://www.economist.com/blogs/economist-explains/2016/10/economist-explains-14—A brief article about the remaining Samaritans of Mt. Gerizim.

http://aa.com.tr/en/middle-east/palestine-s-samaritans-make-pilgrimage-to-mt-gerizim/926999—A news article about the Samaritans today.

Part 3b: Abrahamic Faiths
Comparison and Contrast
Abrahamic Faiths

CHAPTERS:

INTRODUCTION

The three Abrahamic Faiths – Judaism, Christianity and Islam – share a common and often conflicted history. All three religions share a belief in the one God, the God of Abraham, and all claim Jerusalem as sacred. The Dome of the Rock and Mosque of Al-Aqsa sit above the Temple Mount and the Western or Wailing Wall (Figure 1). The Wall is all that remains of the second temple destroyed by the Romans in 70 CE. People go to the Wall to pray and to experience God's presence.

The Dome of the Rock commemorates the place where Muhammad is said to have been taken up into heaven on a Night Journey to speak with God and the prophets. For Christians, the Church of the Holy Sepulcher, also in Jerusalem, marks the place where Jesus is said to have been crucified, buried, and risen from the dead. Jerusalem has left a lasting imprint on the sacred geography of all three Abrahamic faiths.[1]

Similarities and Differences between Judaism, Christianity, and Islam

Throughout much of history, there has been misunderstanding and mistrust between Christians and their religious cousins, followers of Judaism and Islam. Despite much public opinion to the contrary, followers of Judaism, Christianity, and Islam worship the same God. God is referred to by the Arabic word, Allah, in Islam because the Arabic word, Allah, means "the God", and cannot be made plural. The use of Allah underscores the Muslim conviction that there is only one God. Furthermore, Arabic Christians and Jews also refer to God as Allah.

Muslims, Christians, and Jews all trace their history back to the patriarch Abraham, believed to be the first monotheist. Abraham had two sons, Ishmael and Isaac. Ishmael was the firstborn son of

---

[1] For more information on Jerusalem and it's sacred sites and to take 3D virtual tours, see http://jerusalem.com/.

Karol Kozlowski/Shutterstock.com.

Figure 1   Western Wall and Mosque of Al-Aqsa in Jerusalem.

Abraham, by Sarah's handmaid Hagar. Muslims trace their lineage through Ishmael. Jews and Christians trace their lineage through Isaac, the son of Abraham and Sarah.

The three faiths share more in common than simple ancestry. They share a belief in the one God, Creator of the Universe, made known throughout history through prophets. Christianity and Islam both recognize the great prophets of Jewish history (Adam, Abraham, Moses, David, Jesus). All three religions believe strongly in the message of social justice spoken through God's prophets. In addition, they also share a belief that God is active in human history calling people to faithfully enter into a relationship with God. All three have a linear view of history in that there is a point of creation, a purpose for creation, and an end to history. All three traditions believe that angels help to carry out God's purposes; and, many Christians and Muslims believe that demons (nonsubmissive beings) seek to thwart God's efforts.

In all three traditions, there is an emphasis on morality, including the Ten Commandments, and the gracious and merciful nature of God. All encourage a blend of faith and practice. Dietary laws are important in both Judaism and Islam with some common foods to be avoided and an emphasis on animals being properly blessed and humanely slaughtered. Muslims add to their dietary laws an avoidance of alcoholic beverages that the Jewish people do not share.

The issue of God's grace is particularly strong in Christianity; however, all three religious traditions believe in God's mercy and forgiveness. Although Jewish theology is vague on the idea of afterlife, Christians and Muslims share a common belief in the notion of heaven and hell. Christians and Muslims, alike, believe that there will be a day of judgment.

Notion of Messiah

A major difference between Christianity and both, Judaism and Islam, involves the role of Jesus. Christians believe that Jesus is the Messiah and is both fully human and fully divine. He is believed to be

God's Son. Jews and Muslims believe that Jesus cannot be divine, because that would be both idolatrous and impossible. They believe that God cannot be divided in any way and that belief in Jesus' divinity compromises monotheism. Followers of both Judaism and Islam assert that God cannot be birthed nor can God birth an offspring.

Many Christians believe it is obvious that Jesus was the Messiah, and they cannot understand how the Jewish community does not recognize him as such. In addition, there is the assumption that the term "messiah" refers to the same type of figure in all three Abrahamic faiths. Perhaps in looking at the following chart, it will be easier to see the differences by discovering how the term is understood in each religion.

Differing Notions of the Messiah

	Judaism	Christianity	Islam
Nature	Human	Divine	Human
Purpose	Usher in God's kingdom on Earth	Reconcile humankind to God	Serve as ruler who will usher in God's kingdom
Role	✦ Rebuild Temple ✦ Establish an era of justice and peace based on Jewish law	✦ Mediator of God's forgiveness and grace ✦ Sacrifice for human sin (Lamb of God slain for the sins of the world)	✦ Sunnis view as Caliph or ruler of the Muslim world ✦ Shia view Mahdi as the one who kills the anti-Christ
Lineage	Son of David	Son of David Son of God	Descendant of Muhammad
Result	Establish God's Kingdom on Earth based on peace and justice, centered in Jerusalem	Establish God's Kingdom on Earth, defeat Satan, and usher in Day of Judgment	Establish God's Kingdom on Earth centered in Jerusalem for a number of years before defeating Satan and with Jesus usher in the Day of Judgment
Forgiveness	God	God through Christ	God

The nature and purpose of the Messiah differs among the three religious traditions. In both Judaism and Islam, the Messiah (Mahdi) is a human, political figure who acts on behalf of God. In Christianity, the Messiah is both human and divine and brings about salvation. Neither Islam nor Judaism, see the Messiah as having a salvific role; that is left to God.

How does the role of messiah differ in these three faiths? What conflicts might be caused by these differences?

_____

_____

_____

_____

_____

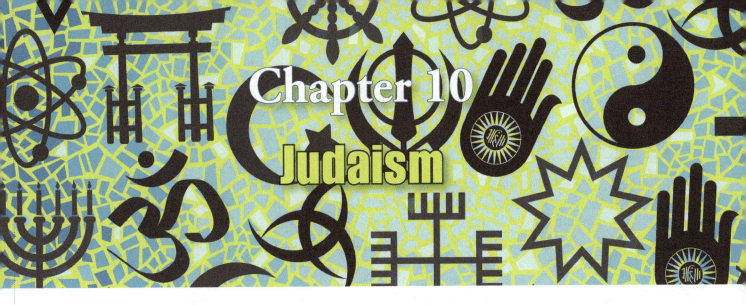

Chapter 10
Judaism

Learning Outcomes

By the end of this lesson, students will be able to

- summarize the similarities and differences between the three Abrahamic faiths;
- briefly outline the history of the Jewish people from the time of Abraham to the end of the 1st century CE;
- identify the basic beliefs of Judaism;
- describe the sacred practices of Judaism including the Sabbath and kosher laws as well as the major Jewish festivals; and
- explain the differences between the major branches of Judaism.

Key Terms

Abraham	Judah (Israel)	Shavuot (Pentecost)
Ark of the Covenant	Kabbalah	Shema
Bar Mitzvah (Bat Mitzvah)	Kosher	Sukkot
Circumcision	Menorah	Synagogue
Conservative Judaism	Mikva	T'fillin
Covenant	Mishnah	Talmud
David	Moses	Tanakh
Diaspora	Passover	Torah
Exile	Purim	Yarmulke
Exodus	Rabbi	YHWH
Hanukkah	Reconstructionism	Yom Hashoah
Hasidim	Reform Judaism	Yom Kippur
Isaac	Rosh Hashanah	Zionism
Ishmael	Sabbath	
Joseph	Seder	

INTRODUCTION

Although Judaism has a smaller global population than many of the other major world religions, its influence on religious thought, morality and ethics, popular culture, and history is profound. Being Jewish is an ethnic, religious, and cultural identity. A person can be ethnically Jewish but not a practicing member of the Jewish faith. Judaism is not a missionary religion; that is, Jews do not actively seek converts from other faith traditions. While Judaism is a relatively small religion, with fourteen million followers worldwide, eighty percent live in either the United States or Israel.

Judaism is a tradition of ethical monotheism. It began with the belief that there is one God and that one God, YHWH, chose the Hebrew people as a "pilot project, a demonstration community."[1] They were "chosen" not for special privileges but rather for unique responsibilities, chief of which is fulfilling the Law, the Torah. In addition, the Jewish people serve as co-creators with God of a just and peaceful world.

VIEW OF HISTORY

In the Judeo-Christian tradition, there is the strong belief that God is active in human history; and, human beings are co-creators with God. In the Genesis 1 account of creation, the writer states that there was evening and there was morning the first day. Does that sound backwards? Shouldn't it be "and there was morning and evening the first day"? No. In Jewish understanding, the day begins with sundown. God is active through the night, and human being awake in the morning to continue what God has already started.

MEMORY

Memory is an important concept in Judaism and Christianity; it is not just a recollection of something that happened a long time ago. Rather, it is a participation in the events of salvation history. In the celebration of the Exodus, the pivotal event of Jewish history, the assertion is made in the celebration of Passover that "we were slaves in the land of Egypt and God brought us out with a mighty hand and an outstretched arm." It is *not,* "our ancestors were slaves," but rather, it is "we." It is this same kind of memory that is the basis of the Christian practice of the Eucharist or Lord's Supper. It is not simply a remembrance of Jesus' death and resurrection; it is a participation in it.

COVENANT, EXODUS, AND EXILE

Beginning in Genesis, the biblical narrative outlines God's involvement in the lives of the Hebrew people and highlights important themes that inform Jewish understanding and identity: covenant, exodus, and exile. A covenant is an agreement between two parties in which both parties have certain

---

[1] Harold Kushner, *To Life* (Little, Brown and Company, 1994), p. 31.

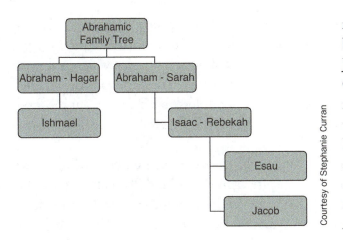

Courtesy of Stephanie Curran

responsibilities to each other. The covenant between God and **Abraham** is the beginning of Judaism (about 2,000 BCE) and is described in Genesis, chapters 12, 15, and 17. In the biblical narrative, God speaks to Abraham and promises that if he will follow where God leads, he will be blessed with many descendants, a great nation, and a land, which God will provide. The sign of the covenant between God and Abraham is **circumcision**. The covenant passes through Abraham's son, **Isaac**, and through Isaac's descendants, Jacob and Esau. Jacob has twelve sons by four different women and these sons become known as the Twelve Tribes of Israel.

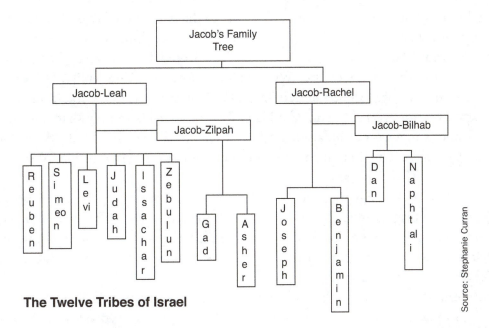

Source: Stephanie Curran

The Twelve Tribes of Israel

Joseph is the firstborn son of Jacob and Rachel. Jacob gives him a special coat and his brothers, fairly or not, believe he is the favored son. What is more, Joseph dreams that his brothers will bow down to him. Rather than keeping these dreams to himself, Joseph relishes telling them to his brothers. The brothers conspire to kill Joseph. Reuben feels a little squeamish about murder and suggests instead that they just leave him in a pit. While Joseph is in the pit, a caravan of Ishmaelites came along, and the brothers sell Joseph to them as a slave.

Once in Egypt, a series of unfortunate events leads to Joseph being imprisoned. However, news of his ability to interpret dreams spreads to Pharaoh whose dreams no one can seem to interpret. Joseph accurately interprets Pharaoh's dreams and tells him that seven years of plenty in Egypt will be followed by seven years of famine. Hearing this news, Pharaoh puts Joseph in charge of preparing for the famine. When the famine comes, Joseph's brothers travel to Egypt to find food. Joseph is handing out the food and recognizes his brothers. Reconciliation ensues, and Joseph tells his brothers to bring their father and their families to settle in Egypt.

Through Joseph, the twelve tribes end up in the land of Egypt. As their numbers grow, a new Pharaoh comes to power. Fearful that the people will conspire against him, the Pharaoh enslaves the Hebrew people. In addition to slavery, the Pharaoh punishes the Hebrew people by the slaughtering of baby boys in order to limit their numbers. **Moses'** mother places him in a basket by the river hoping he will not be slaughtered. Pharaoh's daughter finds Moses who then grew up in Pharaoh's household. As an adult, Moses kills an Egyptian who was mistreating Hebrew slaves. Fearing discovery, Moses flees to the land of Midian.

While Moses is tending the flocks of his father-in-law, Jethro, he sees a strange sight. A bush is burning, but it is not consumed. Moses draws near to the bush and takes off his shoes; confident he is on holy ground. Moses hears God speaking from the bush. God instructs Moses to go back to Egypt, approach Pharaoh and insist on the freedom of God's people. During the exchange between God and Moses, Moses asks for God's identity. "Who shall I say sent me?" God replies, **YHWH**, "The one who brings things into being." These four letters are God's name in Hebrew tradition, and are known as the **Tetragrammaton,** or Ha-Shem, "the Name." God's name is so holy that it is not to be spoken; so, for Orthodox followers of Judaism, God is referred to as Adonai, "Lord." As a sign of respect no vowels are part of the Tetragrammaton. In addition, it is also common for the "o" to be omitted when the English word, G-d, is used.

Moses travels back to Egypt to approach Pharaoh and demand the people's release. Pharaoh refuses and a series of ten plagues afflict Egypt. The tenth plague is the death of the firstborn, including all animals and people. To avoid the "Angel of Death," the Hebrew people are told to put the blood of a lamb over their doorpost. That way, the Angel of Death would pass over. This event is commemorated each year in the celebration of **Passover.**

Moses leads the people out of Egypt and into the wilderness, where they wander for forty years. This event is known as the **Exodus,** and scholars generally think it occurred around 1,250 BCE. The time of wandering is a period in which the people begin to understand their identity and form a second covenant with God at Mt. Sinai. This covenant is not unconditional. God promises to be faithful if Israel remains obedient. The giving of the law at Sinai provides directions for what it means to be obedient. The initial gift of the law was the **Decalogue** or the Ten Commandments.

During their time in the wilderness, the law (**Torah**) is established. The Torah consists of 613 commandments, or **mitzvot**. While in the wilderness, worship takes place in temporary booths, called **tabernacles**. God provides directions for the construction of the tabernacle as well as the **Ark of the Covenant**. The Ark serves as a sign of God's presence with the people and as a receptacle for the stones on which the Ten Commandments were inscribed. At the end of the time in the wilderness, Moses stands on the mountain overlooking the Promised Land. God gives Moses a glimpse, but does not allow him to enter. Moses dies and, according to the Bible, God buries him.

Joshua leads the people from the wilderness into Canaan, the Land of Promise. This period is known as the Conquest; however, the conquest is not a complete one. The Hebrew people divvy up territory by tribe and they live alongside the residents of Canaan, sometimes peacefully, but often, contentiously. The period is characterized by leadership from judges, individual leaders blessed with the spirit of God to provide both the arbitration of disputes and military leadership for one or more tribes. Under the leadership of the judges, a pattern (or cycle) develops that will continue through the monarchy and the period of the prophets. This pattern consists of disobedience, followed by God allowing something bad to happen. At which time, a leader rises up to call the people to faithfulness. Heeding the call, the people repent; God delivers them, and the covenant is renewed. Over time, the leader dies and the people fall into disobedience again. This cycle of covenant making, covenant breaking, and covenant renewal continues for centuries.

After a period of a couple of hundred years, the Hebrew people demand a king. God gives the prophet, Samuel, the task of anointing the first king. **Saul** is the first king, but he falls out of favor with God. Samuel is then asked by God to anoint **David** (around 1,000 BCE). God establishes a specific covenant with David to perpetuate the monarchy and with the descendants of Aaron to perpetuate the priesthood. David is a successful king who unites the tribes into a nation and establishes a capital city in **Jerusalem**. He brings the Ark of the Covenant to Jerusalem, but is not permitted to build the Temple. It is his son, Solomon, who builds the first **Temple**.

After the death of Solomon, the kingdom divides into north and south, and the period of the prophets begins. The Northern kingdom survives until around 722 BCE when its capital, Samaria, falls to the Assyrians. The Southern kingdom survives until about **586 BCE**. At this time, the people of **Judah** are captured by the Babylonians, the temple is destroyed and many of the Hebrew people are taken into exile in Babylon.

The **Exile** is another formative event in Israel's history. It begins the **Diaspora**, or the scattering of the Jewish people outside of Palestine. The Exile lasts for about sixty years. Up to this point in history, the Hebrew people flirted with the gods of their neighbors; however, from the experience of exile, a strict monotheism emerges. In addition, during this period, a new institution arises in Jewish religious life, the **synagogue**. The synagogue was a place of study and fellowship. Religious leadership in the synagogue was provided by a **rabbi**, who functioned as a teacher and guide in interpreting the law. During

the time of the Exile, the Torah is said to have been compiled and serious study and interpretation of the sacred writings began. This emphasis on interpreting the sacred texts continued and strengthened as Rabbinical Judaism developed.

When Cyrus the Great captures the Babylonians in 539 BCE, the Hebrew people are allowed to return to Jerusalem and rebuild the Temple. Ezra and Nehemiah begin the effort. The Romans destroy this second temple in 70 CE, and it is never rebuilt. All that remains of the second Temple is the Western or Wailing Wall, which still remains a sign of God's presence (Figure 1).

Usoltceva Anastasiia/Shutterstock.com.

Figure 1 Women Praying at the Women's Section of the Wailing Wall.

SACRED TEXTS

The Hebrew Scriptures began to be compiled during the time of David and Solomon but did not reach their final form until around 100 CE at the Council of Jamnia. After the destruction of the second Temple, the leadership of rabbis completely replaces the leadership of priests and the system of sacrifice comes to an end.

The Hebrew Scriptures are known as the Tanakh, an acronym for the three divisions of the text:

◆ **T**orah—the Pentateuch, or the five books of Moses (Genesis to Deuteronomy).
◆ **N**evi'im—The Prophets, which include the historical books such as Joshua, Judges, Samuel and Kings as well as the major and the twelve minor prophets such as Isaiah, Jeremiah and Ezekiel along with Amos, Hosea, Nahum, etc.
◆ **K**etuv'im—The Writings include poetry and wisdom literature. Works in this category are writings such as Psalms, Proverbs, Ecclesiastes, Ruth, and Daniel, among others.

In addition to the Tanakh, there are two other bodies of sacred literature in Judaism: the Talmud and the Kabbalah. The Talmud contains commentaries, folklore, and accumulated tradition on the meaning of the law. For the rabbis whose thought is recorded in the Talmud, the question is not, what did God say? Rather, the question is, what did God mean when God said, …? For instance, God said in the Ten Commandments to honor the Sabbath and keep it holy. The question is what does it mean to keep the Sabbath holy? The tradition then develops about what constitutes work, what is part of honoring the Sabbath and what is not. The Talmud is composed of two parts, the Mishnah and the Gemara. The Mishnah developed around the second century CE. It draws together the 613 commandments and the oral law that accompanies them in a topical format. For example, all of the passages about the Passover are gathered together in one collection, as are all of the passages about the Sabbath. The Gemara is the second part of the Talmud, and is made up of commentaries and interpretations on the Mishnah by many of the great rabbis of Jewish history. The Talmud is an example of the value of argument and debate in Judaism. Through discussion, debate, and study, people come to a better understanding of what it means to be faithful to God and God's law. In the Talmud, not only is the "winning" argument recorded, but the additional interpretations are presented alongside the dominant one.[2]

The other collection of writings important in Jewish history is the **Kabbalah**. These writings were compiled during the Middle Ages, but the ideas themselves date back much further. The concern with angels, demons, magical incantations, interpretation of dreams, and speculation on the date of the coming of the Messiah, numerology and fascination with the name of God were all lumped together under the heading of Kabbalah. The most outstanding compilation of Kabbalistic material is the *Zohar*. This material is attributed to Tanna Simeon Ben Yohai, a Jewish leader from the second century CE, but compiled by the Spanish mystic, Moses de Leon. The *Zohar* is concerned with themes such as the nature of God, the existence of evil, and the work of angels in the world; in addition, it is viewed as a commentary on the Torah for those who are spiritually mature. In fact, historically, because of the maturity it required, rabbis asserted that one should be forty years old before beginning a study of Kabbalah. While there are exceptions to the age rule, the requirement upheld in Orthodox Judaism is that the text should always be studied with a rabbi.

---

[2] To read the Talmud in English, see http://www.sacred-texts.com/jud/talmud.htm.

CENTRAL CONCEPTS IN JUDAISM

The central tenet of Judaism is a belief in one God. God is revealed in nature, but is not the same as nature. God is active in human history and is the Creator of the universe. God is knowable and unknowable, holy and merciful. Love for God is at the center of Jewish practice. The central prayer of Judaism is referred to as the **Shema**. Shema is Hebrew for "Hear," the first word of the prayer. "Hear, O Israel, the Lord your God is one. You shall love the Lord your God with your heart, soul, mind and strength." The prayer is found in Deuteronomy 6: 4–9. It is to be taught to children and placed on the doorpost (**mezuzah**); it is to be a sign on one's hand and an emblem on one's forehead (Figure 2). The mezuzah is a cylinder attached to the doorframe that contains the Shema on a tiny scroll. The (**t'fillin**) refers to the bands that Orthodox Jews wrap around their arms during prayer as well as the small box that is placed in the middle of the forehead. The Shema is also to be repeated in the morning and the evening. As such, this prayer is recited at least twice a day.

Figure 2   Orthodox Jewish Male Wearing the Tallit (Prayer Shawl) and t'fillin.

Love for God is shown is through worship and obedience to God's law. The term for Jewish law is **halakha**, which literally means "the path one walks." Jewish law, particularly for the Orthodox, governs all aspects of daily life. Human beings are created to mirror God's qualities of justice, love, wisdom, mercy, and righteousness. Furthermore, Judaism maintains that human beings are potentially perfectible. God limited divine power to give human beings free will and involvement in the creative process. Humans are co-creators with God and share in the responsibility for the condition of creation. By fulfilling the law, humanity upholds its end of the covenant. In Judaism, there is no distinction between the sacred and the mundane. All of life is holy and therefore is subject to the guidance of the law.

The medieval Jewish rabbi, philosopher, scholar, and writer, Maimonides (Moshe ben Maimon, 1,135–1,204 CE), contributed much to the understanding of the application and codification of Jewish law as well as to the intersection of Judaism and Greek philosophy. Maimonides was born in Spain but fled with his family to Egypt because of persecution. He lived in the Arabic world for the remainder of his life serving as a physician, scholar, and writer. He wrote in both Arabic and Hebrew. Two of his most famous works are his commentary on the *Mishnah* and his complete book of Jewish law, the *Mishnah Torah*. The *Mishnah Torah* is a complete codification of Jewish law including the Oral law from the periods both before and after the destruction of the Temple in Jerusalem.[3]

In Judaism, there is no unified view of the afterlife. The emphasis in Jewish practice is on this life and the difference human beings can make in the world. The Jewish idea of *tikkun olam*, or repairing the world, is central to Jewish practice. Human beings work with God to make the world a more peaceful, just, and righteous place for all people. Ethical principles of preserving life and practicing justice are central to Jewish practice. After death, some assert that there is a traditional idea of heaven. Others say

---

[3] For a complete overview of Maimonides including his biography, videos about his life and thought, and translations of his works, see http://www.chabad.org/library/article_cdo/aid/889836/jewish/Maimonides.htm.

that our souls, which were born pure, are purified anew and returned to God. Ultimately, the afterlife is up to God, and human beings are responsible for how this life is lived.

BRANCHES OF JUDAISM

The three major branches of Judaism are the Orthodox, Conservative, and Reform movements. Interestingly, the major differences are not so much in belief but in practice. All assert the belief in one God and following the Torah to make the world a more just and peaceful place. Differences exist primarily in the adaptation of Judaism to modern culture and in the day-to-day practice of the faith. Some of the differences in the branches will become clearer as the focus of the discussion shifts to ritual practices.

The **Orthodox** is the oldest group within Judaism, and the only group until the nineteenth century CE. They attempt to stay as close as possible to the historical core of the faith as outlined in the scriptures as well as the traditions of the Talmud. The Orthodox strictly observe the kosher and Sabbath laws. In worship, the traditional separation of male and female is observed, heads are covered, and Hebrew is the language used. Worship in the synagogue takes place on Saturday morning, and worshippers are expected to walk to the synagogue.

The **Reform** movement began in Germany in the early 1800s. Influenced by the Enlightenment, and an embracing of the belief that the essence of Judaism can adapt to changing times, several rabbis began to rethink Jewish law and its application to modern life. The first Reform temples opened in Germany between 1810 and 1820. Then, in 1843, a group of German Jewish leaders in Frankfort made the following declarations:

- There is a continuation in the development of Judaism.
- The Talmud has no authority for the modern Jew.
- We seek no Messiah, and we know no homeland but the land of our birth.[4]

Reform Judaism spread to the United States very early on; and over time, has become the largest Jewish movement in the United States. The Pittsburgh Platform emerged from a conference in Pittsburgh, Pennsylvania, in 1885 bringing together the United States and German branches of Reform Judaism. The Platform consists of eight agreed upon principles that form the core of what distinguishes Reform Judaism from other branches. To read all eight principles, see https://www.jewishvirtuallibrary.org/jsource/Judaism/pittsburgh_program.html.

For Reform Judaism, worship is on Friday night. Men and women sit together with uncovered heads. The language of the land is the primary language of worship with some Hebrew as well. Kosher food laws and Sabbath regulations are followed less strictly, and for some, not at all. Women fully participate in the life of the synagogue and can become rabbis. However, Israel does not recognize the authority of non-Orthodox rabbis.

Reform Judaism is also very involved in interfaith relations. Intermarriage between followers of Judaism and other faiths has become very common in recent history. Reform Judaism has responded to this by allowing for participation of the non-Jewish spouse in the life of the community and asserting that the Jewish lineage can come through either the father or the mother.

---

[4] Samuel S. Cohon, "The Mission of Reform Judaism." *The Journal of Religion* 2.1 (1922): 37.

Troubled by the extent to which Reform Judaism moved away from traditional Judaism, but still appreciating the need to adapt to modern life and take advantage of secular scholarship and methods in the study of scripture, the **Conservative** movement was founded as a middle ground between Orthodox and Reform. Followers of Conservative Judaism are dedicated to traditional rabbinic Judaism, but unlike the Orthodox, they are more open to restating it in modern terms. Some of the changes that have been made include: acceptance of riding to synagogue for Sabbath worship, but abstaining from driving themselves; and, the acceptance of women into rabbinical schools as candidates for ordination as rabbis. Conservative Judaism, like Reform Judaism, also allows for Bat Mitzvah ceremonies for girls. In its worship, Hebrew is used more extensively. Men are required to cover their heads with the yarmulke, but there is not always strict separation of men and women. Most followers of Conservative Judaism try to follow kosher and Sabbath laws. Jewish faith is passed through the lineage of the mother only in both Orthodox and Conservative traditions.

OTHER MOVEMENTS WITHIN JUDAISM

Reconstructionism is a movement that branched off of Conservative Judaism. Rabbi Mordecai Kaplan founded it in the 1930s. He emphasized Judaism as a culture and a people as well as a spiritual movement. In his view, the traditions exist for the people and not the other way around. He created a new prayer book, removing the portions of the old one he found offensive, particularly those related to supernatural powers. Some of these deletions included the parting of the Red Sea, references to Israel as the "chosen people," and prayers for miracles (such as rain). Women are fully accepted into synagogue leadership in Reconstructionism as well. In fact, it was Mordecai Kaplan who first introduced the practice of bat mitzvah that exists in all but Orthodox communities today.

The term, Zionism, encompasses a variety of movements for a Jewish state. It was spurred by a desire for a homeland and in response to the persecution faced by the Jewish people. Theodore Herzl coined the term, "Zionism," and founded the movement in the late 1890s. He envisioned a place, not necessarily in Palestine, where struggling Jews could go to begin a new life. He didn't believe followers of Judaism who were well off and well assimilated into the cultures of Europe and the United States would be drawn to leave. Later in life, he even went along with and promoted the idea of a Jewish homeland in Uganda. Other Zionists, including Chaim Weizmann, felt that the Jewish state must be in Palestine and should attract the most talented members of the Jewish community. Religious Zionism offered additional reasoning for a Jewish state. For many, the idea of a Jewish homeland would usher in a messianic age. For these individuals, the development of a Jewish state in Palestine was a fulfillment of a religious obligation. On the other hand, some religious Jews felt that the establishment of a Jewish state would lead to secularism and the substitution of religious identity with national identity. After World War II, the state of Israel was established, but differences in Zionist aspirations still remain.

Haredi Judaism is the ultra-Orthodox form of Judaism. Not all ultra-Orthodox followers of Judaism are Hasidim; however, they are one of the largest forms. Hasidic Judaism developed in Poland around 1750. Israel ben Eliezer (1699–1760) taught that God was not to be found in scholarly study but through simple heart-centered faith. Ben Eliezer became known as Baal Shem Tov (Master of the Good Name) and his followers are known as Hasidim. In Hebrew, *Hasidim* means "pious ones"; and, purity and piety are central to the Hasidic lifestyle. The experience of God is central to Hasidic mysticism. Hasidic Jews stress separation of gender roles, are very strict in their practices and are distinguished by their black hats, coats and long beards. Historically, Hasidic Judaism was the dominant perspective in Eastern Europe, but the Holocaust nearly destroyed the movement. Ultra-Orthodox Judaism is on the rise particularly because of their high birth rates. The United States has the largest population of Hasidim worldwide with roughly 200,000 of the 250,000 Hasidic Jews residing here. Most of the Hasidim in the United States live in the New York City area.[5]

In addition to these movements within Judaism, cultural distinctions also exist in terms of dress, diet, etc. **Ashkenazi** is the terms for those who are European Jews; while, **Sephardic** refers to Jews from Spain and North Africa. A strong and historic Jewish community also exists in Ethiopia, particularly in the Gondar region. Judaism in Ethiopia dates back to the time of King Solomon when the Queen of Sheba visited him. She came back from the visit with a child and a strong connection to Judaism. Since that time, a committed Jewish community has existed in Ethiopia, but it has often experienced persecution, been practiced in secret and gone unrecognized within the Jewish community (Figure 3).

Figure 3 Ethiopian Jewish leader carrying a Torah scroll in a religious procession.

JEWISH SYMBOLS

Symbols of Judaism are closely linked to the sacred text and God's presence and action in the lives of the Jewish people. When entering the sanctuary of the synagogue, many symbols are visible. The Ark of the Covenant at the front of most synagogues is where the Torah scrolls are kept (Figure 4).

It is symbolic of the Ark of the Covenant that carried the commandments during the period the Israelites wandered in the wilderness. There are also portable Arks used to carry the Torah scroll in processions. They are cylindrical in shape and often made from wood or precious metals.

In front of the Ark is an Eternal Light that is kept continually lit. The flame may be electric, gas, or oil, and represents the Eternal Light in the Temple in Jerusalem. In addition, it is sometimes said to represent the menorah that was outside the Temple in Jerusalem. The **menorah** is also a

Figure 4 Ark of the Covenant in a synagogue in Morocco.

___
[5] https://www.pbs.org/alifeapart/intro_91.html.

common symbol in Judaism. The traditional menorah in the Temple was a seven-branched candelabra. Several meanings have been ascribed to the menorah. One of the most prominent is that the menorah represents the burning bush through which God spoke to Moses. In addition, it is said to symbolize the Jewish peoples' obligation to serve as a "light to the nations" (Isaiah 42:6). The Hanukkah menorah has nine branches, one in the center to light the other eight in remembrance of the eight nights the consecrated oil burned during the rededication of the Temple after the Maccabean Revolt (Figure 5).

The Tree of Life (Figure 6) is another important symbol in Judaism with multiple meanings. The tree of life is said to represent immortality as well as the wisdom of the Torah. In the mystical Kabbalah, the branches of the tree are said to represent ten attributes of God.[6] In Judaism, there is even a new year for trees, **Tu Bish'vat.**

Perhaps the most well-known symbol in Judaism is the Star of David, also known as the Magen David (Shield of David). Interestingly, little reference is made to the Magen David in early Jewish literature and history. Historically, the six-pointed star created by two interconnected triangles was a symbol of good fortune in the Middle East. Some Jewish scholars attribute theological meaning to the symbol suggesting that the three sides represent God, Torah, and Israel.[7] As a symbol of Judaism, the Star of David was not common until the 1890s when it became of symbol of Zionism (Figure 7).[8]

Figure 5   Hanukkah menorah with other symbols of the festival including a dreidel and doughnuts.

Maglara/Shutterstock.com.

Figure 6   Tree of Life sculpture in front of Beth Shalom Synagogue in Frederick, MD.

Source: Stephanie Curran.

RITUALS AND SACRED PRACTICES

Judaism is a way of life; rituals and sacred practices punctuate the day, particularly for the Orthodox. The daily rituals include prayer three times a day and adherence to the dietary laws. The Sabbath begins at sundown on Friday and ends at sundown on Saturday. Orthodox Jews also participate in the mikvah, or ritual bath, an ancient Jewish purification practice. In addition, rites of passage mark significant transitions in the lives of individuals; and, festivals and holy days are celebrated throughout the year.

---

[6] For more information about tree symbolism within Judaism, see http://www.jewishfolksongs.com/en/tree-of-life.

[7] For more on this see an article by Rabbi Silberberg about the mystical meanings of the Star of David at https://www.chabad.org/library/article_cdo/aid/788679/jewish/Star-of-David-The-Mystical-Significance.htm

[8] https://www.jewishvirtuallibrary.org/magen-david

Kosher

Dietary laws are one of the most widely known Jewish practices; and, they are rooted in the book of Leviticus in the Hebrew Bible. The term for forbidden foods and practices in Hebrew is *tamei*; that is, ritually impure. The dietary laws were not designed for health reasons; rather, they are followed because they are mandated in the Torah. For many, they are seen as a practice of holiness and self-discipline. After naming acceptable and unacceptable animals for consumption in Leviticus 11, God offers Moses a theological framework for the rules.

Figure 7   Israeli flags featuring the Star of David.

> *For I am the Lord your God; sanctify yourselves therefore, and be holy, for I am holy. You shall not defile yourselves with any swarming creature that moves on the earth. For I am the Lord who brought you up from the land of Egypt, to be your God; you shall be holy, for I am holy.*
>
> —*Leviticus 11:44–45*

Major aspects of the **kosher** practices include acceptable and unacceptable foods, methods of preparation and the prohibition against mixing of meat and dairy. Acceptable animals include warm-blooded animals that chew their cud and have cloven hooves (primarily beef, lamb, and goat). Poultry is kosher, except for birds of prey, such as buzzards. Fish, to be kosher, must have fins and scales. Any water creature that doesn't have fins and scales is not kosher (including turtle, frog, etc.). Insects are not kosher, with the exception of four types of locusts.

Preparation is another key aspect of the kosher food laws. Animals must be slaughtered humanely and all blood must be drained from the animal. Various certifying boards exist around the world to determine that kosher standards are being met; each group has its own label identifying a food item as kosher. Another key provision of the kosher food requirements is that meat and dairy cannot be mixed. Meat and dairy are prepared in separate sets of dishes. Some Orthodox followers even have separate refrigerators for storage of meat and dairy products and separate dishwashers for cleaning pots, pans, and serving dishes. Even separate dishtowels and potholders should be used for meat and dairy. The injunctions against mixing meat and dairy stem from three verses in Exodus and Deuteronomy that forbid cooking a kid (baby goat) in its mother's milk. It is permissible to eat fish and dairy together or eggs and dairy, but not poultry and dairy.

A few kosher rules are less well known. For example, much gelatin is not kosher because it is made from collagen found in the bones or hooves of pigs. Gelatin is used to make gel-caps or gel-tabs of some medicines that would then not be kosher. Marshmallows, candy, some pastries and yogurt are not kosher if made with nonkosher gelatin. Kosher gelatin is made of collagen from fish or cattle. Grape products must come from Jewish grape producers to be kosher. This rule stems from the fact that, historically, many communities used grapes and wine in non-Jewish ritual ceremonies and offerings.

Sabbath Practices

The Sabbath begins at sundown on Friday and ends at sundown on Saturday. Orthodox observance of the Sabbath involves rest and worship. Restrictions that apply include no work, no exchanging of money, no driving or use of transportation, and no lighting and extinguishing of fires. For Orthodox followers this final restriction means no cooking, no turning on and off of appliances, light fixtures, or even pushing elevator buttons. At Sinai hospital in Baltimore, a Sabbath elevator continuously stops at each floor for the convenience of observant Sabbath keepers. Over the years, students have had many questions about what happens if … there's a fire, someone has a heart attack, etc. In all circumstances, the value is placed on life. If there is a medical emergency, an ambulance is called and the sick person is taken to the hospital while family follow to the hospital to offer support and care.

The Sabbath begins at home with the lighting of at least two candles in the hour leading up to sundown. The table is set with the candles, a cup of wine and challah bread. Before the meal, a blessing is spoken for the wine and the bread (Figure 8).

While in the Reform tradition worship is on Friday night, Orthodox and Conservative followers of Judaism, worship on Saturday morning. Sabbath worship includes prayers, readings from the Torah, a sermon; and in Reform traditions, sometimes, choirs offer special music. A **cantor** leads the congregation in prayer and can be anyone who has extensive knowledge of the prayers and the melodies used to recite them. In smaller congregations, the rabbi and the cantor may be the same person. In addition to the rabbi and the cantor, a *gabbai,* one who is well versed in the Torah, may stand with the person reading from the Torah to ensure correct pronunciation. In both Judaism and Islam, great emphasis is placed on the reciting of the word of God. Correct pronunciation and intonation are extremely important, and even the rabbi is corrected if a mistake is made. Since the destruction of the Temple in 70 CE, priests no longer serve a ritual function; however, descendants of Aaron and the tribe of Levi continue to be traced to the present.

Figure 8   Sabbath table.

Tomertu/Shutterstock.com.

Rites of Passage

Important rituals mark life transitions in Judaism. Circumcision of baby boys on the eighth day after their birth is the primary ritual surrounding birth. Circumcision is performed either in the home or the synagogue by a **mohel**, a person trained in the surgical procedure. A topical anesthetic is used; and, a specially chosen person holds the baby. The honor of holding the baby is given to a righteous person who has a special connection with the family; it can be a family member, but may simply be a person the family holds in high regard. Traditionally, this person was male, but today, in many synagogues, either gender can serve in this role. Furthermore, in Reform, Reconstructionist, and some Conservative synagogues, a welcoming and naming ceremony is held to celebrate the arrival of baby girls.

Young people become responsible for keeping the covenant for themselves at the age of twelve or thirteen. This transition to becoming an adult member of the synagogue for boys is Bar Mitzvah (son of the commandment). In non-Orthodox congregations, a **Bat Mitzvah** (daughter of the commandment) is celebrated for young girls. The term, Bar or Bat Mitzvah is not the ceremony itself, but rather, the act of becoming a responsible member of the community. A person can become Bar or Bat Mitzvah whether a ceremony is held or not. Typically, the ceremony follows several years of studying the Jewish faith and Torah. As part of the service, the young person reads a passage from the Torah and one from the Prophets. In addition, she or he may offer a brief sermon or speech and as well as recite a blessing. Boys generally celebrate this rite of passage at the age of thirteen, girls at the age of twelve (Figure 9).

As many have seen, if not in person, at least in the movies, Jewish weddings are festive and sacred occasions. The chuppah (canopy over the bride and groom) and the breaking of a glass are perhaps the most well-known customs. Less known but

Figure 9   Bat Mitzvah celebration.

very important to some couples is fasting before the wedding ceremony. Furthermore, prayer is a central part of the ceremony. There are seven blessings for the bride and groom. The couple exchanges rings and share a cup of wine. Divorce is permissible in Judaism. A Jewish certificate of divorce is called a *get*, and it nullifies the wedding contract entered into by the bride and groom. Historically, matchmakers facilitated marriages in Judaism; but, in contemporary society, this is mainly true in ultra-Orthodox communities.

Death is viewed as a natural part of the life cycle. Jewish mourning and funeral practices are rooted in the power of memory and respect for the life that has passed. A prominent feature of many synagogues is a memory board with a plaque that gives the date of birth and death for members of the synagogue. In the anniversary week of the person's death, a light is illuminated in memory.

When a person passes away, a candle is lit next to their body and someone stays with them until burial. The person is buried in a simple shroud in a wooden casket. As returning to the earth is important in Jewish thought, the body is buried directly in the ground, where permissible. After being in the presence of the dead, it is important to wash one's hands (whether or not you have touched the body) to be cleansed of ritual impurity. Cremation is discouraged.[9]

A period of mourning follows the funeral. This seven-day period is known as *shiva* (seven), and it begins the day of the burial. If the death occurs during a religious festival, the shiva is postponed until after the festival. During this period of shiva, mirrors in the home are covered and close relatives do not bathe. Rather than sitting on chairs, mourners sit on the floor or on low stools. The idea is to limit one's own comfort and pleasure. After the period of shiva is over, there are thirty days of less intense mourning that takes place. Those who are grieving offer daily prayers and refrain from going to parties or celebrations. The anniversary of the person's death is an important occasion of remembrance. A candle is lit in memory of the person who passed, and the mourner's prayer, the **Kaddish**, is recited. Tombstones, also, are erected as a way of remembering and honoring loved ones.[10]

---

[9] For a brief video on Jewish burial practices, see https://www.pbs.org/wnet/religionandethics/2004/02/06/february-6-2004-jewish-burial-practices/1794/

[10] To read the Kaddish in Hebrew and English, see https://reformjudaism.org/practice/prayers-blessings/mourners-kaddish

Festivals

Jewish festivals mark important occasions in the life of the community. The Jewish calendar is lunar-based; therefore, the dates of celebrations vary from year to year. However, the structure of the calendar allows for the dates of festivals to always fall within the same two month period each year. The Jewish New Year, or **Rosh Hashanah**, generally takes place in September or October. This festival marks the first days of creation and begins a season of reflection and repent-

Figure 10   Blowing of the Shofar.

ance. Apples and honey are often eaten on Rosh Hashanah in the hope of a sweet new year. The **shofar**, or ram's horn, is blown one hundred times (Figure 10). The ten days between Rosh Hashanah and **Yom Kippur**, or the Day of Atonement, are known as the Days of Awe. This period of repentance and renewal culminates in the fast of Yom Kippur. Yom Kippur is the holiest day of the year. It is common to dress in white to symbolize purity and to hold a special service at the synagogue. In addition, people refrain from work and many completely fast from sundown-to-sundown, abstaining from both food and drink.

Five days after Yom Kippur is **Sukkot** (sometimes known as the Feast of Tabernacles or the Feast of Booths). This fall harvest festival lasts for a week and commemorates the forty years the Hebrew people wandered in the wilderness after the Exodus. During this period, the people lived in temporary shelters. To mark this festival, the faithful create makeshift booths. During Sukkot, four different types of plants are typically gathered to offer praise to God: a citrus fruit, a palm branch, two willow branches and three myrtle branches. Directions for which plants to gather can be found in Leviticus 23:40. Typically people eat in their shelters, and depending on the size of the shelter, the weather, etc., some may even live and sleep in them (Figure 11).

Hanukkah, the Festival of Lights, is one of the most well-known Jewish festivals in the United States, but it is actually a minor festival in Judaism. The festival became more widely celebrated in the United States, in part, because of its proximity to Christmas. The date of this celebration typically falls in very late November or December. The festival is rooted in Jewish history and commemorates the story of the Maccabean Revolt around 163 BCE. At that time, the Syrian ruler, Antiochus Epiphanes, ruled Palestine. He thought the best way to unite his kingdom was through a common Hellenistic culture. He advocated the use of the Greek language throughout his territories, built a statue of Zeus in the Temple in Jerusalem and stole from the Temple treasury. These actions enraged the Jewish people, and Judas Maccabeus led a successful revolt against

Figure 11   The inside of a sukkah, or booth, created by Columbia Jewish Congregation in Columbia, MD. The colorful construction paper garland is a chain of prayers created by the children of the synagogue.

Antiochus. They drove the Syrians out of Jerusalem and reclaimed the Temple. Legend suggests that only a one-day supply of consecrated oil was available for the Temple rededication service. But, miraculously, the oil lasted for eight nights. The festival of Hanukkah is an eight-night celebration of this miracle. To celebrate Hanukkah, Jewish families light the candles of the menorah, increasing one each night. In addition, other traditions include playing the dreidel game, exchanging gifts, and eating fried foods like donuts and latkes (in honor of the oil).

In February or March, one of the most fun, and sometimes even raucous, celebrations is **Purim**. Purim commemorates the period in Persia when Queen Esther saved her people from massacre by Haman, an advisor to the king. The scroll of Esther is read; and, those gathered provide sounds effects, such as booing whenever Haman's name is mentioned, and cheering for Esther. People dress up in costumes; and, carnival-like celebrations are held. Sometimes gifts are exchanged and sweet treats are eaten, like *hamantaschen* (triangle-shaped cookies with a fruit or chocolate filling in the center). Purim is also a time for acts of charity.

The next festival falls during March or April, and is probably one of the most well-known Jewish religious observances; that is, **Passover** (Pesach in Hebrew). Passover is a remembrance of, and ritual participation in, the Exodus from Egypt. As noted earlier in the chapter, during the tenth plague, the angel of death "passed over" the home of the Hebrews as it killed all of the first born male children and animals of the Egyptians. The celebration of Passover lasts for seven or eight days (depending on the form of Judaism). No work is permitted on the first and last days of Passover. A **Seder** meal is eaten the first two nights of Passover, except for in Israel, where the Seder is only on the first night. The order of the service is part of a **haggadah**, a book whose title literally means, "The Telling." A haggadah tells the story of the Exodus and provides an "order of service" for the Passover meal. During the ritual meal, the children ask questions, such as "Why is this night different from all other nights?" Everyone responds with the answer: "We were slaves in Egypt and God brought us out with a mighty hand and an outstretched arm."

All followers of Judaism do not use the same haggadah. Some families have their own version. In the 1950s, Maxwell House coffee published a haggadah that remains popular today. One of the more famous haggadahs is the Sarajevo Haggadah. It is believed to date back to mid-fourteenth Century Spain. For more information on the history of this well-travelled book, see http://www.haggadah.ba/?x=1. A Huffington Post article in 2014 mentions over 25 modern versions including a feminist, a Bob Marley, a vegetarian and a hip-hop haggadah.[11] In addition, some Internet sites offer opportunity to create one's own version, such as www.haggadot.com, or www.personalizedhaggadah.com.

The seder meal is generally composed of several symbolic foods. Since the destruction of the temple, a lamb shank bone is used rather than the meat itself as a symbol and reminder of the sacrifices offered. Interestingly, vegetarians use a beet instead. The red of the beet symbolizes the blood of sacrifice. Greens, particularly parsley, and bitter herbs, such as horseradish are also on the Passover plate. The parsley is dipped in salt water as a reminder of the tears shed during slavery in Egypt and the bitter herbs point to the de-humanizing experience. Haroset is a salad made with fruit, nuts and wine, which is symbolic of the mortar used by the slaves in Egypt during the Pharaoh's building campaign. In addition, its sweetness points to the sweet taste of freedom. In Ashkenazi traditions, the salad is made with apples; but, in Sephardic cultures, dates and figs are the fruits of choice. The final item on the Passover plate is a roasted egg, symbolizing spring and new beginnings. No leavening is used during Passover as a way to

---

[11] https://www.huffpost.com/entry/new-haggadah-passover-2014_n_5104408

remember the fact that the Hebrews left Egypt in such a hurry that they couldn't wait for the bread to raise. The cracker-like bread used during Passover is called matzo. Matzo meal (ground up matzo) is also used in cooking and baking for Passover. A cup is filled, and sometimes a chair is set aside, for Elijah, the prophet who brought relief from trouble and serves as a harbinger of the Messiah.

The period between Passover and **Shavuot**, the celebration of the giving of the Torah, is fifty days. From the second night of Passover until Shavuot, a period known as the Counting of the Omer is observed. An omer was a unit of measure. During the Temple period, an omer of barley was brought as an offering to the Temple. Since the destruction of the Temple, this time between Passover and Shavuot is marked by the reciting of a blessing each night.[12] The Greek term for the festival of Shavuot is "**Pentecost**" because of the reference to it occurring on the fiftieth day. The Jewish celebration of Pentecost is a remembrance of the giving of the Law at Sinai and is marked by an all-night reading of the Torah for the faithful. It is also a time to refrain from work and spend time in prayer.

❧ Choose a Jewish festival or ritual to explore a little more and write two-three sentences about what you learned.

_____

_____

_____

_____

_____

THE HOLOCAUST

The Jewish community has suffered for its faith throughout history. From the destruction of the Temple and the slaughter of many by the Romans, to the Spanish Inquisition and the pogroms in Eastern Europe, they have been forced into ghettos and experienced limited participation in their communities. However, perhaps the most extensive and horrific persecution in modern history is the genocide of the Holocaust.

An estimated six million Jewish men, women and children were killed during the Holocaust along with many others deemed "unfit" by Hitler, including gypsies or Roma, homosexual men, Jehovah Witnesses, those of Polish and Slavic descent, and people with disabilities. The effects of the Holocaust were physical, emotional, intellectual, and spiritual. For many followers of Judaism, their faith in God was shaken. How could the God who brought them out of the land of Egypt allow them to be tortured and killed? If God is active in human history, why not intervene and stop the suffering? Much writing and reflection on the meaning of this event can be found in the Jewish community. Every year a memorial service, **Yom HaShoah**, is held for those who were lost. The following is part of a prayer written by Elie Wiesel at the end of his book, *One Generation After*:

---

[12] For an example of how to do the Counting of the Omer ritual, see https://www.ritualwell.org/counting-omer.

> *I no longer ask you for either happiness or paradise; all I ask of You is to listen and let me be aware of Your listening.*
>
> *I no longer ask You to resolve my questions, only to receive them and make them part of You.*
>
> *I no longer ask You for either rest or wisdom, I only ask You not to close me to gratitude, be it of the most trivial kind, or to surprise and friendship. Love? Love is not Yours to give.*
>
> *As for my enemies, I do not ask You to punish them or even to enlighten them; I only ask You not to lend them Your mask and Your powers. If You must relinquish one or the other, give them Your powers. But not Your countenance.*
>
> *They are modest, my requests, and humble. I ask You what I might ask a stranger met by chance at twilight in a barren land.*[13]

A visit to the Holocaust Museum in Washington, DC, is an important way to remember and reflect, not only on the tragedy, but also on the events, fears, propaganda, and social conditions that allowed the Holocaust to take place.

☯ Explore the Holocaust Museum web page including the page of survivor testimonies and reflections. http://www.ushmm.org/remember/the-holocaust-survivors-and-victims-resource-center/survivors-and-victims/survivor-testimonies.

Share a few sentences about what you discovered as well as any insights you had as a result of browsing the site. How do you think Hitler and the Nazis were able to convince ordinary people to commit such horrific actions?

____

____

____

____

____

JEWISH FEMINISM

One of the most important contemporary movements within Judaism is Jewish feminism. Jewish culture is matrilineal and historically patriarchal. In other words, a person is Jewish if born of a Jewish mother. At the same time, men have historically had the most influence in Jewish religious practices. Several issues present challenges for Jewish feminists.

One challenge is the patriarchy and sometimes violence against women in the Hebrew Scriptures. Phyllis Trible, a biblical scholar, writes of four of these texts in her now classic book, *Texts of Terror*. Another challenge for Jewish feminists is a ritual one. Many of the rites of passage at birth, puberty, etc. were only for boys. Obviously, women don't want to be circumcised; however, Jewish feminists since the

[13] Elie Wiesel, *One Generation After* (Schocken Books, 2011), p. 189.

nineteenth century have been creating rituals to mark significant life passages for women. Bat Mitzvahs were discussed earlier in the chapter; however, it is interesting to read about some of the additional rituals developed over the years including a Simhat Bat ceremony to welcome baby girls.[14]

A Jewish feminist magazine, *Lilith*, was first published in 1976. It continues to be a voice for Jewish women. The magazine is named after Lilith who tradition says was the first wife of Adam. Lilith's identity is derived from the Genesis 1 account of creation in which God is said to have made male and female in God's own image. Lilith asserted her equality, according to legend, and thus ensued an argument between she and Adam. Lilith fled the garden rather than submit to Adam. As Jewish tradition developed, Lilith was characterized as a demon who punishes women and children. Lilith is a strong, independent woman who fought alone to assert her equality. She became a woman in exile.[15] Another example of strong, independent, faithful Jewish women is a group formed in 1988. This group of Jewish women from around the world formed Women of the Wall, an organization promoting the ability of women to pray, read Torah, wear prayer shawls and receive the priestly blessing at the Western Wall of the Temple (Kotel).[16]

JUDAISM IN THE UNITED STATES

In chapter two, we explored the early religious diversity in the United States. The longest continually functioning Jewish community is Congregation Mikveh Israel in Philadelphia, Pennsylvania. The community was formed in the 1740's. The longest standing Jewish synagogue in North America is the Touro synagogue in Rhode Island. Yet, a Jewish presence in the Caribbean, as well as what would become the United States, dates back at least to the 1650s.

Followers of Judaism make up a little over 2 percent of the population of the United States; however, Jewish influence is far greater than its size. Many of America's comedians are Jewish. Adam Sandler, in his "Hanukkah Song," runs through a whole litany of Jewish celebrities. Moreover, Stephen Prothero, in his book, *God Is Not One*, writes "Whenever anyone anywhere puts on a pair of Levi's, sips a cappuccino from Starbucks, spends the night in a Hyatt, powers up a Dell computer, or performs a Google search, they have a Jewish entrepreneur to thank."[17]

☯ Think of an example of Judaism in popular culture. Share a link to the reference, if available. Does the reference accurately reflect what you have come to learn about Judaism?

_____

_____

_____

_____

_____

[14] For more information on Jewish feminist rituals, see the article, "Ritual: A Feminist Approach" at https://jwa.org/encyclopedia/article/ritual-feminist-approach.

[15] To read the first article from Lilith about "The Lilith Question," see http://lilith.org/articles/the-lilith-question/.

[16] For more information about Women of the Wall, see their website http://womenofthewall.org.il/.

[17] Prothero, Stephen. *God Is Not One* (HarperCollins, 2010), p. 247.

WEB RESOURCES FOR FURTHER STUDY

http://www.chabad.org/library/article_cdo/aid/889836/jewish/Maimonides.htm—Excellent resource for all things Maimonides including video clips, biographies and translations of his works.

https://www.jewish-funerals.org/about-us/about-kavod-vnichum/—A great resource about Jewish burial and mourning practices.

https://www.jewishvirtuallibrary.org/jsource/Talmud/talmudtoc.html—Great link for reading the full text of the Babylonian Talmud online in English.

http://www.jewfaq.org/index.htm.

http://lilith.org/—A Jewish feminist magazine with great articles and blogs.

http://www.pbs.org/alifeapart/index.html—A documentary and information about Hasidic Judaism with a great introduction to the basics.

http://www.reformjudaism.org/history-reform-judaism-and-look-ahead-search-belonging—A great overview of the history of Reform Judaism from its beginnings to the present.

http://www.zohar.com/—This link is a great resource for exploring the Kabbalah. It also includes the translation of the Zohar.

http://www.kabbalah.info/engkab/mystzohar.htm#.WfXxRxNSxok—A great site for general information on the Zohar, the central text of Kabbalah.

Chapter 11
Christianity

Learning Outcomes

By the end of this lesson, students will be able to

- summarize the life, ministry, and central teachings of Jesus;
- explain the major teachings of Christianity while acknowledging there are differences among various branches;
- characterize the development of the Christian scriptures and the criteria for canonization;
- analyze key events in the history of Christianity and characterize the main differences among the three major divisions of the faith;
- identify the sacraments and describe variations in their practice or understanding; and
- recognize the major festivals of the Christian year
- discuss modern movements in Christian traditions particularly those that developed in the United States.
- characterize the global shifts in Christian populations in recent years.

Key Terms

Advent	Fundamentalism	Paul
Apocrypha	Gospel	Pentecost
Apostle's Creed	Grace	Pentecostalism
Baptism	Icons	Pope
Beatitudes	Immaculate Conception	Purgatory
Constantine	Incarnation	Reconciliation Atonement
Consubstantiation	Lent	Resurrection
Council of Trent	Liturgy	Rosary
Easter	Lord's Supper (Eucharist)	Sacrament
Ecumenism	Martin Luther	Sermon on the Mount
Epiphany	Ordinary Time	Sin
Epistles	Original Sin	Substitutionary Atonement
Eucharist	Papal Infallibility	Transubstantiation
Evangelicalism	Parables	Trinity
Filioque	Patriarch (in Orthodox tradition)	Vatican II

INTRODUCTION

Christianity is the religious tradition with which many students are most familiar. Yet, many only have a surface knowledge of the tradition of which they are a part. As with all religious traditions, there are variations in practice between branches and sects (sometimes to the point that one group has a hard time accepting another group as being "true" followers). This is also true of Christianity. We will look at the basic elements of Christianity recognizing that each sect has its own interpretation of both teachings and practice. One of the important lessons from this chapter is that Baptists, Catholics, Coptic Orthodox, Latter-day Saints, and Presbyterians are not different religions; they are different sects within the same religion—Christianity.

JUDAISM AT THE TIME OF JESUS

Christianity emerged from the fertile soil of Judaism. It focuses on the life, ministry, death, and resurrection of Jesus. Jesus was a Jewish man born in Palestine sometime between 4 BCE and 4 CE. He lived during a time of turbulence in which the Jewish people were frustrated with Roman rule. The Pax Romana was enforced by strict suppression of any threat to Rome's power and authority. Four small Jewish sects played a significant role in first century Judaism. Out of roughly 3.5 million Jews at that time, these groups formed a small but influential percentage of the population.

One of these groups was a small, apocalyptic sect known as the Essenes. The Essenes were a separatist group that established a community at Qumran, in the caves near the Dead Sea. Many scholars think they are responsible for preserving the *Dead Sea Scrolls*[1] (Figure 1). The Essenes believed the kingdom of God was imminent and would be ushered in by both a priestly and kingly messiah. The messiah would restore purity to temple worship and reestablish the throne of David. The messiah they sought was a purely human servant of God who would establish God's kingdom on earth. This group was wiped out by the Romans in the First Jewish Revolt between 66 and 70 CE.

The second group, the Sadducees, made up a very small but wealthy and influential group. They were despised by some within the Jewish faith because many saw them as aligned with the Romans. Because of this alignment, they were perceived as having a lot of political and religious influence in Jerusalem before 70 CE. The group's name comes from the Hebrew, *Zaddokim*, which derives from the priestly line of Zadok. "Both Josephus and the Gospels describe the Sadducees as a conservative group that rejected certain 'newer' theological and philosophical ideas. Specifically, they are noted for rejecting the role

Figure 1   Cave at Qumran where the Dead Sea Scrolls were found.

Sopotnicki/Shutterstock.com.

---

[1] For more information on the Dead Sea Scrolls, see http://www.deadseascrolls.org.il/learn-about-the-scrolls/introduction.

of Fate in human life as well as belief in afterlife and resurrection of the dead."[2] They only considered the five books of the Torah as authoritative.

The Pharisees constituted the largest sect of the four groups, having around 6,000 members. The Pharisees gathered under the direction of a teacher and spent time in community, fellowshipping and studying together.[3] The Pharisees were known for their concern for purity in daily life; their broader view of scripture that included the Torah, Prophets, and Writings; and, their belief in the afterlife and the physical resurrection of the body. Out of their concern for purity, they advocated a broader interpretation of the law that included an "oral" law. This "oral" law eventually grew into the Talmud, the second most important text in Judaism.

The last group is a collection of smaller sects that advocated violent resistance to the Romans. It included the *Sicarii*, or daggermen, who used assassination to get rid of leaders they believed were collaborating with the Romans; it also included the Zealots. The Zealots received their name because they were "zealous" for the law. They advocated armed rebellion against the Romans. Luke's gospel describes one of Jesus' disciples as Simon, the Zealot.[4]

All of these groups are mentioned in the Gospels, the books describing the life, ministry, death, and resurrection of Jesus. Like these groups within Judaism, Jesus and his disciples did not see themselves as starting a new religion, but rather, as renewing the tradition of which they were a part.

HISTORICAL JESUS

In recent years, there has been intense interest in seeking to know the "historical Jesus." Few doubt the historicity of Jesus; what many scholars and students of the New Testament want to know is: what can we know about the Jesus of history? The Jesus Seminar, founded in 1985, was the most well known of these groups. The group sought to use literary, historical, and archaeological data, to understand as closely as possible what Jesus actually did and said.[5]

The New Testament gospels are the primary source of information for the life and ministry of Jesus. Two gospels, Matthew and Luke, describe Jesus' birth but each has a slightly different emphasis. The chart below demonstrates the aspects of the narrative that are held in common as well as the unique aspects of each gospel account.

The gospels of the New Testament have little information about Jesus' childhood and young adult years. The only story in the biblical text of his youth is Luke's account of Jesus in the Temple at around the age of twelve (Luke 2:41–52). The next major event in Jesus' life that is recorded is his baptism (described in Matthew, Mark, and Luke) at around the age of thirty. According to these three gospels, Jesus was baptized by the prophet, John the Baptist, in the Jordan River (Figure 2).

During his baptism, a dove is said to have descended from heaven and a voice declared "This is my Son, the Beloved, with whom I am well pleased."[6] After his baptism, the **Synoptic Gospels** (Matthew, Mark, and Luke), so called because they are similar in style and content, say that Jesus was tempted by

---

[2] Michael L. White, *Jesus to Christianity*, p. 78.

[3] Ibid, p. 79.

[4] Luke 6:15.

[5] For more information on the Jesus Seminar, see https://www.westarinstitute.org/projects/the-jesus-seminar/.

[6] Matt. 3:17; Mark 1:11; Luke 3:22.

Comparison of Birth Stories

Matthew	Luke
✦ Born in Bethelahem	✦ Born in Bethelahem
✦ Born of Mary and the Holy Spirit	✦ Born of Mary and the Holy Spirit
✦ Born at home	✦ Born in stable
✦ Angel visits Joseph	✦ Angel visits Mary
✦ Genealogy of Joseph precedes birth narrative – traces Jesus back of Abraham	✦ Genealogy of Joseph is after baptism
✦ Wise men visit	✦ Shepherds visit
✦ Flight to Egypt	✦ Census
✦ Born in time of Herod, around 6 BCE	✦ Born while Quirinius was governer, around 6CE
✦ Family returns to Nazareth after time in Egypt	✦ Family returns to Nazareth about a month later
✦ No mention of Temple	✦ Jesus presented in Temple

Satan in the wilderness for forty days. Having successfully completed each of Satan's tests, Jesus began his ministry.

In all four **canonical gospels** (those found in the Christian New Testament), Jesus calls twelve disciples to follow him and share in his ministry. Throughout this ministry, Jesus is said to have performed miracles and taught in **parables** (short teaching stories from everyday life). In his preaching, he called people to repent from **sin** because God's kingdom was coming near. **Sin** is understood as unfaithfulness to God, while **repentance** is a turning away from sin and turning toward God. Jesus' ethical teachings are out-

Figure 2 Christian Pilgrims experiencing baptism in the Jordan River Image.

lined in what is often called the **Sermon on the Mount**, found in Matthew 5–7.[7] The sermon begins with the **Beatitudes** (i.e., "Blessed are the poor in spirit, for theirs is the kingdom of heaven.") which promise spiritual rewards to those who follow the strict ethical principles outlined in the verses that follow. Included in the Sermon on the Mount are the challenging teachings of loving one's enemies and turning the other cheek.

Jesus' teachings were not popular with the religious and political leadership of the day. In fact, according to Luke's gospel, Jesus was run out of his hometown after his very first sermon (Luke 4:14–30). He spent three years traveling throughout the Galilee teaching, healing, and preaching. In the final week of his life, according to the gospels, Jesus rode into Jerusalem on a colt (or a donkey depending on the gospel account) to much fanfare and praise. But, by the end of the week, the tide of public opinion had turned against him.

---

[7] Luke records a similar but shorter sermon (6:17–49); but, since it is preached on a flat place rather than a mountain, it is often called the Sermon on the Plain.

In order for a gospel to have been considered for the Christian canon, it had to have an account of Jesus' death and resurrection. The narrative of his arrest, trial, and death are referred to as the **Passion**. Each gospel has some variation in detail, but all describe a final meal with his disciples (**Last Supper**), betrayal by Judas, arrest and trial, denial by Peter, and finally death by crucifixion. In the Synoptic Gospels, the Last Supper is a Passover meal; while, in John's gospel, the Last Supper occurs before the Passover begins. In John, Jesus is crucified as the Passover lambs are being slaughtered in preparation for the holy days of Passover.

After Jesus' death on the cross, the gospels record his hurried burial just before the Sabbath. On the third day, a group of women traveled to the tomb and were surprised to find the stone rolled away and the tomb empty. An angel told them not to be afraid and asked them to tell the disciples that Jesus had risen from the dead. The gospels, in their present form, all record appearances of Jesus to his disciples offering comfort and a call to ministry. In Matthew's gospel, Jesus charged his followers with the task of going out and making disciples, baptizing them in the name of the Father, the Son and the Holy Spirit."[8] This call to evangelism is one practice that set Christianity apart from Judaism. Although the split was gradual and varied by region of the Mediterranean, many scholars date the formal split between Judaism and Christianity to the Council of Nicea in 325 CE.[9]

PAUL'S ROLE OF SPREADING CHRISTIANITY TO THE GENTILES

Christianity was certainly rooted in the life, teachings, death, and resurrection of Jesus. At the same time, the apostle Paul is sometimes referred to as the founder of Christianity because he led the effort to spread Christianity beyond the Jewish community. Although fully Jewish and a Pharisee of Pharisees by his own admission,[10] Paul (then known as Saul) had an experience of the Risen Christ on the road to Damascus. He was blinded by a bright light and the voice of Jesus asked, "Why are you persecuting me?" Saul went from being a persecutor of followers of Christ to Paul, an apostle of Christ.[11] It wasn't long before Paul and the leaders of the church in Jerusalem, Peter and James, were engaged in an intense debate over whether one had to become Jewish to be a follower of Christ. Paul asserted that baptism replaced circumcision, and that as a follower of Christ, one no longer needed to follow Jewish dietary restrictions (Figure 3). Paul began his ministry to the **Gentiles** (those who were not Jewish) travelling from place to place across the Mediterranean world. Eventually, Paul, Peter, and James reached an agreement. Over the next several centuries, the church spread and established centers in Alexandria, Antioch, Asia Minor, Constantinople, Damascus, Edessa, Ephesus, Greece, Jerusalem, Pella, and Rome. Christians, in these centers, did not always agree on theology and practice, but they shared a faith in and a struggle to understand the mystery of Jesus and his power to save.

Figure 3 Painting of the Apostle Paul.

Zvonimir Atletic/Shutterstock.com.

---

[8] Matt. 28:19.

[9] For a good discussion of the split, see "The Parting of the Ways" by Anne Amos for the Council of Jewish Christian Relations at http://www.jcrelations.net.

[10] Phil. 3:5

[11] For the story of Saul's "conversion", see Acts 9.

THE CHRISTIAN SCRIPTURES

The canonization of the New Testament scriptures took nearly 400 years, as the church came to determine what writings were to be included, and what writings were not. Paul's letters to various churches were the earliest Christian writings (dating from about 50–60 CE). The gospels were put to paper between 70 and 100 CE and later. The delay in recording the gospels came largely from the belief by Jesus' early followers that he would return and establish the kingdom of God before their deaths. As time went on, and the return of Christ was clearly delayed, the community felt a need to record narratives about the life, teachings, death, and resurrection of Jesus.

As differences of opinion existed about the purpose and nature of Jesus, the canonization process and the development of creeds were two ways the early church established orthodox teaching. Marcion was the first to suggest a Christian **canon** (or authoritative collection of writings). He believed that the Hebrew Bible was irrelevant to Christianity and that only Luke's gospel and Paul's letters should be part of the canon. The Hebrew Bible was ultimately included in the Christian canon and Marcion's view was rejected.

Gnosticism was a philosophical system circulating in the Greco-Roman world in the first centuries of the Common Era. Gnostics viewed the world as being divided between spirit and matter. Matter was evil, as was the deity who created it; and, Spirit was good. Gnostics taught that a teacher passed secret knowledge (gnosis) to students concerning how to move from the physical world to the spiritual world. For Christian Gnostics, this teacher was Jesus. Because the physical world was considered "bad," Christian Gnostics did not emphasize the idea of the Incarnation (God made flesh); rather, they emphasized the secret, rather cryptic teachings that Jesus passed to his students as the way to heaven. Salvation, for Christian Gnostics, was not through the death and resurrection of Jesus, but rather, through the teachings of Jesus. Many Gnostic gospels have been unearthed detailing some of these teachings.[12]

Other early Christians, such as Montanus, Priscilla, and Maximilla, collectively known as Montanists, taught that a canon was unnecessary because the Holy Spirit would continue to teach and guide the Christian community. They drew their views mostly from John's gospel; and, in particular, the passage in which Jesus promised to send the Holy Spirit to serve as a teacher and advocate (John 14:26).

The canonization process did not occur in a back room somewhere over a weekend, rather it was a process that developed over time as Christian leaders utilized various writings, discussed, and sometimes argued over, their veracity, relevance, and significance. Ultimately, what is known as the New Testament today, is made up of four gospels, twenty-one letters, an Act of the Apostles; and the apocalyptic writing, called "Revelation." In addition to the gospels that were included in the canon, there were a number of other gospels, known as "**noncanonical gospels**," and additional writings that were not included.

Two types of gospels circulated in the early church: sayings gospels and narrative gospels. Only narrative gospels were included in the Christian canon because one of the criteria for a gospel's inclusion in the canon was that it had to describe the death and resurrection of Jesus. Mark is believed to have been the first gospel written, while John is viewed as the last of the canonical gospels. All four gospels include an account of Jesus' death and resurrection. Only two, Matthew and Luke, address the birth of

---

[12] Some Gnostic gospels include the Gospel of Thomas, the Gospel of Philip, the Gospel of Mary, the Gospel of Judas, etc. To read more about the Gnostic gospels as well as read their English translations, see http://www.pbs.org/wgbh/pages/frontline/shows/religion/story/pagels.html and http://www.earlychristianwritings.com/.

Jesus; and the three **Synoptic gospels** (Matthew, Mark, and Luke) describe Jesus' baptism. Despite a drive to determine what was **orthodoxy** (correct teaching) within early Christianity, the church leaders preserved not one gospel, but four different gospels, each with its own interpretation of who Jesus was and what he came to accomplish.

In addition to gospels, other types of Christian literature included epistles (letters to early Christian communities and leaders), **acts** (narratives about the leaders and heroes of the early church), and **apocalypses** (highly symbolic accounts of God finally triumphing over evil). While the canonization process took place over a period of time, certain criteria can be seen as having played a role in which writings were ultimately chosen. These criteria included association with an **apostle** (that is a witness to the resurrected Christ), the age of the document (all of the writings included were written between 55 and 120 CE), the soundness of a writing's doctrine, and how widespread the use of the writing was in the early Christian community. "Widespread use" references diverse centers of Christianity throughout the ancient world (such as Alexandria, Antioch, Ephesus and Rome), all drawing meaning and relevance from certain texts.

There are variations between the Bibles of Catholics, Protestants, and Eastern Orthodox Christians. For instance, the Apocrypha is included as part of the canon for Roman Catholics and Eastern Orthodox traditions, but not for Protestants. Also, there are 151 Psalms in the Eastern Orthodox bible and 150 in the Roman Catholic and Protestant versions.[13] The books of the New Testament are the same in all Christian traditions; however, the writings of the Old Testament (or Hebrew Bible) vary. For Roman Catholics, there are forty-six books in the Old Testament. Orthodox Christians typically have forty-nine and Protestants have thirty-nine. Part of the reason for this can be demonstrated in the following graphic.

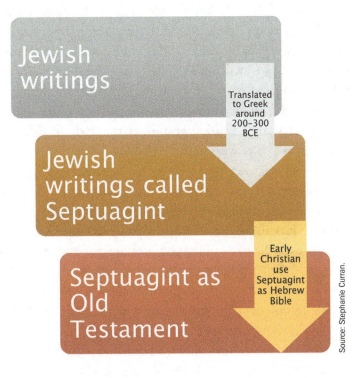

Jewish writings

Translated to Greek around 200–300 BCE

Jewish writings called Septuagint

Early Christian use Septuagint as Hebrew Bible

Septuagint as Old Testament

Source: Stephanie Curran.

---

[13] For a chart of the various versions and the writings of the Hebrew Bible/Old Testament, see https://etimasthe.com/2018/08/29/comparison-of-the-books-of-the-old-testament-in-various-christian-traditions/.

In the third century BCE, a group of scholars translated a collection of Hebrew writings to Greek. Tradition states that there were seventy scholars who worked on this translation; therefore, it is called the Septuagint. Early Christians used the Septuagint as their version of the Jewish scriptures. When the Jewish canon was finalized in 100 CE, a few of the writings in the Septuagint were not included in the Hebrew Bible. However, these writings remained part of the Old Testament in the Christian Bible until the time of Martin Luther. Luther believed that the Hebrew texts which were in the Septuagint but not the Hebrew Bible (Tanakh) were useful for study, but should not be included in the Christian canon. He set these texts aside putting them in a section called the Apocrypha. Some Protestant Bibles have the Apocrypha, it is usually found in between the Old and New Testaments.

The original language of the Old Testament is Hebrew; and, the New Testament is written in Greek. There are various translations and paraphrases of the Scriptures today. There are no original manuscripts of any of the books of the Bible. All that remain are copies of copies of copies of manuscripts. A translation seeks to develop a consensus on which is the most likely original wording of a passage and then attempts, as directly as possible, to translate from Greek or Hebrew to whatever language into which it is being translated. Alternate wording is often given in the footnotes. A paraphrase, on the other hand, seeks to convey the general meaning in the common language of the people and is, therefore, subject to a greater degree of interpretation.

CENTRAL TEACHINGS OF CHRISTIANITY

The first of the central teachings in Christianity is the divine Sonship of Jesus; Jesus is the incarnation of God—that is, God made flesh. The belief that Jesus was both fully human and fully divine led to the development of the doctrine of the Trinity. This doctrine is the basis of the primary disagreement between Jews, Muslims and Christians. The Jewish faith does not give Jesus any special status, while in Islam Jesus is affirmed as a prophet. What Judaism and Islam cannot accept is the divinity of Jesus or the idea that God can be divided in any way. Even for Christians, the doctrine of the Trinity is perplexing and difficult to explain. Illustrations of water having three forms (steam, liquid, and ice) and the clover having three orbs in one leaf have been used to explain the concept of the Trinity. At times, confusion can be heard in the language of some Christian groups, particularly in using the titles of "God" and "Jesus" interchangeably in hymns and prayers.

The central core of love is another key component in Christian teaching. Jesus' teaching on ethics and love is summarized in the Sermon on the Mount found in Matthew, Chapters 5–7, and begins with a series of statements known as the Beatitudes, which affirm that those who suffer in the present life will receive their reward in heaven. It is also in this passage where Jesus says that he did come not to abolish the Law, but to fulfill it. He goes to the heart of the commandments and takes them another step further in a series of teachings known as the Antitheses. "You have heard it said…, but I say to you… (Matt. 6). For example, Jesus says "you have heard it said, 'do not kill,' but I say to you, anyone who harbors anger toward another will be liable to judgment." Jesus then summarizes the law in the two great commandments central to Judaism: love for God and love for neighbor.

A third teaching of Christianity is that humanity is flawed; and, we cannot save ourselves. Christianity has long lived with a tension between grace and works. Because Christianity affirms that we are reconciled with God through grace, there is nothing the believer can do but receive the gift. At the same time, Christianity, like all religions, is an action-oriented faith. While actions do not save the faithful, the believer's actions are a response to the grace that has been freely given. Two views of atonement can be seen in the Christian tradition with both views represented in the gospels. **Atonement** is the belief that it is through Jesus Christ, that human beings are reconciled with God and one another.

◆ **Substitutionary Atonement** is the view represented in the Gospels of Matthew, Mark, and John and held by the majority of Christians. In this view, Jesus died in the place of sinners, as a substitute for humanity who deserved death as the consequence of sin. Jesus is the sacrificial Lamb of God. Interestingly, in John's gospel, Jesus is said to have been crucified at the same time the Passover lambs were being slaughtered.

◆ **Reconciling Atonement** maintains that it was not God's intention for Christ to die. Rather, he died because of human sin manifest in the political and religious leadership of the day feeling threatened by him. In this view of atonement, the response to the innocent death of Jesus should be one of repentance. This view holds that Christ could not have been given to God to cover humanity's sins because he was given by God to show the depth of God's love for humanity. The gospel of Luke presents this view of salvation.

Finally, Christians affirm that Christ will return. Various understandings exist in the church as to how this will take place. Some advocate a "rapture" event, popularized by the *Left Behind* series. Others do not accept such a view and simply assert that at some unknown time in the future, Christ will come again. When that happens, there will be a time of judgment, and the kingdom of God will be fully established on earth as it is in heaven. Christianity generally holds a linear view of history; that is, there is a single point of creation; from there, humanity progresses through history to a particular moment when the world will come to an end.

HISTORY OF CHRISTIANITY

Christianity began as a sect within Judaism and remained such for a couple of hundred years. Some scholars even assert that it did not formally split from Judaism until the Emperor, Constantine, made Christianity the official religion of the Roman Empire in 313 CE. However, at least hundred years before Constantine, Christianity was made the state religion of the small kingdom of Edessa (in modern day Syria). Edessa became a center of Christianity when Christians fled Jerusalem during the revolt of 66–70 CE. This revolt ended with the destruction of the temple by the Romans. Christians in Edessa had a significant role in developing the hymns of the early church, particularly St. Ephrem.[14] The Syriac Orthodox Church is rooted in this ancient tradition and practice of Christianity.

One of the major struggles in the early years of Christianity was over how to understand the role and nature of Jesus. Was Jesus both human and divine? If so, how are those two natures related? Did the two natures merge into one, or do they remain separate but side by side in the person of Jesus? What was the nature of the relationship between the three members of the Trinity? Does the Holy Spirit originate from both the Father and the Son or only from the Father? The questions may not seem as important today, but they were quite significant in the first few centuries after Jesus' death and resurrection.

---

[14] For more information on Ephrem (or Ephraim) and his hymns, see http://www.ccel.org/ccel/ephraim.

Councils and Creeds

When Constantine made Christianity the official religion of the Roman Empire, money and power enabled the Church to grow and become more organized. Constantine's mother, Helena, was instrumental in having churches built in Jerusalem and other centers throughout the empire. In 325 CE, Constantine called Christian bishops to gather in Nicea (in modern Turkey) to settle the question of whether Jesus was both fully human and fully divine. One of the outcomes of this council was the Nicene Creed, which affirmed that Jesus was of "one substance" with the Father: "God from God, Light from Light."[15]

Another creed that also developed during this time period, was the Apostle's Creed.[16] Its origins are a little murkier with some saying that it developed in an early form before Nicea. However, the first record of the wording of the creed comes from around 390 CE. Both the Nicene Creed and the Apostle's Creed counter the claim of Christian Gnostics who believed that Jesus was pure spirit, not flesh. In the creeds, it is emphasized that Jesus was "born of the Virgin Mary, suffered under Pontius Pilate, was crucified, dead and buried"; all very physical and human actions. The holy catholic church mentioned in the creed is not the Roman Catholic church alone; rather, here, catholic means universal.

> **Apostle's Creed**
>
> I believe in God the Father Almighty, Maker of heaven and earth:
>
> And in Jesus Christ his only Son our Lord, Who was conceived by the Holy Ghost, Born of the Virgin Mary, Suffered under Pontius Pilate, Was crucified, dead, and buried: He descended into hell; The third day he rose again from the dead; He ascended into heaven, And sitteth on the right hand of God the Father Almighty; From thence he shall come to judge the quick and the dead.
>
> I believe in the Holy Ghost; The holy catholic Church; The Communion of Saints; The Forgiveness of sins; The Resurrection of the body, And the life everlasting. Amen.
>
> *Source: Project Gutenberg, Book of Common Prayer and the Scotish Liturgy from 1912.*

Non-Chalcedonian Churches

Roughly a hundred years later, a new debate took place over how the human and divine natures existed together in the person of Jesus. Nestorius, archbishop of Constantinople, asserted that the two natures existed side by side in the person of Jesus, like oil and water. Cyril of Alexandria, another bishop, was on the other side of the argument. He countered that the two natures merged in the person of Jesus, like water and wine. As the debate intensified, Emperor Marcian, called another council in 451 CE, this time in Chalcedon also located in modern Turkey. Marcian suggested a compromise between the two positions, but neither side was happy. The council resulted in the first split in Christianity. The non-Chalcedonian Churches, those who didn't accept the compromise, continue to believe the two natures comingle. These ancient churches are vital and lively traditions that flourish today. They include the Armenian, Coptic Orthodox, Ethiopian and Eritrean Orthodox, Indian Orthodox, and Syriac Orthodox Churches (Figure 4).[17]

---

[15] From Nicene Creed, for full text of the creed, see https://www.ccel.org/creeds/nicene.creed.html.

[16] Apostle's Creed text from https://www.ccel.org/creeds/apostles.creed.html.

[17] For a profile of five of these communities in Atlanta, see the study sponsored by the Pluralism Project at http://pluralism.org/wp-content/uploads/2015/08/Allen_Orthodox_Churches_2004.pdf.

Figure 4 Photo of the Christmas Procession of the Ethiopian Orthodox Churches in Addis Abeba, Ethiopia, January 2016. Priests carry the Ark of the Covenant through the streets as crowds follow, singing.

☯ Explore the website of one of these branches of Christianity. Some examples of sites to explore include: http://www.armenianchurch-ed.net/; http://www.stmarkdc.org/; http://syrianorthodoxchurch.org/; http://www.ethiopianorthodox.org/english/indexenglish.html; or http://mosc.in/the_church. Write down one or two interesting facts you learned about one of these branches of ancient Christianity.

_____

_____

_____

_____

_____

The Great Schism

Another 600 years passed before the next major split in the Church occurred. At the turn of the millennium, tensions came to a head between the Eastern and Western branches of the Church over issues both religious and political in nature. The political tension involved both the Crusades and the governance of the

Church. Many date the split of the Eastern and Western Chalcedonian Churches to 1054 CE when Pope Leo IX excommunicated the Patriarch of Constantinople; but, that was only a small part of a division that continued to increase as the years passed. The Western church began the Crusades to take the "Holy Land" from Muslim control in 1095. In 1204, Crusaders pillaged Constantinople on their way south adding fuel to the fires of separation. The Western Church solidified the power of the papacy, however, the Eastern Church did not believe that power should be centralized in the office of the Bishop of Rome, the Pope. Eastern Orthodox Church (as the Eastern Church came to be known) believed that theological decisions rested in church councils. Moreover, authority in church matters should be shared by a group of Patriarchs.

Theological differences developed early. One such difference was over the relationship between the three persons of the Trinity and, in particular, the origin of the Holy Spirit. At issue was the Western idea of filioque. Filioque is the belief that the Holy Spirit proceeds from both God, the Father, and Jesus, the Son. The Eastern Orthodox Church believes that the Holy Spirit originates only from the Father. A second difference developed in later years regarding the Immaculate Conception of Mary. The Immaculate Conception is the belief that Mary was without original sin. Roman Catholics believe that it is essential for Mary to have been born without original sin in order for Jesus to be without original sin. The Eastern Orthodox Church rejects the belief in the Immaculate Conception of Mary. They see no need for Mary to be without original sin, because they do not believe in original sin. Rather, the Eastern Orthodox tradition believes that humans bear the consequences of Adam and Eve's sin (i.e., death), but not the guilt for their sin. Individuals are responsible only for their own sin. A third theological difference is in the Orthodox belief in **theosis**, or deification. The Eastern Orthodox Church believes that, through God's grace and a person's faith and practice, individuals can be united with God. According to the Abbott of the Holy Monastery of St. Gregorios, humans "have as our final aim to unite with holy God Himself. This is the purpose of the creation of the universe. This is what we desire. This is our joy, our happiness, and our fulfillment."[18]

Differences also exist in custom, sacred practices, and art forms. The language of the Eastern Orthodox Church was Greek, but the Roman Church used Latin. In addition, the Eastern Orthodox Church follows the calendar instituted by Julian in 46 BCE; however, the Western Church follows the Gregorian calendar, a more widely used calendar named for Pope Gregory XIII in 1582 CE. Because of this, Orthodox dates for Christmas and Easter are often different from Western dates. Another difference related to sacred practice is that the Eastern Orthodox church rejected the idea of priestly celibacy. In Orthodox traditions, priests may marry before ordination. Those who are given the task of patriarchs, bishops, and metropolitans, however, come from the orders of celibate priests and monks. Icons are a unique art form in Orthodox tradition (Figure 5). Icons are sacred images of Jesus, Mary, and the saints; they can also be of

Figure 5   Ancient Icon of Mary, Jesus, and John.

Oleg Golovnev/Shutterstock.com.

---

[18] Archimandrite George, *Theosis: Deification as the Purpose of Man's Life.* https://www.greekorthodoxchurch.org/theosis_contents.html.

Christian symbols, such as the fish. Icons were used from the beginnings of early Christianity as a way to teach the faith and as focal points for attention in prayer and meditation. Panels (or screens of icons), called an **iconostasis**, are found in the front of many Orthodox churches.

The Reformation

The next major division within Christianity occurred in 1517, when Martin Luther posted his ninety-five theses on the door of the church in Wittenberg, Germany. The Reformation was a movement both within, and, later outside of the Roman Catholic Church. Martin Luther was a Roman Catholic monk whose goal was to invite discussion, particularly over the issue of indulgences. Indulgences were opposed by many reformers within the Catholic tradition, particularly among the monastic community. **Indulgences** were the practice of making a donation to the Church to have a special service done to shorten a person's time in purgatory. Purgatory is viewed as a "waiting room" of sorts, a place of purification for the consequences of sin, before entering heaven. The length of time one is in purgatory is dependent on an individual's actions in life. Later, Protestants came to reject the whole idea of purgatory. Some confusion still exists in Protestant Christianity about the role of indulgences. Some have misunderstood indulgences as payments for forgiveness of sin. This is absolutely not the case. In Catholic tradition, as in Protestant tradition, it is only God through Christ who can forgive sins. Although sins are forgiven, God is holy. Before entering God's holy presence, one must be purified from the consequences of sin. Purgatory is the place in which one is purified.

A second theological issue was over the tension between works and grace. Martin Luther asserted that salvation was by grace alone. He even went so far as to question the value of the New Testament book of James, which seemed to stress the importance of works as a sign of grace. Again, there has been some confusion among Protestants over this theological argument. Roman Catholics believe that human beings are saved by grace as well. In the Council of Trent, the Roman Catholic Church asserted that we are saved by grace alone.[19] The experience of grace leads the believer to work toward sanctification. Protestants, particularly in the Holiness traditions, also emphasize this idea of sanctification. **Sanctification** is the process by which believers become more like Christ.

Luther also emphasized the view that practices of the Church should be rooted in Scripture (*sola scriptura*). Moreover, he thought it was important for individuals to read and interpret scripture within the context of the community of faith. This aspect of the Protestant Reformation depended on three things: that people had their own copy of the scripture, that the scriptures were translated into the language of the people, and finally that people could read. The first challenge was that the scriptures to this point in history were hand copied by monks. The time consuming process of hand copying meant that limited numbers of copies existed. Those that were created were very expensive. When the printing press entered the scene in Europe, copies of the scriptures were easier to obtain. The second necessity was the translation of the Bible from Latin to the language spoken by the people, whether that was English, French, German, Chinese, and so on. Great tension existed in the Roman Catholic Church over the translation of the Scriptures. Ultimately, translations were created throughout the Christian world. Luther, Wycliffe, and others worked tenaciously on the process. Finally, people needed to be able to read their own language; so, education was vital. Many early schools in Europe focused on young

---

[19] To read this part of the documents from the Council of Trent, see http://history.hanover.edu/texts/trent/ct06.html.

people learning to read by reading passages from the Bible. Ultimately, individual interpretation of the Bible resulted in the development of many branches of the Protestant family tree.

In addition, the Protestant Reformation became known for the idea of the priesthood of all believers; that is, everyone has a responsibility to share in the ministry of Christ. That being said, Luther did not reject the idea of the ordination of the clergy. The term "priesthood of all believers" developed a hundred years or more after Luther. It was Phillip Jakob Spener who first talked about a "spiritual priesthood," the idea that individuals should be responsible for their own spiritual practice and development.

Protestants rejected the idea of priestly celibacy and eventually affirmed only two sacraments: baptism and the Eucharist. Luther was quickly joined by other reformers, including John Calvin and Ulrich Zwingli. Calvin is best known for his systematic theology, *Institutes of the Christian Religion*, and his introduction of the doctrine of predestination. **Predestination** is the view that God has already seen or determined who will be saved. This doctrine is rooted in the idea that God is in control of all that happens.

The Anglican Church also separated from the Roman Catholic Church during this time period. The separation came about, in large measure, because Henry VIII wanted an annulment; but, the Pope would not grant him one. Henry VIII also wanted to appropriate church property and enhance the royal treasury. As a result, Pope Paul III excommunicated Henry VIII, and Henry VIII responded by excommunicating the Pope. The Anglican Church shares much in common with the Roman Catholic tradition in terms of theology; differences are primarily over matters of authority.

During this same time period, the Roman Catholic Church also experienced reformation. The most obvious outcomes of the Catholic Reformation were documented in the Council of Trent. The **Council of Trent** was held between 1545 and 1563 in Trento, a city in Northern Italy. In the Council of Trent, the church reaffirmed the authority of the Pope, formalized the belief in transubstantiation (the substantive change in the bread and wine once blessed), addressed corruption in the church, and emphasized the importance of an educated priesthood.

Two additional councils have been influential in the modern development of Roman Catholicism. Vatican I (1869-1870) affirmed the doctrine of papal infallibility. **Papal infallibility** is the view that when the pope speaks ex cathedra (that is, from the official office) his teachings are without error. Papal infallibility has only been utilized twice. The belief in the Immaculate Conception of Mary was included as infallible though the doctrine was established earlier in 1854. In addition, the Assumption of Mary was declared an infallible doctrine in 1950. No teachings since those have been deemed infallible. Pope John XXIII presided over **Vatican II** from 1962 to 1965. Some major changes that came from Vatican II include the use of the people's language in the **liturgy** and participation in meetings on Christian unity. Additional statements related to religious liberty and the equality of all people.[20]

Anabaptists or Radical Reformers

Some reformers felt that Luther and Calvin didn't go far enough in their calls for change. For example, Luther and Calvin continued the practice of infant baptism. The Anabaptists, like Menno Simons, Conrad Grebel, and Jacob Hutter, called for baptism to be delayed until a person made a profession of faith. They also emphasized congregational autonomy and opposed bureaucratic church structures. Many were pacifists and called for a separation of church and state. Descendants of these Anabaptist reformers are the Amish, Brethren, and Mennonite traditions. As the Protestant movement continued, various groups

---

[20] To read more about Vatican II and its outcomes, see http://vatican2voice.org/4basics/sixteen.htm

emerged including Baptists, Congregationalists, Methodists, and Nazarenes. Today, numerous types of Baptists exist, such as American Baptists, Freewill Baptists, General Baptists, and Southern Baptists. In the 2006 Yearbook of American and Canadian Churches, 217 different Protestant denominations are listed.[21] In addition to the variety between denominations, there is also great variety within each tradition.

SACRED PRACTICES

Understanding the nature of Christ, the purpose of his ministry, and his relationship to God encompassed much of Christian thought; however, central to Christian life is worship, study, prayer, and service. Christianity is lived out in ancient and modern forms of devotion to God, through Christ, and the power of the Holy Spirit.

Monasticism

Very early in Church history, individuals began to separate themselves from daily life to focus solely on spiritual disciplines. Some retreated to the desert, while others perched on pillars. Those who lived atop pillars were called **stylites**. The earliest stylite was St. Simeon of Syria.[22] Moreover, a number of men and women isolated themselves in the desert, in caves, or in small buildings to practice their faith in isolation. On the other hand, communities of monastics soon formed as well, living together in monasteries and ministering to surrounding towns and villages. One of the earliest Christian monasteries is St. Catherine's monastery in the Sinai desert (Figure 6).

Figure 6 St. Catherine's Monastery in the Sinai desert.

Monks and nuns, of both the Eastern and Western traditions, have served as spiritual guides for pilgrims, reminders of Christ's call to simplicity and faithfulness, and reformers of the church. In addition, they have served their communities by starting schools and hospitals, and ministering to the physical and spiritual needs of others.

Sacraments

Sacraments are rituals that connect people to the sacred; and, in Christian tradition, enable worshippers to experience the power of God's grace. In both Orthodox and Roman Catholic traditions, seven sacraments are recognized. However, most Protestant traditions practice two sacraments: baptism and Eucharist (also known as Communion or the Lord's Supper). Some Protestant traditions have additional rituals that act as sacraments though they don't bear that label. For example, in most Pentecostal traditions, in addition to water baptism, the baptism of the Holy Spirit is essential. The baptism of the Holy

[21] http://hirr.hartsem.edu/research/fastfacts/fast_facts.html#denom. For a more complete list, see https://www.pewforum.org/2015/05/12/appendix-b-classification-of-protestant-denominations/
[22] For an interesting story of a modern-day stylite, see https://www.huffpost.com/entry/katskhi-pillar-monk-georgia-maxime-qavtaradze_n_3950192.

Eastern Orthodox	Roman Catholic	Protestant
Baptism	Baptism	Baptism
Eucharist	Eucharist	Eucharist*
Chrism	Confirmation	
Confession	Confession	
Healing (unction)	Healing (unction)	
Marriage	Marriage	
Ordination	Ordination	

* Also known as Communion or the Lord's Supper

Spirit is manifest in the speaking of tongues (**glossolalia**). In Catholic, Orthodox, Anglican, Church of the Brethren, and some other Protestant traditions, footwashing is often practiced at least once a year, often during Holy Week as part of celebrations of the Last Supper. Although a meaningful and significant ritual, footwashing is not a sacrament.

Baptism is rooted in the ancient Jewish practice of **mikvah** (a cleansing or purification ritual involving immersion in water). In Christian tradition, baptism is also for the forgiveness of sin and an incorporation into the Body of Christ (the Church). Baptism is a ritual reenactment, and a participation in, the death and resurrection of Jesus. As Jesus was baptized by John in the Jordan River, Matthew's gospel reports that after the resurrection, Jesus encouraged his disciples to "make disciples of all nations and to baptize them." (Matt. 28:19)

Within Christian tradition, baptism has taken two forms: immersion and sprinkling. Immersion involves submersion in water; while with sprinkling, the priest or pastor cups water from the baptismal font and administers droplets of water on the head of the person being baptized. From the early centuries of the church, infant baptism has been a common practice. Orthodox, Catholic, Episcopal, Lutheran, Methodist, Presbyterian, and United Church of Christ communions all practice infant baptism. Anabaptist, Holiness, Pentecostal, and Nondenominational Christians practice baptism at the "age of accountability"; that is, when a person chooses to be baptized. Many traditions that baptize infants do so by sprinkling; however, most Orthodox Christians immerse infants (Figure 7).

Figure 7 In Orthodox baptism, infants are anointed with oil and immersed in the baptismal font.

In the Roman Catholic and Protestant traditions that practice infant baptism, children later confirm their faith through the act of **confirmation**. Confirmation takes place around the age of twelve or thirteen. The young people who will be confirmed take a series of classes about the faith, then make a decision on whether to come before the congregation and confirm the faith for themselves.

The second primary sacrament in the life of the church is the Eucharist. This ritual is also known as Communion or the Lord's Supper in Protestant traditions. The practice is rooted in Jesus' Last Supper with the disciples in which he declared the bread as his body and the wine as his blood (Figure 8). Many parts of the Christian family celebrate the Eucharist weekly, some even daily; however, others practice it on a less frequent basis, such as once a month or every three months.

Different forms of Christianity have distinct views of the elements. Orthodox, Catholic, and Anglican/Episcopal doctrines understand the blessing of the bread and wine by the priest to lead to a substantive transformation in the elements. This view is known as **transubstantiation** and asserts that, when blessed, the bread and wine become the body and blood of Christ. During the Protestant Reformation, Luther shared the

Figure 8 Mural of the Last Supper done by Giacomo Raffaelli in 1816 as a copy of DaVinci's famous work.

Catholic view that there is a substantive change in the elements, but he asserted that they also remain bread and wine. His view is called **consubstantiation**, and it asserts that there is a mystical change, but not a full transformation. Other forms of Protestantism hold a **symbolic view** of the elements and assert that there is no substantive change that takes place when the elements are blessed.

Liturgical Year

Every year, the Church cycles through the birth, ministry, death, and resurrection of Jesus. Orthodox, Roman Catholic, Episcopalian, and most mainline Protestant denominations follow the seasons of the church year. These churches also typically follow a three-year cycle of readings, called a **lectionary**. Each year focuses on one of the Synoptic Gospels (Matthew, Mark, or Luke). Readings are also given for the Old Testament, Psalms, and Letters. Typically, readings from the Gospel of John and Acts are part of the Easter season. One or more of the scripture passages for each Sunday of the lectionary are usually read in the service and serve as the basis for reflection in the homily or sermon offered by the pastor. Each season of the church year has a color that corresponds to it. The colors are often displayed in the altar cloth, the minister's or priests stole, and the paraments on the pulpit and lectern.

Advent begins the liturgical year in late November or early December. This period is a season of repentance and preparation during the four weeks before Christmas in anticipation of Christ's birth. Common

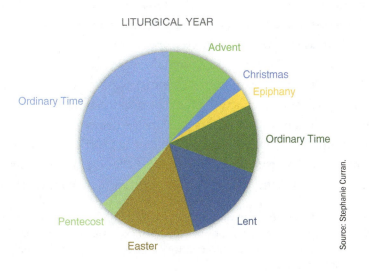

elements of worship related to Advent are the Advent Wreath as well as an advent calendar with daily readings (and often a piece of chocolate). The Advent Wreath is made up of five candles, four outer candles, and then the Christ Candle in the middle that is lit on Christmas. One of the outer candles is lit on the first Sunday of Advent and an additional one is lit for each successive Sunday until Christmas. **Christmas** is a period of twelve days that celebrates the birth of Jesus. The dates for Christmas and Easter are slightly different in the Orthodox Churches than in Western traditions because the Orthodox Church follows the Julian calendar (as mentioned earlier in the chapter). Following Christmas is Epiphany, a season that reflects on the revelation or manifestation of Jesus as the Christ. The first reading of Epiphany is the story of the coming of the wise men to honor the Christ child. Epiphany is followed by a period of ordinary time until Lent. Services in ordinary time focus on Christ's ministry, and the liturgy in Roman and Orthodox traditions follows the standard format.

Lent begins the next season of repentance. Ash Wednesday is the first of the forty days in Lent. Forty, of course, is symbolic of Jesus' time in the wilderness. The counting of the forty days does not include Sundays, because each Sunday is understood to be a celebration of Christ's resurrection. On Ash Wednesday, worshippers are reminded of their need for repentance and the reality of their mortality. Some will fast from certain foods during Lent or take on an additional spiritual discipline. The final week of Lent is often called Holy Week. This week begins with Palm Sunday and Jesus' triumphal entry into Jerusalem. The week of services also includes Maundy Thursday, which commemorates the Last Supper Jesus shared with his disciples, and Good Friday, which reflects on the arrest, suffering, and death of Jesus. Orthodox and Roman Catholic traditions also have a Holy Saturday service in which a light is brought out of the darkness in anticipation of the celebration of the resurrection on Easter Sunday. Easter lasts for fifty days and culminates in the celebration of Pentecost. Pentecost is sometimes referred to as "the birthday of the church," and focuses on the gift of the Holy Spirit and the spreading of the Good News to all nations. The events of Pentecost are recorded in Acts 2. Following Pentecost is a longer season of ordinary time. This longer stretch is punctuated by various feast days for saints and martyrs of the church. The last Sunday of the liturgical year is Christ the King Sunday. It is the Sunday before the first week of Advent. Then, the cycle begins anew.

Devotional Practices

A variety of devotional practices are utilized as an individual and community of believers seeks to grow in faith. Bible study, weekly worship and prayer are primary devotional practices in all Christian communities. In addition, many traditions also utilize specific prayer practices such as a routine of daily prayers (referred to as praying the hours),[23] the use of rosary beads to mark prayers and remember the mysteries of Christ, and *lectio divina*. *Lectio divina* is the repetition of a scripture passage as a way to let go of preconceptions about the text and to open one's mind to a new word.[24] The practice of the Stations of the Cross is common in the Roman Catholic tradition; it consists of fourteen images depicting the final hours of Jesus' life.

An important misconception to debunk is that Catholics and Orthodox worship Mary and the saints. Mary and the saints are not worshiped; rather, they are understood as intercessors. Prayers to Mary don't replace prayers to God; in fact, often, they are in addition to them. In much the same way as someone would

---

[23] For more about praying the hours, see http://www.phyllistickle.com/fixed-hour-prayer/ or http://www.usccb.org/prayer-and-worship/liturgy-of-the-hours/. There is even an app you can download to assist you: http://divine-office.com/.

[24] For more information on the practice of lectio divina, see http://www.ignatianspirituality.com/ignatian-prayer/the-what-how-why-of-prayer/praying-with-scripture.

ask their beloved Aunt Bea to prayer for them because she is believed to be close to God and a devout person of prayer; so Mary and the saints are often asked to pray on behalf of a person in need (Figure 9).

Pilgrimage

From the early days of Christianity, pilgrimage has been a practice of journeying to a sacred space as a means of spiritual growth. Pilgrimages to Jerusalem, Bethlehem, or Rome are perhaps the first that come to mind. When travel was not possible, the labyrinth served as means of internal pilgrimage. The labyrinth on the floor of Chartres Cathedral is a good example of this practice; this labyrinth is thought to have been created in the thirteenth century (Figure 10).

Pilgrimages to hermitages, sites of divine healing, and literary pilgrimages punctuate various periods of history and may be specific to cultural expressions of faith. The pilgrimage to Lourdes in France and the pilgrimage to Our Lady of Guadalupe in Mexico are two examples of the intersection of faith and culture as well as places of healing. The Camino de Santiago, or Way of St. James, is another popular pilgrimage route that winds through France and Spain. Chaucer, author of *The Canterbury Tales*, wrote a tale of fiction in which a variety of pilgrims, each with his or her own reasons for taking the journey, interact with one another on the Way. A significant aspect of pilgrimage is the internal spiritual growth that comes from making the journey.

Music

Many people express their faith through music. From "Amazing Grace" to "Handel's Messiah," music has played a central role in Christianity. Beginning with the hymns of the Syrian St. Ephrem in the fourth century, if not earlier, music has enabled the faithful to express their devotion and affirm their belief. African American spirituals voiced the hope for freedom. Christian hip-hop and punk rock artists seek to connect the message of the faith with contemporary musical forms. Popular music from every genre articulates faith from the artist's perspective; a brief sampling ranges from Lady Gaga's "Judas," and Kanye West's "Jesus Walks," to Carrie Underwood's "Something in the Water."

Source: Stephanie Curran at San Francis Xavier Mission, Tucson Arizona in July 2019.

Figure 9   St. Kateri Tekakwitha is the first indigenous American saint in the Roman Catholic Church. She was an Algonquin-Mohawk laywoman, who was also known as the Lily of the Mohawks. She is buried in the San Francis Xavier Mission in Tucson, AZ.

Jaime Pharr/Shutterstock.com.

Figure 10   Labyrinth on the floor of Chartres Cathedral.

❧ Explore a genre of Christian music with which you are unfamiliar. The options are endless, but some ideas include Taize, Gregorian Chant, Christian Punk, Christian Hip-Hop, African American spirituals, Orthodox Church hymns, or revival hymns of the nineteenth century. Choose a song to listen to and write about. Which song did you choose? What drew you to the song? What is the song's central message?

Alternatively, explore examples of Christian art from any culture or time period. Select one work of art to describe and explain how it demonstrates an aspect of Christianity.

_____

_____

_____

_____

_____

CHRISTIAN SYMBOLS

Many Christian symbols reflect a variety of traditions and cultures. The two most commonly thought of symbols are the cross and the fish. The cross takes many forms and shapes depending on the form of Christian tradition and the specific meaning behind the image. Although the crucifix of the Roman Catholic tradition typically has Jesus hanging on the cross, crosses in Orthodox and Protestant traditions are generally empty (Figure 11).

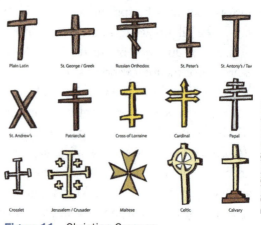

Figure 11   Christian Crosses.

Another Christian symbol is that of the fish. The fish, or ichthys (the Greek word for fish), was an acrostic of the phrase "Jesus Christ, Son of God, Savior" in Greek. The fish was also a symbol based on the teachings and miracles of Jesus. Jesus fed the crowds with five loaves of bread and two fish; he also called the early disciples to be "fishers of people (Figure 12)."

Figure 12   Christian ichthys symbol.

☮ Choose a Christian symbol, such as a specific type of cross, the dove, bread, the shepherd's staff, the ChiRho, Alpha, and Omega, and so on. Research the meaning behind the symbol and share what you discovered.

_____

_____

_____

_____

_____

CHRISTIANITY IN THE UNITED STATES

Christianity was introduced in North America through the efforts of missionaries and immigrants from all different branches of Christianity. Moreover, the United States experienced two Great Awakenings, or spiritual revivals, as well as the development of its own unique forms of Protestantism. Although Christianity was not the state religion, Protestantism became deeply embedded in the cultural life of the United States. As social movements, such as abolition, temperance, suffrage, and workplace reform movements took shape, Christianity and appeals to the Bible were utilized by proponents on all sides of the issues. This reality is still the case in the political landscape of the United States.

Evangelicalism

Luther first used the term "evangelical" to define his movement in keeping with the Greek root, "euangelion" which translates as "gospel" or "good news." Some Lutheran churches still have "Evangelical" in their name, such as the Evangelical Lutheran Church of America. However, "the evangelical movement" was propelled by the Second Great Awakening of the early 1800s led by Charles Finney. This movement emphasized four ideas: the centrality of the Bible, the importance of Christ's sacrifice on the cross, the need for conversion, and social activism. The social activism of Evangelicalism led to involvement in the movement for temperance, social justice, and abolition.

Evangelicalism is not the same as Fundamentalism. The term, "fundamentalism," is overused in describing conservative and sometimes radical movements both within and outside of Christianity. Individuals in these movements have been known to express violence and hatred toward anyone whose beliefs or practices don't match those of the movement. However, historically in Christianity, the term arose in the early twentieth century in response to the liberalism and biblical criticism of the late 1800s and early 1900s. Darwin's theory of evolution, and its teaching in schools, was another catalyst for the formation of the fundamentalist movement. Christian fundamentalism asserted that there were certain "fundamentals" on which Christians could not compromise. These tenets included a literal understanding of the Bible and an affirmation that the Bible is without error or contradiction; the belief in the Virgin Birth; substitutionary atonement; the bodily resurrection of Jesus; and, the premillennial second coming of Christ. In addition to these theological principles, fundamentalists refused to associate or cooperate with any individuals or groups who did not share their concern for moral and doctrinal purity. Concern for moral purity led them to seek to preserve, or impose, laws that supported their moral teaching. For example, fundamentalists supported Prohibition and wanted to keep the "blue laws" which forced businesses to remain closed on Sundays. Fundamentalism, as a movement, continues in the United States and is, in part, inspired by a fear that Christian influence is waning in contemporary culture.

Nineteenth and Twentieth Century Christian Movements in the United States

The nineteenth and twentieth centuries served as fertile soil for the growth of some very unique and distinct Christian sects. Many of these movements were revivalist in tone and emerged from the Second Great Awakening. Some were focused on the second coming. Some emphasized the power of the Spirit; others, the power of the mind. The sampling below is not comprehensive, but does give a flavor for the variety of the movements.

Christian Science

Christian Science began in the latter part of the 1800s and centered around the spiritual philosophy of Mary Baker Eddy. Blending science, theology, and health practices, Mary Baker Eddy stressed the power of the mind to connect with God; and thereby, experience spiritual and physical healing. Her teachings were outlined in her major work, *Science and Health with a Key to the Scriptures*, published in 1875. This text is an outgrowth of years of studying how God healed her, and describing the "science of healing" she experienced. She also founded *The Christian Science Monitor*, a newspaper that continues to be read widely today.

Christian Science teaching is rooted in the Bible, and *Science and Health* serves as a companion text. Eddy taught that Jesus' healing miracles can be replicated today. Healing comes from God, rather than medicine. Jesus is viewed as the Son of God and his human example enables him to mediate between God and human beings. Baptism and Eucharist are understood spiritually rather than as physical rituals. A follower practices baptism on a daily basis by purifying the mind and acting in pure and holy ways. Eucharist is understood as a spiritual connection with God through prayer and thought. Human beings are created in God's image and bear God's likeness within them. Sin, suffering, and death are a result of separating oneself and one's thoughts and actions from God who is within each individual.

Christian Scientists meet in reading rooms around the country where they read the Bible and passages from *Science and Health*. These two texts are the "pastors" of the church. Individuals within the community serve as readers, but there are no ordained clergy. Often, weekly testimonial meetings are also held to share experiences of healing or insights gleaned through a person's spiritual practice.

Although not all, many Christian Scientists refuse medical treatment. This refusal has caused some legal controversies over the years; particularly, in cases involving parents who have not sought medical care for their children. Christian Scientists are not alone in facing these dilemmas. Many faith healing traditions experience the same critical decisions, as well as legal ramifications, for being true to their beliefs.[25]

---

[25] See http://www.pewforum.org/2009/08/31/faith-healing-and-the-law/ for an excellent overview as well as a few specific cases related to this tension between faith and government.

Church of Jesus Christ of Latter-Day Saints

Born of a young boy's quest for which of the many denominations of Christianity is the correct one, the Church of Jesus Christ of Latter-Day Saints (LDS) has grown into a global movement with well over fifteen million members.[26] LDS have suffered persecution and misunderstanding for much of the church's history. The roots of the faith began in 1820, when Joseph Smith received his first vision at the age of fourteen. However, it was not until 1823 when the angel, Moroni, told him of the golden tablets that would eventually become the Book of Mormon.

The Church utilizes both the Bible and the Book of Mormon as their sources of truth. Basic tenets of the faith include a belief in salvation through Jesus Christ (who is believed to be God's first creation), the Trinity as three separate persons, and a need for individual repentance. LDS practice baptism by immersion. Communion is practiced in weekly services utilizing bread and water. Thirteen Articles of Faith summarize the core beliefs of the tradition.[27]

Two controversial practices that have caused much contention include the practice of polygamy and the baptism of the dead. The practice of polygamy (plural marriage) came to Joseph Smith in a revelation in 1843. At first, neither Brigham Young, who would become the leader of the movement after Smith's death in 1844, or Smith's wife, Emma, were in agreement with the practice. However, Young eventually accepted the practice and had a total of twenty wives. In 1862, an anti-polygamy law was passed in Congress, but it would be several years before it was enforced in any way. In 1890, Wilford Woodruff, who was President of the Church of Jesus Christ of LDS, officially rescinded the practice of polygamy in the Church. A division in the church resulted from Woodruff's repeal of the practice; now only fundamentalist groups who have broken away from the main church continue to practice plural marriage.

The second controversial practice is the baptism of the dead or baptism by proxy. In Latter Day Saint tradition, a person can undergo baptism in place of someone who has died. LDS believe that this baptism allows the person who has died to either accept or reject the baptism. The practice is rooted in John 3:5, a passage that asserts that to be saved a person must be born of water and the Spirit. LDS followers believe that it is their responsibility to offer baptism to those who did not have the opportunity to accept or reject it. LDS value family and mission. Beautiful temples dot the landscape across the country including this one in Washington, DC (Figure 13).

Figure 13   LDS Temple in Washington, DC.

Joe Ravi/Shutterstock.com.

---

[26] http://www.ldschurchtemples.com/statistics/.
[27] To read the Thirteen Articles of Faith, https://www.comeuntochrist.org/articles/articles-of-faith.

Seventh Day Adventist

The next two movements to be discussed both began in anticipation of Christ's Second Coming. Seventh Day Adventists emerged from the Millerite movement. The Millerites believed Christ's Second Coming would take place in 1844. When that failed to happen, the Millerites disbanded. Emerging from the disappointment, James and Ellen White and others studied the scriptures and determined that in 1844, Jesus began the final phase of his ministry in heaven.

Adventists share much with other Protestant traditions including a belief in the Trinity, Jesus' atoning sacrifice on the cross, and the practice of baptism; yet they are unique. One distinguishing feature of this movement is its emphasis on Saturday as the Sabbath. They also follow diet restrictions, such as refraining from consuming pork, caffeine, or alcohol. Many are vegetarian. Ellen White was very interested in healing practices and opened a clinic in Michigan as part of her ministry. From these beginnings, Adventist hospitals have been built around the world.[28] Ellen White was also a writer and evangelist and did much to spread Adventist teachings.

Jehovah's Witnesses

Another movement focused on the second coming of Christ is the Jehovah's Witnesses. This movement was founded a little later than the Seventh Day Adventists, but shares the anticipation of Christ's return and the belief that his second coming will inaugurate the reign of God on earth. In the late 1890s, Charles Taze Russell, a native of Pittsburgh, began to meet regularly with friends to study the Bible. They published their views in *The Watchtower* magazine. Russell came to believe that Christ would return in 1914. His view was later amended to reflect his understanding that Jesus began his reign in heaven in that year. Like the other movements discussed in this section, Jehovah's Witnesses are very committed to evangelism and have grown into a global movement.

Jehovah's Witnesses share a belief with other Christians in the saving work of Christ. At the same time, they do not equate Jesus and God and do not believe in the Trinity. They believe that their allegiance is only to God and that they are citizens of his kingdom; therefore, they do not pledge allegiance to any flag, serve in the military or vote. They respect the authority of government but remain politically neutral. At the Second Coming, Jehovah's Witnesses believe that 144,000 will rule with God in heaven. The remainder of the faithful will live in a paradise on earth. Witnesses do not believe in hell. The punishment for sin is simply death and separation from God; there is no eternal torment. Worship in Jehovah's Witness tradition takes place in kingdom halls and involves prayer and study as well as singing and preaching.

Birthdays and holidays, such as Christmas and Easter, have pagan origins; therefore, Witnesses do not celebrate them. They do, however, celebrate the memorial of Christ's death at Passover and believe in the power of the resurrection. Another practice that is somewhat unique to Jehovah's Witnesses is their refusal of blood transfusions. This refusal is based in passages from the Hebrew Bible forbidding the consumption of blood.[29]

---

[28] For more information on Adventist beliefs, see https://www.adventist.org/en/beliefs/.

[29] For more information on Jehovah's Witnesses views on blood transfusions, see https://www.jw.org/en/jehovahs-witnesses/faq/jehovahs-witnesses-why-no-blood-transfusions/#?insight[search_id]=60716253-a236-47bc-b95a-a0a0c1ea2bdd& insight[search_result_index]=2 Practices of bloodless surgery have been developed in response to this restriction.

Pentecostalism

Pentecostalism is a broad movement taking many forms and is rooted in the ancient Christian belief in the continuing revelation of the Holy Spirit. It emerged from the Holiness movement that produced the Church of God (Anderson, Indiana), the Church of the Nazarene, the Methodist Church, and the Salvation Army among others. Holiness traditions emphasized the role of sanctification or growing in Holiness. In addition to water baptism by immersion, Pentecostals are characterized by a belief in a second baptism, that of the Holy Spirit. For them, the sign of this baptism is speaking in tongues (**glossolalia**).

Figure 14 Aimee Semple McPherson service.

The history of Pentecostalism is rooted in the Azuza St. Revival in Los Angeles beginning in 1906. Out of this revival, many branches of Pentecostalism emerged including: the Church of God in Christ, the Church of God (Cleveland, Tennessee), the Pentecostal Holiness Church, and the Foursquare Church. The Foursquare Church was founded by Aimee Semple McPherson, a dynamic evangelist who founded the Angelus Temple in Los Angeles in 1923. She was a passionate preacher who held services every night for packed crowds of thousands. One service lasted a legendary fourteen hours (Figure 14).

One of the fascinating things about the early Pentecostal movement is that it was much more inclusive than the rest of society at the time. Men and women served as leaders of this movement that embraced people of all social classes and races.

☙ Search the web page for a denomination you are interested in learning more about. Write down one interesting fact you learned about the movement.

_____

_____

_____

_____

Ecumenism

The word "**ecumenism**" comes from the Greek word *oikoumene*, which is translated as "the whole inhabited earth." The modern movement for church unity between various denominations began in the early twentieth century with the formation of working groups from several Protestant denominations. The working groups focused on Life and Work (social justice issues) and Faith and Order (doctrine and governance). The goal was a unity of witness and practice. After World War II, the World Council of Churches was formed. This organization remains the most prominent expression of Christian unity in the world with over 300 member churches including Catholic, Orthodox, and Protestant traditions. The goals of the movement are to foster discussion, share Eucharistic fellowship, and promote evangelism and mission.[30] In terms of doctrine, one of the most important developments from the World Council of Churches was the document, *Baptism, Eucharist and Ministry*, which was adopted in the 1982 meeting of the Faith and Order Commission. The document explores shared understandings of the sacraments of baptism and Eucharist as well as the ordination of pastors and priests.[31] Cooperative agreements between denominations, such as the Christian Church (Disciples of Christ) and the United Church of Christ, have emerged out of these common understandings.

Nondenominationalism and the Emerging Church Movement

Since the 1960s, a distrust of social institutions has been permeating the culture of the United States. Some feel that the institutionalized forms of Christianity can no longer meaningfully address the challenges of living out the faith in our day and time. Nondenominational churches are somewhat difficult to study as a whole because there is no one point of origin. Roughly 35,000 nondenominational congregations exist in the United States today with an estimated ten million members.[32] Although some began before 1950, most formed from the 1980s to the present. Willow Creek Church is perhaps the most well-known nondenominational congregation. Bill Hybels founded this congregation in a suburb of Chicago in 1975. The congregation continues to grow; and, in April 2016, received zoning approval to build a new 193,000 square foot campus. They average about 20,000 in worship on Sunday mornings.

Another contemporary movement of the Christian faith in the late twentieth and early twenty-first centuries is the "emerging" church. This is a global phenomenon that rejects the idea of church buildings in favor of smaller house-type churches. They emphasize practice and community rather than buildings and structures. One organization of this movement is the Emergent Village which has both US and UK branches. It is dangerous to categorize this movement because it is so new and continues to adapt; but, there are a few things that can be said about it. It emphasizes being a follower of Jesus rather than a member of a church. It is prophetic and seeks to disrupt the status quo of society and the church as a social institution. It practices in small groups that form cells or house-type churches. Creative worship, theological discussions, and a service/mission orientation are central to its practice. The goal is to make the teachings of Jesus alive and relevant in the twenty-first century.[33]

---

[30] For more information on the World Council of Churches, see https://www.oikoumene.org/en/about-us.

[31] To read the full text of Baptism, Eucharist and Ministry, a pdf is available at https://www.oikoumene.org/en/resources/documents/commissions/faith-and-order/i-unity-the-church-and-its-mission/baptism-eucharist-and-ministry-faith-and-order-paper-no-111-the-lima-text.

[32] http://hirr.hartsem.edu/cong/nondenom_FACT.html.

[33] For a good overview of this movement, see this article from Christianity Today: http://www.christianitytoday.com/ct/2007/february/11.35.html.

LIBERATION AND FEMINIST THEOLOGY

The twentieth century also saw the rise of theologies of liberation rooted in Jesus' sermon in his home synagogue. In Luke 4, Jesus asserts that he has come to fulfill Isaiah's prophecy and "to proclaim good news to the poor. He has sent me to proclaim freedom for the prisoners and recovery of sight for the blind, to set the oppressed free, and to proclaim the year of the Lord's favor."[34] Latin America was home to the first of these movements which emphasized "base communities" (*comunidades eclesiales de base* in Spanish) of Christians who gather for worship, bible study, and social action on behalf of the poor and oppressed. Gustavo Gutiérrez and Juan Luis Segundo were some of the earliest Catholic theologians of the movement in the 1970s.

Liberation theology spread simultaneously to the African American community with the publication in 1970 of James Cone's, *A Black Theology of Liberation*. Asian and African theologies of liberation also grew. Aloysius Pieres published *An Asian Theology of Liberation* in 1988, and Josiah Ulysses Young, III published *A Pan-African Theology: Providence and the Legacy of the Ances*tors in 1992. South African struggles against apartheid also led to further works of African Liberation Theology such as the writings of Nelson Mandela, Archbishop Tutu, and Allan Boesak.[35]

Feminist, Mujerista, and Womanist theologies also emerged in the twentieth century. These movements explore the history of women's leadership in Christian history as well as new interpretations of biblical texts from the perspective of women. They affirm liberation from oppression and full participation in the community of faith for women. Reconstructionist feminist theologians work to recreate the history of women in the early church. Pioneers of reconstruction of the work of women include Letty Russell and Elisabeth Schussler Fiorenza. Other feminist writers proposed a more radical feminist theology and focused on developing new rituals and practices meaningful to women. Landmark works in this vein are Rosemary Radford Ruether's, *Sexism and God-Talk* and *Women-Church*. Ruether also has worked to blend feminism and ecological justice. Mujerista theologians focus on liberation for Latina women; Womanist theologians, on the other hand, focus on liberation for women in the African American context.

Full inclusion in the community of faith for members of the lesbian, gay, bisexual, and transgender (LGBT) community is another form of liberation theology in the church. In the 1990s, in response to the isolation experienced by so many LGBT persons, the pain caused by loss of many to acquired immune deficiency syndrome (AIDS), and the affirmation that the faith community should be open to all, queer theology began to develop. "Recognition of difference in solidarity is central to queer theology. It acknowledges that black, white, disabled, poor, rich, male, female, and transgendered queers are oppressed in different ways and that some of us are involved in the oppression of our fellow queers."[36] Although some communities of faith have fully embraced those of all sexual orientations, others still struggle with the full inclusion of members of the LGBT community in the fellowship of faith.

---

[34] Luke 4: 18–19.

[35] For more information on Liberation Theology and those who are doing its work, see http://liberationtheology.org/.

[36] Elisabeth Stuart, *Religion is a Queer Thing* (Pilgrim Press, 1998), 3.

GROWING CENTERS OF CHRISTIANITY TODAY

The greatest growth in Christianity today is being experienced outside of the European and American spheres. The growing centers today are Africa, Asia, and Central and South America. Although Willow Creek Church in Chicago averages a worship attendance of 20,000 on Sunday, the Yoido Full Gospel Church in Seoul, South Korea has 830,000 members and over twenty-five weekly services. Yoido Full Gospel Church is an Assemblies of God affiliated church that began in a living room in 1958 and grew to a peak membership of a million.[37] The growth has not been without controversy; their founding pastor and his son were charged in 2014 with embezzlement. Although he remains pastor emeritus, the founding pastor, David Cho, no longer heads the church.[38]

In 1910, two-thirds of the world's Christians lived in Europe. "Today, only about a quarter of all Christians live in Europe (26%). A plurality – more than a third – now are in the Americas (37%). About one in every four Christians lives in sub-Saharan Africa (24%), and about one-in-eight is found in Asia and the Pacific (13%)."[39] Much of the growth of Christianity is happening in Pentecostal movements in the global south.

☻ Explore this report from the Pew Forum, *Global Christianity: A Report on the Size and Distribution of the World's Christian Population* at http://www.pewforum.org/2011/12/19/global-christianity-exec/. Write down one new fact you learned or something that surprised you from the report.

_____

_____

_____

_____

WEB RESOURCES FOR FURTHER STUDY

http://www.earlychristianwritings.com—A website offering access to translations of many ancient documents in the early church—canonical and non-canonical texts as well as offering a section on historical Jesus theories.

http://www.oikoumene.org/—The homepage for the World Council of Churches.

---

[37] For more information on this controversial congregation, see their website http://english.fgtv.com/.

[38] For more information on the scandal see this article from Christianity Today: http://www.christianitytoday.com/gleanings/2014/february/founder-of-worlds-largest-megachurch-convicted-cho-yoido.html.

[39] http://www.pewforum.org/2011/12/19/global-christianity-exec/ page 1.

http://www.pbs.org/wgbh/pages/frontline/shows/religion/—The Frontline series "From Jesus to Christ: The First Christians" offers a variety of information about the life of Jesus, the early church, and the history and development of Christianity.

Individual denominational sites:

https://www.ame-church.com/—African Methodist Episcopal.

http://www.abc-usa.org/—American Baptist.

www.ag.org—Assemblies of God.

www.disciples.org—Christian Church (Disciples of Christ).

www.episcopalchurch.org—Episcopal.

www.elca.org—Lutheran.

www.oca.org—Orthodox.

www.pcusa.org—Presbyterian.

www.sbc.net—Southern Baptist.

www.ucc.org—United Church of Christ.

www.umc.org—United Methodist.

Chapter 12

Islam

...son, students will be able to

...nt events in the life of Muhammad;

...ation and composition of the Qur'an;

...ars of the Faith and describe their practice;

... various branches of Islam including Sunni and Shi'a;

... by Muhammad in regard to the treatment of women and ...jab; and

...lam impacts the daily lives of followers including food restric-...d marriage, and so on.

Abraham	Id-al-Adha	Muslim
Abu Bakr	Imam	Qibla
Adhan	Ishmael	Qur'an
Ali	Islam	Rabi'a
Allah	Jihad	Ramadan
Fasting	Jinn	Shahadah
Fatima	Ka'aba	Shariah
Gabriel	Khadijah	Shirk
Hadith	Kufr	Sufism
Hajj	Minaret	Surah
Hijrah	Mosque/Masjid	Ummah
Hijab	Muezzin	Wudu
Id-al-Fitr	Muhammad	Zakat

INTRODUCTION

The word, *Islam*, derives from the Arabic word, *Salaam*, which means "peace." Islam is a religion of peaceful submission to the will of God. A Muslim, therefore, is one who submits to God. Muslims worship Allah, which is an Arabic word meaning, "the only One to be worshipped." Allah cannot be made plural and emphasizes the oneness of God. It is the same word that Arabic-speaking Christians and Jews use for God.

One of the greatest misconceptions about Islam is that the majority of Muslims live in the Middle East. Not true. The largest population of Muslims is in Indonesia, and the vast majority of all Muslims live outside of the Middle East in Asia, Africa, Europe, and the United States. With the rise in terrorism around the world and misconceptions about Islam in abundance, this chapter is one of the most important in the book. Having an accurate understanding of Islam and those who practice it is critical for dialogue and the building of relationships between Muslims and non-Muslims in this country and around the world.

THE LIFE OF MUHAMMAD

The prophet Muhammad was born in Mecca around 570 CE. He was part of the powerful Quraysh tribe. His father died before he was born, and his mother died when he was only six. An uncle, Abu Talib, raised him. As an orphan, Muhammad developed a lifelong commitment to those who are marginalized in society, as well as a deep concern for equality and justice. As he grew up, he engaged in business and trade. He took caravans of goods throughout the Middle East and came into contact with a variety of people, including followers of Judaism and Christianity.

When Muhammad was twenty-five, a widow named Khadijah hired him to take a caravan of goods to Syria. She was impressed with the work he did and admired his integrity. In time, she asked him to marry her. Muhammad accepted her proposal and their families facilitated the marriage. Together, they had several children. Unfortunately, only one daughter, Fatima, survived to adulthood. Throughout his life, Muhammad was plagued by spiritual questions and often went on retreat to the mountains to think and pray. In 610 CE, Muhammad went on retreat to Jabal al-Nur (the Mountain of Light) just outside of Mecca. Inside the cave, called al-Hira, he received his first revelation of the Qur'an (Figure 1).

As he was praying in the cave, the angel Gabriel appeared to him and commanded him to "Recite." Muhammad insisted that he could not recite. He did not read or write. Three times the angel commanded him to recite. Finally, Muhammad was so overwhelmed that he began to speak what became the first verses of the Qur'an. He was terrified and ran home; he worried that he was losing his mind. However, Khadijah encouraged him and suggested a visit to her cousin, who was a Christian. Her cousin, Waraqa, encouraged Muhammad and assured him that the words he had received were from God. At the same time, Waraqa warned Muhammad that prophets were often persecuted for their messages.

Figure 1 Muslims waiting to pray at the cave, al Hira, where Muhammad received his first revelation.

Artpixelgraphy Studio/Shutterstock.com.

For two years, Muhammad only shared his revelations with Khadijah and Waraqa. When Muhammad began to more widely share his revelations, they were not well received by the people of Mecca. Muhammad preached equality and spoke out against the high interest rates under which the poor suffered. In addition, he preached monotheism in a largely polytheistic society. Even so, his influence grew, and the leaders of Mecca feared that Muhammad threatened their power. A boycott was put in place forbidding trade with Muslims, including selling them food. Muhammad began to make alliances with leaders in Medina. During this boycott, Khadijah passed away.

One of the most significant events in the life of Muhammad is his "Night Journey" from Mecca to Jerusalem, where it is said that he ascended into heaven. It is said that the Prophet Muhammad was taken by the angel Gabriel up to heaven where he found himself in the presence of God. On the way, he greeted many of the prophets from Adam to Moses; and, on his return trip he stoped to converse with them. According to the **hadith** (traditions of the prophet), when asked if he saw God, Muhammad replied, "God is covered in light, how could I see him?" The Dome of the Rock and the Mosque of al-Aqsa in Jerusalem are built in honor of this important Night Journey (Figure 2).

In 622 CE, the situation in Mecca was becoming unbearable because of the boycott. Many of the community were dying from starvation while others suffered financial ruin. In addition, Muhammad's life was threatened. Muhammad's followers began to slip out of the city and the migration to Medina (**Hijrah**) was underway. It is from the date of the Hijrah that the Muslim calendar begins. In Medina, Muhammad's message fell on receptive ears, and he built the first **masjid** (place of prostration) for prayer. The layout of many mosques today are based on the original floor plan of this one in Medina (Figure 3).

Over the next eight years, battles ensued between the followers of Muhammad and the Quraysh in Mecca. Finally, in 630 CE, Muhammad marched toward Mecca with 10,000 followers. The leadership of Mecca surrendered and Muhammad took the city with no further bloodshed. By the end of his life, Muhammad had united the Arabian Peninsula. In 632 CE, after a brief illness, Muhammad passed away.

Corbis Historical/Getty Images

Figure 2 Dome of the Rock, Jerusalem.

Hikrcn/Shutterstock.com.

Figure 3 Mosque of the Prophet in Medina. Muhammad is buried underneath the green dome.

SCRIPTURE AND TRADITION IN ISLAM

The sacred text of Islam is the Qur'an. The name for the text comes from four different Arabic roots, including the one for "reciting." Every word of the revelation was memorized and recited by the prophet and his followers. The Qur'an is written in first person, as Muslims believe that it is literally the words of God spoken through the angel Gabriel to Muhammad. The Qur'an has 114 surahs (or chapters). It is written in Arabic and translations will often have the Arabic next to the language in which it has been translated. It is an honor to memorize the entire Qur'an and many Muslims seek to accomplish

this act of devotion. A fascinating aspect of this practice is that when memorized, a devotee can pick up and recite from any point in the text. Muhammad received these revelations over a period of twenty-three years. Muhammad, as well as many of his followers, were not educated; however, memorized stories and poems were an important part of Arabic culture. The oral revelations were carefully memorized and recited in the community. Over time, followers began to write them down. After the death of the prophet, and to prevent claims of new revelations from false prophets, Zaid ben Sabit, Muhammad's most trusted scribe, compiled the surahs into one volume (Figure 4).

Figure 4   Two young boys read from the Qur'an.

The Qur'an is treated with great respect. One should be in a state of ritual purity when touching the sacred text. The text must be recited correctly to prevent changes in meaning. For example, a change in the pronunciation of a vowel can lead to misinterpretation of the word. A very similar practice is employed in Judaism for reading from the Torah. Both should be recited in their original language and without error.[1]

❧ Choose a surah from the Qur'an to read. A good site for this is http://quran.com/. At www.quran.com you can also hear the passage recited in Arabic. What passage did you choose? What is the main theme of the passage? What three words would you use to describe it?_____

_____

_____

_____

_____

In many religious traditions, alongside the sacred text, there is a collection of traditions that are held in high regard. In Judaism, there is the Tanakh and the Talmud. In Buddhism, there is the Pali Canon and the Sutras. In Islam, there is the Qur'an and the Hadith. Hadith are sayings by, and stories about, Muhammad that were recorded by his followers. Although there is no argument about the truth of the Qur'an, many arguments take place over the authenticity and use of the hadith.

---

[1] To listen to the recitation of the Qur'an in Arabic along with an English translation, visit http://www.recitequran.com/1:1.

One of the hadith stories is about Muhammad's night journey and why Muslims pray five times a day. In the account, Muhammad is on the way back from the seventh heaven when he sees Moses. Moses asks Muhammad what God told him. Muhammad replies that God instructed him to have the people pray fifty times a day. Moses can't believe it and says to Muhammad, "You have to go back up. That will never work." Muhammad travels back up to visit God. On the way back down, Moses stops him and asks, "Well, what did God say." "He changed it to 10 times." Again, Moses replies, "I know these people. They are a stubborn and stiff-necked people. Ten will never work. You're going to have to go back up." Muhammad ascends and descends one last time. Moses again questions Muhammad, who responds by saying that God negotiated the number down to five. Moses asserts, "Even five is too many." Muhammad responds by saying that, "If you want to make it less, you're going to have to go up this time." So, the number of times to pray each day is five.

CENTRAL TEACHINGS OF ISLAM

The core of the Islamic faith is the belief in one God, Allah, who cannot be divided in any way. The Shahadah (statement of faith) in Islam is: "There is no God, but God; and Muhammad is the messenger of God." God is the all-knowing, all-powerful Creator of the universe. God is just, merciful and compassionate. Muslims assert that God has ninety-nine names or attributes, such as Al-Noor (the Light) or Al-Khaliq (the Creator); reciting these attributes is a devotional practice.

The second part of the creed focuses on the role of the prophets. Muhammad is the final prophet in a long line of prophets. Adam, Abraham, Moses, and Jesus are all believed to be prophets of God and all are shown respect. A common practice when a prophet's name is spoken is to invoke a blessing on the prophet (peace be upon him or them). No prophet is considered divine. Muslims believe that the role of the prophet is to renew the message of the oneness of God and to call people to worship God not only in word, but also in deed. Prophets call people to faithfulness. Muhammad is viewed as the best example of what it means to be human. In this sense, it is significant that Muhammad was a husband and father. He engaged in business dealings, governance, and military leadership. Through his life example, Muslims believe they can see what it means to live faithfully.

The relationship between human beings and God is characterized by submission. To believe is to totally submit to the will of God. There are two major sins in Islam: shirk and kufr. Idolatry (**shirk**) is associating anything with God other than God. It is giving anything or anyone partner status with God. Muslims do not create images or representations of any of the prophets. If a prophet is depicted, he does not have a face. This is a way to avoid any confusion that it is God alone who is worshiped and not any representative of God. The veil that separates humanity from God is a human creation rather than placed there by God. It is the job of a Muslim to remove the barriers that keep her or him from total dependence on God.

Kufr goes hand in hand with shirk and is variously translated as "ingratitude" or "unbelief." By denying something commanded by God, one is committing kufr. Many actions can be described as kufr including hypocrisy, denial of God, misusing God's name, or seeking to justify something as okay that God expressly forbids.

Muslims believe in angels and demons, including Satan. Angels are servants of God who submit to God's will and do God's bidding. Demons, including Satan, are nonsubmissive beings who try to turn people away from God. People who fall prey to Satan's influence will ultimately go to Hell. **Jinn** is a term for invisible beings created by God before human beings. They can either be submissive beings or nonsubmissive beings. If they are nonsubmissive, they, like Satan, are liable to judgment. Jinn can also take various forms to trick people.

Time is linear in Islam with a specific point of creation, and a time when the world will come to an end. After a period of time in the grave, all humans will be bodily resurrected and assembled for a final judgment. What is experienced in the afterlife is a reflection of how a person behaved in this life. For the just and merciful, there is heaven. For sinners and nonbelieves there will be hell. A debate exists in the Muslim community about whether or not believers, who are deemed "sinners," go to hell permanently. The argument that all believers will go to heaven is based on the view that God is more merciful than wrathful. However, others argue that if hell wasn't permanent, God would have said so more explicitly in the Qur'an. Either way, ultimately, it is God who judges.

FORMS OF ISLAM

Sunni-Shi'a Split

After the prophet's death, disagreement erupted over who should succeed the prophet as both a political and religious leader in the Islamic community. One group believed that the successor should be elected by the community (the **ummah**); another group believed that the successor should be divinely appointed. Those who believed the successor should be divinely appointed assert that it was **Ali**, the cousin and son-in-law of the prophet, who should succeed him. The disagreement eventually led to a split within Islam. The Sunnis were led by **Abu Bakr**, Muhammad's close friend; and the Shi'ites led by Ali, the son-in-law of the Prophet. Sunnis are by far the largest group of Muslims; they make up about 85%–90% of Muslims worldwide. Further subdivisions also exist in each of these movements. Sunni sects include Hanafi, Shafi, Maliki, Hannbali, and Salafi (Wahhabi). The main differences among these groups deals with interpretation of Islamic law (**shariah**). Shi'a Islam is divided into five major groups: Ithna Asharis (also known as Twelvers, who recognize twelve Imams), Ismailis, Zaydis, Alevis, and Alawites. Sunni and Shi'a agree over many theological and practical ideas. The largest area of difference is in the authority of the imam or clerical leadership. Shi'as invest greater authority in the office of cleric.

Sufism

Sufism is the contemplative, and sometimes, ascetic practice of Islam which developed very early in Islamic history. Sufis are not a separate branch; one can be a Sunni Sufi or a Shi'a Sufi. The origins of Sufism are unclear and the history often debated. However, the term "sufi" is from an Arabic word meaning "wool." Sufis were those who wore prickly woolen garments. The goal of Sufism is union with God; imagination and creativity contributed to Sufi practice, particularly in the form of songs and poetry. Rumi is probably the best-known Sufi poet. His poem, "The Reed," highlights one of the major themes of Sufi poetry, which is the desire to reconnect with God. The poem speaks of how the reed has been plucked from the reed bed and longs to go back to its source.[2]

---

[2] To read Rumi's poem, see https://onbeing.org/poetry/song-of-the-reed/.

Sufis view God as the Beloved and emphasize drinking deeply of God's profound mercy and compassion. Sufis also emphasize tolerance and service to others. Historically, Sufis have reached out to mystics of all faiths as they strive together to experience a connection with God. Some of the **Sants** (Hindu and Muslim mystics) in India who influenced the development of Sikhism were Sufi, such as Kabir.

☯ Explore the poetry of Sufi mystics such as Rumi, Hafiz, or Rabi'a. A good site to check out is: https://www.poetseers.org/spiritual-and-devotional-poets/sufi-poets/. Which poem did you read? What imagery did you notice in the poem? What was its theme?

_____

_____

_____

_____

_____

One branch of Sufi monasticism is the Mevlevi order, or Whirling Dervishes. They use a form of dancing prayer called *sema*. During the dance, the goal is to harmonize with the movement of the whole universe and to pray and give thanks to God for all good gifts. At the beginning and end of the **sema** (dance), the dancer crosses his arms over his chest representing the oneness and unity of God. The drum, the reed flute, and a three-stringed instrument (rebab) provide the music for each of the four musical movements.

Wahhabism and Salafi Islam

Wahhabism developed in Saudi Arabia in the eighteenth century. It was founded by Muhammad ibn 'Abd al-Wahhab (1703–1792). Wahhab sought to renew and purify Islam by emphasizing doctrinal orthodoxy. He took the sin of shirk (idolatry) to an extreme insisting that honoring teachers, celebrating the birthday of Muhammad, and going on pilgrimages to holy sites (other than Mecca) were idolatrous. Wahhabism may have remained a very small group with a minimal impact on Islam if it were not for the adoption of this understanding of the faith by some in the Saudi royal family.

Wahhabism has essentially merged with the Salafi movements that developed in the late nineteenth and early twentieth centuries. Salafi movements insist that they are following the practices of Muslims dating back to the first three generations after the Prophet Muhammad. Multiple Salafi movements exist today; and, each views their own form as the "true" expression of Islam. They generally resist contemporary

Figure 5 Sixteenth century Turkish painting of Whirling Dervishes.

Everett—Art/Shutterstock.com.

influences and are opposed to honoring saints and teachers. A tendency of Salafi movements is to be isolationist avoiding association with those who do not share their views. In addition, most are peaceful; only a few advocate violence as a means to counteract non-Muslim governments. Those Salafi movements that act out violently often target other Muslims and non-Muslims who intervene in Muslim lands.[3]

SACRED PRACTICES OF ISLAM

Islam is a way of life; and therefore, faith cannot be separated from practice, particularly the practice of the Five Pillars of the Faith. In addition, faith influences the way one eats, dresses, and conducts business. The rules guiding these day to day aspects of life in Islam are called shariah. Interpretations of shariah often differ by culture. Moreover, various Islamic scholars also have specific views on how shariah is interpreted.

Five Pillars of Islam

Shahadah

The Shahadah is the central statement of faith in Islam. It affirms the oneness of God and the role of Muhammad as the final prophet. It is found over the door of many mosques (masjids) and is often recited daily in prayer. When the muezzin calls people to prayer, the Shahadah is part of that call. A muezzin is the one who calls people to prayer often from a prayer tower called a minaret. To become a Muslim, a person recites the Shahadah with conviction as a witness and testimony of faith (Figure 6).

Figure 6   Mosque door in Lanham, MD with Shahadah inscribed above it.

Source: Stephanie Curran, August 2019.

Prayer

Faithful Muslims pray five times a day: early morning, midday, afternoon, sunset, and nighttime. Before prayer, Muslims perform ablutions (wudu) by washing hands and arms, rinsing the mouth and nose, then washing the face and feet. If water is not available, purification can be done with clean dirt or sand by touching the palms to the earth and ritually touching the forehead and hands. Whether with water or earth, the intention is to be ritually pure in the presence of Allah. The place of prayer can be any clean surface. Muslims often use prayer rugs with colorful designs. When possible, Muslims pray at the masjid (place of prayer); otherwise, prayers are done at home. When praying, worshippers face the holy city of Mecca. The prayer direction is marked at the masjid and one can also find the qibla (direction of prayer) through an app on a smartphone. Each prayer involves movement (standing, bowing, prostrating, and sitting) and recitation of passages from the Qur'an in Arabic. Women and men typically pray separately to avoid distraction. An additional prayer practice is to use beads to recite the ninety-nine names or attributes of God, such as the Compassionate, the Just, and the Merciful (Figure 7).

---

[3] Yasir Qadhi, "On Salafi Islam." https://muslimmatters.org/2014/04/22/on-salafi-islam-dr-yasir-qadhi/.

Fasting

During the entire month of Ramadan, Muslims observe a fast from dawn to sundown. During the daytime hours, the observant fast from food, liquids, smoking, and sexual activity. Muslims follow a lunar-based calendar, so Ramadan can fall any time during the calendar year. Sometimes it is in the heat of summer with very long days; other times, it is in winter when the days are shorter and cooler. Currently, the month falls during the summer. Those who are sick, pregnant, or nursing, young children and the elderly are all exempt from the fast. If the sickness is temporary, an individual may make up the missed days later. The fast commemorates the first revelation of the Qur'an to the Prophet Muhammad. One spiritual discipline that is sometimes taken up during the month is reading through the entire Qur'an and/or working to memorize it.

Figure 7   During Ramadan 2014, a man at Noor Masjid in Nairobi uses prayer beads.

The fast has multiple purposes. Chiefly, it is a way to submit to God. It also helps one to control the body, intensify one's spiritual practice, and identify (at least briefly) with those who do without because they have nothing to eat or no clean water to drink. The month is also a time for giving charity, including the zakat, or tithe.

The fast begins each day just before dawn. Before the first light appears each day, it is advisable to eat a small meal and then speak the intention to fast for the day. At the end of the day, the fast is broken with the **iftar**. Tradition is to break the fast initially each night with dates and water. Dates are said to have been one of Muhammad's favorite fruits. After the fast is broken, family and friends often gather to share in a communal meal.

Toward the end of the month, on the twenty-seventh day of Ramadan, the holiest night of the year is observed. It is called the Night of Power (**Laylat al-Qadr**) and commemorates Muhammad's first revelation to "Recite." One of the best ways to observe this night is to spend it reciting from the Qur'an, either communally at the masjid or at home. When the month draws to a close, one of the two major Islamic feasts is observed. The three-day festival is called Id-al-Fitr (Eid-al-Fitr) and is the first time that observant Muslims eat during daylight hours since the start of Ramadan. Id (Eid) begins with special community prayers. People dress up, give charity, exchange gifts, and enjoy the company of family and friends (Figure 8).

Figure 8   Eid al-Fitr celebration in East Harlem, New York, July 2015.

Zakat

Zakat is the tithe given to those in need. It is not a tax, but an obligation of any Muslim who has *nisaab*, or wealth beyond one's living expenses. It is a way of expressing the belief that everything a person has comes from God and a portion should be given back to God and to those in need as a way to foster self-discipline and deter greed. Zakat is 2.5% of one's excess wealth. Fellow Muslims are provided for first. Once all Muslims have what they need, struggling non-Muslims receive the benefits of the tithe. Historically, zakat could also be used to buy freedom for a slave. It can be given directly to the needy or dispersed through an Islamic charity or masjid. The zakat does not go for upkeep of the masjid or to pay a salary for the imam; other contributions fund the running of the masjid originating from separate gifts.

Hajj

The fifth pillar is **hajj**, the pilgrimage to Mecca. Every Muslim hopes to be able to make the pilgrimage once in a lifetime if they are physically and financially able. The centerpiece of the pilgrimage is the **Ka'aba**, a shrine said to have been built by Abraham (Ibrahim) and **Ishmael** to mark the place where Abraham was ready to sacrifice his son. Muslims believe that Abraham was prepared to sacrifice his first son, Ishmael, because of God's desire. God stopped Abraham and provided a ram to sacrifice instead. This event is remembered annually in the Islamic festival of **Id-al-Adha** (Eid al-Adha), the Feast of Sacrifice, which marks the end of the month of Hajj. Historically, Muslims believe that Abraham, and after his father's death, Ishmael, performed the annual pilgrimage.

Over time, the Arabian Peninsula turned to polytheism and many idols were placed around the Ka'aba. However, pilgrimage remained an annual event, though not in keeping with the tradition of Abraham and Ishmael. When Muhammad returned to Mecca from Medina, he cleansed the Ka'aba of idols and restored the purity of the Hajj. Muslims continue to follow the pilgrimage practice as it was observed by Muhammad (Figure 9).

The ideal time for pilgrimage is in the twelfth month of the Islamic calendar. Each year, hundreds of thousands of people from all over the world embark on this life-changing journey. Before beginning the Hajj, the pilgrim makes amends for all wrongs and repays all debts. Arriving in Mecca, all males change into the *ihram* (attire) of the pilgrim. The ihram symbolizes purity and the physical changing of clothes conveys the intention to enter into this spiritual practice. The ihram consists of two white cloths, one covering the body from the waist down and the other draped over a shoulder. All men wear the ihram to demonstrate social and religious equality. Women wear modest dress.

Figure 9 Pilgrims gather for prayer around the Ka'aba.

The pilgrimage commemorates the faithfulness of Abraham and begins in the tent cities of Mina, just outside of Mecca. From there, people travel to Mt. Arafat. It is here that Muhammad preached his final Hajj sermon. Followers spend the afternoon praying and reciting surahs from the Qur'an. They gather pebbles from a valley halfway between Arafat and Mina. Upon their return to Mina, pilgrims renounce the devil by throwing seven pebbles at each of three pillars as they seek forgiveness for sins committed. Seven is the number that symbolizes infinity and represents the need for continual repentance. In remembrance of Abraham's sacrifice, they also sacrifice a goat or sheep and give the meat to the poor.

Returning to Mecca, they gather to pray at the Ka'aba. The black stone was said to have been white when God sent it down from heaven; however, the sins of humankind turned the stone black. Pilgrims circle the Ka'aba as they pray; touching the stone is said to erase sin. On the pilgrimage, men and women pray together. The well of Zamzam, where it is said that God provided water in the desert to Hagar and Ishmael when the young boy was dying of thirst, is close by. In her supplications for water, Hagar ran back and forth between two hills here in the desert seven times. Followers drink from the well; and, they often carry small jars of the water back with them when they return to their homes. When the pilgrimage is complete, the travelers may choose to visit the mosque in Medina built by the Prophet and climb up to the al-Hira cave where Muhammad received his first revelation.

Communal Worship

The place of worship in Islam is the masjid, or mosque. Several years ago, a false rumor circulated indicating that the word, *mosque*, comes from the Spanish word for mosquito and that the term originated during the Crusades as a hateful term. This rumor has been dispelled by many Islamic scholars.[4] The Arabic word for the place of prayer is **masjid**. Mosque is an English rendering of the term. In the United States, many masjids are called Islamic Centers or Societies addressing their role as places of prayer, fellowship, and study.

Friday is the day when Muslims, who are able, gather at the masjid for communal prayer. It takes the place of the noon prayer and often includes a sermon or message. Anyone can lead prayers; however, this generally means any man can lead prayers. Men and women typically pray separately at the masjid with the women often behind a screen or curtain to avoid distraction. However, Muslim feminists have been advocating for change in these practices asserting that the prophet did not forbid women from leading prayers for the community or praying side by side with men.[5]

Many masjids have similar architectural features. The front of the prayer room faces toward Mecca and has a **mihrab**, or niche, to mark the direction of prayer (**qibla**). If large enough, the mihrab is where the imam stands and sits to lead prayers. Many masjids also have a dome, symbolic of the heavens, and a minaret, or tower. The minaret is the place from which the call to prayer (adhan) is broadcast in largely Islamic communities and serves as a visual reminder of the faith, much like a steeple is for Christian churches (Figure 10).

Figure 10   Imam sits in the mihrab leading prayers at a mosque in the Netherlands.

[4] See this discussion of the hoax, https://muslimspeak.wordpress.com/2009/01/15/the-meaning-and-evolution-of-the-word-mosque/.
[5] For an excellent discussion of this debate, see http://ingridmattson.org/article/can-a-woman-be-an-imam/

Dietary Restrictions

Muslims also follow specific dietary restrictions. Food that is acceptable to eat is called **halal**; food that is forbidden is **haram**. Muslims are not to eat pork or pork products. Animals must be blessed and humanely slaughtered in an approved fashion. It is forbidden to drink or consume blood. Alcohol and all intoxicants are also forbidden. Most seafood is permissible. Gelatin is often made from pork; therefore, unless specifically marked halal, anything containing gelatin such as fruit-filled pastries, marshmallows, and medicine encased in gel capsules is forbidden (Figure 11).

Figure 11   Halal food label.

Mushan/Shutterstock.com.

Hijab

Modest dress is required of both men and women. The covering of the head with a scarf and refraining from wearing clothes that show the arms or legs is termed, hijab, or modesty in dress. The word, **hijab**, has also come to be used to specifically refer to the head scarf worn by many Muslim women. The full covering and the heavy burqas are more culturally specific, rather than required by the Qur'an or the Hadith. The **burqa** covers the whole body with a mesh screen over the eyes for a woman to see through. The **niqab** is also a veil; but, unlike the burqa, it does not cover the eyes. For most Muslim women, the extent of their covering is a personal choice; however, there are some families and countries who require it. On the other hand, France, the Netherlands, and Belgium ban the burqa.

❧ Read an essay on hijab from. Here are a couple of good examples: http://thisibelieve.org/essay/1337/; https://thisibelieve.org/essay/82514/. If you are more interested in the burqa or full covering, try these essays during France's 2010 campaign to ban the burqa. https://www.cnn.com/2016/08/25/europe/burkini-ban-protest-london-french-embassy/index.html, https://www.huffpost.com/entry/why-i-hate-the-burqa----a_b_669953 or http://religion.blogs.cnn.com/2010/08/23/muslim-women-who-wear-the-hijab-and-niqab-explain-their-choice/. After reading an article from the perspective of those who wear hijab, reflect on what hijab means in a sentence or two. Should the burqa be banned? Why or why not? _____

_____

_____

_____

_____

Jihad

Jihad is perhaps the most controversial term in Islam, yet one of the most important. It refers to struggle or striving. The term, primarily, references the struggle to live faithfully and strive to follow the faith, even in difficult circumstances. Souheila, the author of a *This I Believe* essay on hijab, describes her practice of wearing hijab as a form of jihad.[6]

Separate terms exist in the Qur'an that reference war. One such word in Arabic is al-harb. In the Qur'an, rules exist for how to conduct war. War is justified for self-defense when an aggressor comes against the community or to free Muslims from oppression. War cannot be fought against other Muslims (terrorists claim their targets are not "truly Muslim"), against unarmed combatants, or against civilians.[7]

Dating and Marriage

In Islam, high value is placed on marriage and producing children; many see marriage as the obligation of a devout Muslim. Dating is traditionally forbidden in Islam; and, marriages are generally facilitated by the parents. Dating is prohibited to try to discourage sexual relations before marriage and to promote respect for each other.[8] Even so, the practice of facilitated marriages is fading among Muslims in the West. Marriage is not a sacrament in Islam, but a mutually beneficial contract between equals. In fact, a contract is made between the bride and groom that includes conditions for divorce as well as financial provisions. Islam had prenuptial agreements long before it was fashionable in the West. Both men and women have the right to initiate divorce according to the Qur'an, which also prohibits forcing a woman to marry against her wishes.

When a Muslim couple marries, the civil service is all that is legally required; however, many couples also have a religious ceremony and reception as well. Most of the marriage customs are influenced by the cultural background of the bride and groom. One practice that is common across several cultures is the drawing of henna tattoos on the hands of the bride (Figure 12).

Altin Osmanaj/Shutterstock.com.

Figure 12 Henna tattoo adorns bride's hand.

Death and Burial

In Islam, the dead are buried as soon as possible after death. The family washes the body and wraps it in a clean white cloth.[9] Embalming is to be avoided; and, ideally, the individual is buried directly in

---

[6] For an excellent description of jihad and the hijacking of the term by extremists, listen to Bobby Ghosh's TED talk at https://www.ted.com/talks/bobby_ghosh_why_global_jihad_is_losing?language=en.

[7] For helpful information on jihad, see http://islamicsupremecouncil.org/understanding-islam/legal-rulings/5-jihad-a-misunderstood-concept-from-islam.html.

[8] For an interesting look at facilitated marriage among UK Muslims see https://www.themuslim500.com/guest-contributions-2016/getting-married-british-muslim-style/

[9] A Muslim woman in Charlotte, North Carolina, teaches classes a couple of times a year on how to wash the body of a loved one in preparation for burial. To read about some of the intricacies of the practice, see http://wfae.org/post/how-muslims-wash-bury-their-dead.

the ground. A simple coffin can be used if it is a requirement in the area in which the family lives. As Muslims believe in the physical resurrection of the body on the Day of Judgment, cremation is avoided. Prayers are performed over the body asking that God receive the deceased. The mourning period is three days. However, if it is a spouse who has died, the mourning period lasts a little over four months.

Banking and Finances

Islam has a system of banking and finance that is based on the core values of equality, cooperation, and community. Charging interest or any burdensome fees is forbidden in Islam. According to the Institute of Islamic Banking and Insurance, "Islamic economics is a complete system of social and economic justice. It deals with property rights, the incentive system, the allocation of resources, economic freedom, decision-making and the proper role of government."[10] Islamic banking emphasizes shared profits and shared risk. Both the person providing capital, and the person receiving the benefits of that capital are viewed as equal partners in the transaction. A just contract is negotiated rather than a wealthy lender dictating the terms of an agreement to a poor debtor.

ISLAM AND WOMEN

Many in the West view Islam as being oppressive to women. Some of these misconceptions are based on inaccurate information about the teachings of Islam as outlined in the Qur'an. The restrictive nature of society in some predominantly Islamic countries, particularly in the Middle East, reinforces that image. However, many of these restrictive practices, such as women being forbidden to drive in Saudi Arabia or women being forbidden to go to school by the Taliban, are culturally based practices rather than practices inherent to Islam.

When Islam developed, it was actually ahead of its time in regard to the treatment of women. In pre-Islamic Arabia, the practice of female infanticide was common. Muhammad forbade such a practice. In addition, as in most other societies of the day, including Jewish and Christian, women could not inherit property. From the very beginning, Muhammad allowed women to inherit property and to control their own financial resources. Also at the time of the Prophet, Arab men could marry as many women as they wanted; and, they could divorce with a simple word, while extending no provisions for the woman. Muhammad limited the number of wives a man could have and insisted they be treated equally. He also gave women the right to divorce and to negotiate the marriage contract. Women are allowed to keep their income and are not required to use any of their income in support of the family. Although all of these provisions are provided in the tradition, not all women know their rights, or are able to claim them, because of the repressive societies in which they live.

Islamic Feminism

Feminism is local. That is, it is embedded in the cultural and religious traditions where it arises. Islamic feminism is not the same as Christian feminism, nor is it the same as Hindu feminism. Egypt was the fertile soil in which feminism began to develop in Islam in the 1920s. However, it wasn't until the 1990s that the term Islamic feminism became more widespread.[11] Great diversity of thought exists in

---

[10] http://www.islamic-banking.com/.
[11] Margot Badran, "Islamic Feminism: What's in a Name?" 242–43. http://www.feministezine.com/feminist/international/Islamic-Feminism-01.html.

these movements. Some are more religious, others more secular. Many root their views in the equality and social justice found in the Qur'an and in the teachings of Muhammad. As mentioned earlier, Muhammad asserted that women had rights that were not granted to them in other societies of the day.

One particular area in which Islamic feminism is most visible is in the call for women to have the right to lead prayers for the entire community. In addition, many call for men and women to be able to pray side by side in the prayer room at the masjid. These calls have been received with mixed reactions from both men and women in Islam. Between 2010 and 2011, women organized pray-ins in mosques across the United States. Sometimes, they would form rows behind the men in the main prayer room for prayers; other times, they would pray alongside the men. An additional concern among many women in Islam is the space set aside for women to pray. These spaces are often substandard compared with men's spaces. Some women's spaces are even in basements and smell of mildew. African–American mosques, in the tradition of W.D. Muhammad, are more likely than other African–American mosques to have women praying in the same room as men. Moreover, mosques lead by American-born imams are less likely to have a divider separating men and women.[12]

❧ Take a moment to explore http://www.islamandfeminism.org/-start-exploring.html or https://www.musawah.org/. Share one interesting insight from the reading._____

_____

_____

_____

ISLAMIC ART

Islamic art is known for its calligraphy and geometric patterns. In Islam, artists generally refrain from depicting people or animals. The focus is primarily on beautiful mosaic tiles and elaborate calligraphy, often of verses from the Qur'an. The mosaic tile designs are based on vectors and angles, circles and triangles with the design repeated in specific sections (Figure 13).

Calligraphy has been a part of religious art in many religious traditions. It can be found in embellished texts of medieval Bibles and Japanese and Chinese writing. However, calligraphy is perhaps the most characteristic form of Islamic art. Training for

Source: Stephanie Curran, August 2019.

Figure 13 Inlaid mother of pearl mosaic from the Diyanet Center in Lanham, MD.

[12] Actual statistics can be found at https://womensenews.org/2014/04/mosques-relegate-womens-prayers-the-basement/.

calligraphers is extensive and the style is often unique to a particular region, such as the Middle East, or Spain and Morocco. The pens were made from reeds and the tip, or nib, is cut in specific ways to change the shape or thickness of the lettering.[13] Many museums across the country have excellent collections of Islamic art and calligraphy (Figure 14).

Figure 14   Calligraphy of "In the Name of God, the Most Gracious, the Most Merciful."

◐ Explore images of Islamic art by searching for images of Islamic art on the internet or visiting a gallery in your area. Select an image and describe it in your own words._____

_____

_____

_____

ISLAM IN THE UNITED STATES

The presence of Islam in North America is not a new phenomenon. As mentioned in Chapter 1, Islam has been here since before the United States was founded. The faith came not only with the slaves, but also with merchants engaged in spice, tea, and coffee trade. The first European American convert to Islam was Alexander Russell Webb, who was born in 1846. He grew up a Presbyterian in upstate New York. From a young age, he struggled with the idea of the Trinity; and, in his twenties abandoned Christianity. Following the Civil War, he flirted with atheism and alternative forms of spirituality. In the 1880s he began communicating with a Muslim reformer in India, Ghulam Ahmad. He eventually formally converted to Islam.[14]

The Muslim community in the United States is extremely diverse and it includes African Americans, Southeast Asian Americans, Arab Americans, and European Americans, among others. Many are native born, others are converts, and

Figure 15   The Diyanet Center in Lanham, MD is one of the most beautiful mosques in the United States.

---

[13] See http://www.vam.ac.uk/content/articles/c/calligraphy-in-islamic-art/ for more detail about the materials and styles of Islamic calligraphy.

[14] Edward E. Curtis, IV. *Muslims in America: A Short History* (Oxford: Oxford University Press, 2009), 25–27.

still others are new immigrants. Most masjids across the United States are diverse communities constituting a mix of all types of Muslims.

Islamville, South Carolina, is a small community of about 300 people in York County in the northern area of the state. It was founded over thirty years ago by a group of native-born African American Muslims. Following the Paris attacks in November, 2015, many false allegations were made about this community being a terrorist camp. In a December 2015 article in the *Charlotte Observer*, York County Sheriff Bruce Bryant, invited all who believed such false allegations to visit Islamville with him. Sheriff Bryant has known the people of this community for twenty-five years and is committed to protecting them.[15] Community members have recently expressed concerns about the rising rhetoric in the 2016 political campaign.[16]

WEB RESOURCES FOR FURTHER STUDY

http://www.icna.org—Website of the Islamic Circle of North America, an organization founded in 1968 to serve as a supportive community for Muslims in North America.

http://www.isna.net—This site is from the Islamic Society of North America based in Plainfield, IN, and has some great resources about interfaith relationships and the green initiative to promote environmentally friendly practices in masjids.

https://onbeing.org/programs/omid-safi-and-seemi-bushra-ghazi-the-spirit-of-islam/—Great program on Islam with two leading American Muslims, Omid Safi and Seemi Bushra Ghazi.

http://www.oxfordislamicstudies.com/Public/about.html—This site, edited by John Esposito, offers extensive resources for understanding the terms, beliefs, and practices of Islam. It is also a good site for reading passages from the Qur'an.

http://www.pbs.org/opb/historydetectives/feature/islam-in-america/—Interesting feature on the history of Islam in America.

http://www.pbs.org/video/-contrary-gender-equality-islam1/—Excellent video about gender equality in Islam.

www.islamview.org—Look in the articles section for some great information. This site is from the Islamic Center of Blacksburg.

---

[15] Bass Jack, "Trump Needs to Visit S.C.'s Islamville," *The Charlotte Observer*, December 16, 2015, http://www.charlotteobserver.com/opinion/op-ed/article50117590.html.

[16] "Enclave," *Christian Century*. Vol. 133:6, March 16, 2016, 9.

Part 4: Emerging Religious Traditions

CHAPTERS:

Chapter 13
Paganism

Learning Outcomes

By the end of the lesson, students will be able to

- ☛ explain the history and beliefs of pagan traditions.
- ☛ describe the characteristics common to many pagan traditions.
- ☛ list and define the major pagan festivals.
- ☛ differentiate between Wicca and Druidism.
- ☛ describe unique characteristics of Hellenistic and Scandinavian paganism.
- ☛ analyze what is drawing followers to these movements today.

Key Terms

Beltane (Beltaine)	Lammas/Lughnasdh	Reincarnation
Coven	Litha	Samhain
Divination	Mabon	Wicca
Druid	Magick	Yule
Gerald Gardner	Ostara	
Imbolc	Pagan	

INTRODUCTION

Over the last several decades, ancient religious traditions have experienced a revival. Though much of the ancient practice remains shrouded in mystery, new life has been infused into them by people longing for a connection with the sacred and its manifestation in the world around us. Some refer to these movements as neo-pagan traditions because of the adaptation of the ancient traditions. This term encompasses a variety of traditions from Wicca and Druidry to Asatru and Hellenistic Polytheism. The revival of these ancient traditions began in the late 1800s to mid-1900s.[1] Though there are few reliable statistics, the

---

[1] For an in-depth timeline, see http://lycianwicca.info/The_Lycian_Sanctuary/Pagan_Timeline/Pagan_Timeline.html

movements continue to grow and maintain themselves in the United States, Europe, and Australia. The 2008 American Religious Identification Survey estimates suggest there are roughly 700,000 Pagans in the United States.[2] This number represents a significant increase since 1990.[3] Followers of Asatru, a Norse pagan movement, are building the first temple to the Norse Gods in over a millennium in Iceland.[4] While this chapter cannot possibly be comprehensive of all modern pagan movements, it will explore a variety of the larger traditions.

GENERAL CHARACTERISTICS

Though somewhat dangerous given the variety of traditions, a few general characteristics of these movements can be identified. The term **pagan** comes from the Latin word, *paganus*, which means "of the countryside." Many pagan traditions are deeply rooted in the agricultural cycle and the land. Because they originated in the indigenous practices of a particular region, they share many characteristics in common with the indigenous religions discussed in Chapter 3. Most pagan movements believe in **animism**, the view that all life is sacred and spiritually interconnected. In addition, most pagan traditions are polytheistic with a pantheon of both male and female deities. The exception to this generality involves goddess movements, such as the Feminist Craft and Dianic Wicca, which only focus on the female aspects of divinity. **Divination** is also a common element of these traditions as the practitioners seek to discern the best course of action by consulting spirits and ancestors. A desire for wholeness and self-understanding also characterize many of these movements, exemplified in the ancient Greek saying, "Know thyself." Pagans believe that the capacity for both good and evil reside within us. Personal choices dictate whether the energy people generate is positive or negative. Furthermore, whatever a person does returns back on the individual, much like the Eastern view of karma. Worship typically takes place out of doors rather than in a building with the sacred space ritually created. The ritual life of Anglo-Saxon, Celtic and Norse pagan traditions centers around the Wheel of the Year with each form having its own variants.

WHEEL OF THE YEAR

The Wheel of the Year is the annual cycle of rituals that follows the seasons, particularly in Wicca and Druidism. The solstices and equinoxes are observed in Anglo-Saxon, Celtic, Hellenistic, and Norse traditions (Figure 1).

Samhain

Samhain is sometimes called, the Pagan New Year; it is the time when the division between the physical and spiritual world is at its thinnest. The celebration remembers ancestors and is also a time for divination. The word, *Samhain* (pronounced Sah-win), is a Gaelic word, that indicates summer's end. Samhain occurs on October 31 or November 1. The jack-o-lantern traditionally associated with Halloween derives from an Irish myth in which Jack spent eternity wandering the earth. Jack-o-lanterns were originally carved from

---

[2] https://commons.trincoll.edu/aris/publications/2008-2/aris-2008-summary-report/

[3] http://religionandpolitics.org/2012/06/20/the-plight-of-pagans-in-the-military/.

[4] http://america.aljazeera.com/opinions/2016/1/a-norse-temple-for-the-21st-century.html.

turnips, but the larger pumpkin is much easier to shape. Fall decorations of carved pumpkins and gourds figure prominently in Samhain. Food is also placed out for the ancestors, often at an ancestral altar with pictures and mementos that serve as reminders of them. Tarot cards and runes are used for divination. As with many New Year festivals, there is an aspect of "out with the old and in with the new". An example of a ritual that highlights this aspect of Samhain is to light a bonfire, then write behaviors, thoughts, or attitudes to let go of on scraps of paper and throw them into the fire while circling the fire clockwise. Samhain leads into the darkest part of the year (Figure 2).

Figure 1 The Wheel of the Year depicting in relation to the cycles of the moon.

Yule

Yule begins December 21st and is the twelve-day celebration of the Winter Solstice, the darkest point in the year. In a yin/yang sense, it is remembering the light in the midst of darkness. The Romans celebrate it as Saturnalia. The festivities involve gathering with family and friends and feasting. Some traditions that many Christians have adopted from Yule are evergreens and holly, as well as the yule log. The Norse celebrated the Winter Solstice as the return of the sun. Similarly, in Celtic traditions, the Sun God, Lugh, becomes human and marries the Goddess. For Welsh pagans, Yule and the Summer Solstice are the two holidays in which the Oak King and the Holly King battle for control. The Holly King wins during the summer battle and reigns until Yule, when the Oak King rules supreme.

Figure 2 Samhain celebration in Midland, MI. The lighting of candles is part of the celebration of the new year.

Wassail is another ancient tradition associated with Yule. It is a spiced wine that is used for toasting. In English tradition, people would go from house to house, singing, visiting and sharing the toast.

Imbolc

Imbolc is the next festival and occurs on February 2nd; the name comes from a Celtic word meaning, "ewe's milk." The birth of new calves and lambs is just beginning. This festival is also called Candlemas or Brigid's Day. The Maiden aspect of the goddess is revered; and, candles and bonfires are lit to warm the earth in hopes of an early Spring. Groundhog Day also grows out of this tradition as animals begin to emerge from hibernation. Additionally, it is a time of initiation and purification (Figure 3).

Figure 3   Imbolc altar featuring milk, candles, and an image of a lamb.

Figure 4   A traditional maypole dance during a May Day celebration.

Ostara

Ostara is the Spring Equinox and falls around March 20th. It is a celebration of fertility and new birth. The name, Ostara, comes from the Germanic goddess, Oestre, the goddess of the dawn. Eating spring greens and coloring eggs are common customs. The festival is also a time to cleanse oneself of toxins and seek blessings for new endeavors. Planting seeds or trees and going on a hike through the woods are additional ways of honoring the sacred during Ostara.

Beltane

Beltane (or Beltaine) is also known as May Day. It is celebrated around May 1st and is a continuation of the celebration of fertility and new life. The origin of the name of the festival dates back to the Celtic fire god, Bel. Beltane itself means "bright fire." Traditionally, bonfires were lit as part of this festival and cattle were driven among and around the fires to bless them. Young men and women would sometimes leap over the fires as well. The fertility aspects of the ritual are visible in the tradition of dancing around the maypole, which is an ancient phallic symbol (Figure 4). As they are entwined during the dance, the pole represents the God and the ribbons the Goddess. Beltane is also a time for pagan weddings, or handfastings. Flowers are celebrated during this festival with a common tradition being to fill a basket of with flowers and take it to someone who is in need of healing or care. Beltane is another time of the year ideal for the practice of divination as it is on the same cross-quarter as Samhain.

Summer Solstice

The Summer Solstice is also known as the Midsummer Festival, Alban Hefin, or Litha. The sun is at its brightest, and the day is the longest of the year. Picnics and other gatherings are common on this day as the first fruits of the season are enjoyed. Bonfires and staying up all night to welcome the sun are also a part of this celebration. The Summer Solstice is one of the most sacred festival for Druids. The festival marks the beginning of the waning season when the sun's light ebbs as it nears the Winter Solstice. The herb, mugwort, is often associated with the Summer Solstice because of its cleansing and healing properties.[5]

---

[5] For more information on mugwort during the summer solstice, see https://www.circlesanctuary.org/index.php/circle-magazine/sample-articles/ritual-tools-sacred-work-with-mugwort

Lammas/Lughnasdh

This festival is really two different celebrations depending on the pagan tradition. **Lammas** is the Saxon bread festival; whereas, **Lughnasdh** is a Celtic festival of the sun God, Lugh. Held around August 1st, it is the first of the harvest festivals.

The festival is a time to complete projects, harvest grain and herbs, and offer baked bread to the goddess. Picnics and summer games are also a part of the celebration. For Druids, this festival can be a time for weddings.

Mabon

Sometimes called, the Pagan Thanksgiving, **Mabon** festival marks the Autumn Equinox. It is the second of the three harvest festivals culminating in Samhain. It is a time to give thanks, celebrate the harvest, and discard that which is not needed. This practice of letting go of that which is not needed includes material possessions as well as thoughts, negative feelings, ideas and behaviors.

☯ Choose a pagan festival to learn more about. Websites to use in this exploration include, but are not limited to, https://thecelticjourney.wordpress.com/the-celts/wheel-of-the-year/ or http://www.thewhitegoddess. co.uk/the_wheel_of_the_year/. Which festival did you explore? What is the essence of the celebration? What is a sample ritual, practice, food, or activity for this festival?

_____

_____

_____

_____

_____

INDIVIDUAL TRADITIONS

Although some traits are generally true of many pagan traditions, each has its own unique history and expressions. In this section, some of the most visible pagan traditions are explored.

Anglo-Saxon and Celtic Traditions: Wicca and Druidism

One of the first revivals of Pagan traditions came through the pathways of Wicca and Druidism, or Druidry. Though these traditions will be explored separately, they share roots in Anglo-Saxon and Celtic cultures dating back centuries in Ireland and the United Kingdom.

Wicca

The Old English root of the word, **Wicca**, is *wic* meaning to bend or shape. The term is also linked to *wikk* which means "magic" and *witega*, "seer" or "prophet." Other theories suggest the connection between Wicca and the word, *witgan*, "to know" and the Norwegian word, *vitja,* to turn away. Doreen

Valiente, in her article, "The Derivation of the Word 'Witch,'" asserts, "A witch was a seer, a knower, an averter of evil." The modern Wiccan movement is often traced to Gerald Gardner, but it is also alluded to a little earlier in the writings of Hugh Ross Williamson in 1947.[6]

Wicca, as a reconstruction of the Old Religion of Europe, began in the United Kingdom and spread to the United States and other parts of Europe as well as Australia. The characteristics of Paganism discussed earlier in the chapter certainly apply to Wicca. Most forms of Wicca worship the divine in the form of both goddess and god and emphasize the Wheel of the Year. Divination and magick, the art of causing change through the use of energy, are also building blocks of the practice. This understanding of magick is rooted in the belief that "reality is a field of energies that congeal, temporarily, into forms. In time, all 'fixed' things dissolve, only to coalesce again in new forms, new vehicles."[7]

The goddess has three forms representative of the cycles of the moon. The waxing moon is the maiden; the full moon, the mother; and the waning moon, the crone. The goddess goes by many names including Gaia, Diana, and Aradia, among others. She is rooted in the earth and its cycles and seasons; ultimately, She is the source of life. Some Wiccans even worship the Egyptian goddess, Isis, as a primary manifestation of the mother Goddess. The male aspect, the God, also goes by many names including Cernunnos, Pan, Herne, the Horned God, and the Green God. The male aspect of aspect of divinity is often represented as having hooves touching the earth and horns reaching toward the sky.

Wiccan ethics is rooted in a poem called, The Rede, which asserts "And it harm none, do what ye will."[8] The ethic involves avoiding harm to oneself, others, and the created world. Wiccans honor all life forms. Alongside the intention to do no harm, Wiccans also hold to the Three-fold Law which states that whatever you do will return to you in threes: "Three times bad, three times good" in the words of The Rede. Essentially, the energy a person sends out is the energy received back multiplied. Individuals are responsible for their own actions; no demon or devil can be blamed for an individual's choices.

Typically, Wiccans also believe in reincarnation. The cycle of birth, death, and rebirth is seen naturally in the four seasons as well as in a person's life. One's spirit lives and dies, then is refreshed and born again. In each lifetime, an individual learns new lessons. Some Wiccans believe in a place called Summerland where the soul is rejuvenated before being born again.

Some Wiccans are solitaries; that is, they practice alone. Others join together in small groups for fellowship and ritual. These groups are known as covens. A sacred text is not followed by those in the Wiccan traditions; rather, each practitioner has his or her own Book of Shadows. The **Book of Shadows** is a collection of folk lore, herbal remedies, magick spells, ritual material, and the wisdom that comes through life experience. It is often handwritten and passed down from one generation to the next (Figure 5).

Worship typically takes place outdoors. A circle is cast to mark the space as sacred. A broom is used to symbolically sweep away impurities. An altar in the center holds symbols of the five elements of earth, air, fire, water and spirit. The **pentacle** (or pentagram) is a five-pointed star representing these five elements with a circle surrounding it to signify the interrelationship of all the elements. Prayers are also typically offered to the four directions as the circle is cast.

To become Wiccan there is commonly an initiation ceremony. Many Wiccan circles or covens are egalitarian, but some have various hierarchies of initiation including priestess/priest and high priestess/high priest.

---

[6] Doreen Valiente, "The Derivation of the Word 'Witch,'" http://www.paganlibrary.com/reference/derivation_of_witch.php.
[7] Starhawk, *The Spiral Dance* (San Francisco: HarperCollins, 1979), 32.
[8] The Wiccan Rede accessed at https://wicca.com/celtic/wicca/rede.htm.

Eco-centered Feminist Paganism

Some forms of Wicca either primarily or exclusively emphasize the worship of the Divine Feminine. They developed, in part, as a response to oppressive patriarchy present around the world. Dianic Wicca is a goddess-centered spiritual practice begun by Z. Budapest in 1971 when she formed the Susan B. Anthony Coven Number One, a women-only coven in Southern California. This coven is today known as the Circle of Aradia. Starhawk, another feminist Craft leader in California, wrote *The Spiral Dance* in 1979. These two women are the most well-known leaders in the feminist Wiccan movement, which focuses on women's empowerment. "The image of the Goddess inspires women to see ourselves as divine, our bodies as sacred, the changing phases of our lives as holy….Through the Goddess, we can discover our strength, enlighten our minds, own our bodies, and celebrate our emotions."[9] While these movements do not exclude the male, they are unapologetically rooted in the power of the feminine.

Figure 5   Pentacle and handwritten Book of Shadows.

Druidry

The ancient **Druids** were centered in Western Europe probably 2,500 years ago. A common image associated with Druids is cloaked figures mysteriously circling Stonehenge in England (Figure 6). Sources suggest that ancient Druids were poets, philosophers, priests, and physicians. Some were probably also scientists and inventors who probably practiced alchemy. However, the modern Druid movement can be dated to the 1960s. Two different developments mark these contemporary beginnings. In 1963, a group formed at Carlton College to protest mandatory chapel. They called their

Figure 6   Stonehenge at sunset.

group, The Reformed Druids of North America. The following year in England, Ross Nichols formed the Order of Bards, Ovates and Druids. Before the formation of these modern groups, Druidry had largely become a fraternal order with little emphasis on Druidism as a spiritual practice.[10] Because of these fraternal roots, it is often thought that Wicca is for women and Druidry for men. Not so. Both men and women practice Wicca and Druidry today.

---

[9] Starhawk, 24.
[10] Phillip Carr-Gomm, *What Do Druids Believe* (Granta Books, 2006).

Druidry focuses on three human aspirations: wisdom, creativity, and love. As a religious tradition, the core is a belief in the sacredness of life. Little dogma guides the movement. Some Druids are monotheists; whereas, others are polytheists. Further, Christian Druids also exist who practice Christianity and the Druid path simultaneously. While human beings are rooted in the earth, an Otherworld exists that is just as equally real. Our spirits can travel to this world through meditation, trance, and dreams; and, ultimately, at death our soul travels there. The oak tree is a common Druid symbol because it is rooted in the earth, but its limbs reach high. Many, but not all, Druids believe in the cycle of birth, death, and rebirth as a natural course of events. Modern Druids hold some values drawn from Eastern traditions, such as ahimsa (nonviolence), karma, and the interconnectedness of all living things. The individuality and separateness of Western cultures is seen as illusion.[11] Folktales and odes are often utilized in the quest for wisdom.

Ethical practice is central to Druidry. Two books that focus on Druid ethics were published in 2008: *Living with Honour* by Emma Restall Orr and *The Other Side of Virtue* by Brendan Myers. While no formal creed or code exists, certain ethical principles rooted in relationship form the foundation of the way Druids live in the world. These ethical values include responsibility, self-reflection, integrity, courage, honor, generosity, and trust.[12] Primary spiritual practices include seasonal celebrations, healing rituals, pilgrimages, meditation, and spirit journeys (either through shamanic trance or hypnosis).

Hellenistic Polytheism

Hellenistic Polytheism is a revival of the worship of ancient Greek gods and goddesses. It is sometimes called Olympianism, Hellenismos, or Dodekatheism (worship of the twelve Gods). Many of these deities, including Diana, Gaia, and Pan, can also be found in Wicca and other Pagan traditions. The renewal of Hellenistic Polytheism occurred in the 1990s. The movement came to my attention in the last year or so thanks to a student who practices this path. The practice is based on reverence for the Greek deities as well as respect for oneself and others. The sacred texts are not viewed as dogma and consist primarily of the ancient poetry, philosophy and wisdom of the ancient Greeks, including the Homeric Hymns. The writings of Homer, Hesiod, Ovid, Plutarch, and Xenophon.[13]

The Hellenic ritual calendar is lunar-based and follows the waxing, full, and waning moon. As in other forms of paganism, home altars are very common. Offerings to the gods represent the love and attraction of the worshiper. The gods don't demand worship; individuals are completely free. Offerings represent a recognition of the beauty and goodness of the deity. They are a way of bonding with the sacred, or kharis. Offerings in this tradition, as in many other religious traditions, are not understood as a business transaction but rather a gift, an expression of devotion.[14] Worship also involves purification with water (khernips) and prayers of praise and supplication.

---

[11] For more on the beliefs of Druids, see http://www.druidry.org/druid-way/druid-beliefs.

[12] For more information on Druid ethics, see http://www.druidry.org/druid-way/what-druidry/ethics-values-druidry/ethics-values-druidism.

[13] For a comprehensive reading list, see http://baringtheaegis.blogspot.nl/p/reading-list.html.

[14] For a full discussion of the purpose of offerings, see http://www.hellenicgods.org/offerings-to-gods-in-hellenismos.

❂ Explore the meaning and symbolism of various offerings to the gods at http://www.hellenicgods.org/offerings-to-gods-in-hellenismos or http://baringtheaegis.blogspot.com/2012/07/overview-of-my-daily-practice.html. Describe the meaning and purpose of offerings and worship. Choose one item that is offered and describe its purpose in a sentence or two.

_____

_____

_____

_____

_____

Norse/Scandinavian Paganism

Another strain of paganism comes from Norse and Scandinavian pantheons and mythology. A number of traditions fall into this category including Asatru, Odinism, and Heathenism. Some Norse groups have been associated with white supremacist movements; however, it is equally important to note that not all followers of Norse paganism are racist.[15] Some Norse groups, such as Heathens United Against Racism, actively work against racist elements of the tradition. Asatru and other Norse traditions are rooted in the worship of the Norse and Icelandic deities, including the Father of the Gods, Odin, and his son, Thor. **Odin** is a complex figure, much like Shiva in Hinduism. While he is the god of war and death, he is also the god of music and magic. **Thor**, known for his symbol of the hammer, is linked with thunder, healing, and protection. Thor also has a magical belt and is associated with the oak tree. **Baldur** is another son of Odin and his wife, **Frigg**, and the god of the sun. He is killed by **Loki**, the trickster in Norse mythology, who causes all kinds of trouble. Loki is also a shape-shifter, and the father of the goddess of the Underworld, **Hel**. In addition to being Baldur's mother, Frigg is a nurturing figure who is the goddess of weaving and spinning as well as wisdom. The other important goddess is **Freyja**. Like Odin, she is a deity of opposites. On the one hand, she is the goddess of love and fertility, and on the other, the goddess of war and death.

Norse mythology and folklore is rooted in a body of literature made up of _Eddas_ and sagas. The two major types of _Eddas_ are poetry and prose. The writings primarily date from 800 to 1,400 CE. Many of the writings are anonymous, but some were composed by Snorri Sturluson, an Icelandic scholar of the thirteenth century. The Eddas and sagas served as inspiration for some of Wagner's operas and Tolkien's _Hobbit_ and _Lord of the Rings_ series.[16]

Norse cosmology is very complex with nine different realms of existence. In addition, the view of death and afterlife is varied and unclear. Perhaps the most well-known term from Norse mythology is

---

[15] For more information on Odinism and its relationship with white supremacy movements, see
https://www.theatlantic.com/international/archive/2017/11/asatru-heathenry-racism/543864/,
https://www.splcenter.org/fighting-hate/intelligence-report/1998/new-brand-racist-odinist-religion-march, and
http://wildhunt.org/2014/04/cnn-ties-accused-white-supremacist-killer-frazier-glenn-cross-to-odinism.html.
[16] For more information and to read the Poetic _Eddas_, see http://www.sacred-texts.com/neu/poe/.

Valhalla, or the hall of the fallen, where great warriors are said to go at death. References to the underworld as the place of the dead are also prevalent in Norse literature. The view of the soul in Norse traditions is similar to the Chinese view of the soul splitting after death. In Norse tradition, one part goes to the underworld where it is honored as an ancestor and another part is reborn in a person's descendants. The third part of the self or soul is an animal helper similar to those found in other indigenous traditions. This animal helper influences the characteristics and personality of an individual.[17]

Norse festivals also follow the seasons, but include additional celebrations and festivities beyond the solstices and equinoxes. Rituals mark agricultural festivals and rites of passage; they include an offering of food or drink, **blót**, and a series toasts, *sumbel*. A common offering is ale, mead or beer poured on the ground representing the connection and bonding between people and the deities. The spoken word in the form of an intention, an oath or a boast is seen as very powerful and carries the weight of a promise. Personal spiritual practices include relaxation, journeying (a form of vision quest), divination and magic. The use of runes is a common practice in Norse tradition. Runes are symbols from an early Germanic alphabet said to have been revealed to Odin. The word, rune, derives from a Germanic word that means both "letter" (as in alphabet) and "mystery." The symbols were usually carved into wood or stone. Each letter symbol is associated with a sound. These sounds have magical purposes and can be put together in the form of chants to achieve a particular goal, such as fertility, prosperity, clearing obstacles, harmony in relationships or healing. The runes can also be cast as a means of divination. To do this, the runes are cast from a bag onto a cloth. The runes that land face up are the ones to particularly focus on. In addition, various spreads or diagrams are used to place the runes in a particular order for a reading. Generally, the more tiles the layout requires the more detailed the reading (Figure 7).

Figure 7   A collection of rune stones.

Borys Vasylenko/Shutterstock.com.

Contemporary Shamanism

Contemporary Shamanism is rooted in healing of the body, mind, and spirit. It is not a particular religion so much as it is a healing practice. Like shamans in specific indigenous religions, contemporary shamans seek to mediate between the physical and spiritual realm. They traverse the paths of consciousness to lead themselves and others to deeper understanding and a place of healing. Key to shamanic practice is the ability to enter altered states of consciousness through drumming, dreaming, plant based hallucinogens, meditation, sweat baths, and other practices. In these states of heightened awareness, it is believed that one can see things more clearly and gain wisdom to transform one's own life as well as the

[17] See this article from Dan McCoy on "Death and the Afterlife" at http://norse-mythology.org/concepts/death-and-the-afterlife/.

lives of others. Rather than being rooted in a particular culture, Contemporary Shamanism is often a solitary practice; however, modern shamans emphasize the need to use the wisdom they gain to benefit the community.

☯ As you reflect on this chapter, write down one new thing you learned as well as one question you would like to explore further. Also, share what factors you think draw people to these movements today.

_____

_____

_____

_____

_____

WEB RESOURCES FOR FURTHER STUDY

http://www.asatru.org/index.php—This is the homepage for the Asatru Alliance and has a wealth of information about the history and practice of Norse Paganism.

http://baringtheaegis.blogspot.com/p/the-beginners-guide-to-hellenismos.html—Great blog with articles on Hellenismos, worship of the Greek pantheon.

https://www.circlesanctuary.org/—Website for a pagan circle in Wisconsin that includes many resources about pagan traditions.

http://druidry.org/druid-way/—Great site from the Order of Bards, Ovates and Druids that has an immense amount of information about Druid beliefs and practice.

http://www.hellenicgods.org/projectstatement—A resource page with multiple links to information on the worship of the Hellenic deities.

https://hrafnar.org/articles/dpaxson/norse/trac/—A site with numerous articles on Norse Paganism.

http://www.neokoroi.org/religion/—A site maintained by a group of Hellenic pagans with lots of good introductory material.

http://www.shamanscave.com/—This site offers articles and information on Contemporary Shamanism.

http://www.sharedwisdom.com/article/modern-shaman—An article on Modern Shamanism.

https://wicca.com/—Also called the Celtic Connection, this site has information on Wicca, the Rede, and the Wheel of the Year.

http://wildhunt.org/—News and commentary from the pagan community.

http://www.witchvox.com/—A Wiccan news and networking site with lots of interesting information.

Chapter 14
New Religious Movements

Learning Outcomes

By the end of this chapter, students will be able to

☛ distinguish between the sociological definitions of cult and sect;

☛ characterize the social conditions most favorable to the establishment and growth of new religious movements (NRM);

☛ describe the factors that determine whether a NRM will stand the test of time; and

☛ name the founders, countries of origin, key writings, and basic beliefs of major NRM.

Key Terms

Auditor and Auditing	Helena Blavatsky	Rastafarianism
Bab	ISKCON	Rev. Sun Myung Moon
Baha'i	L. Ron Hubbard	Scientology
Baha'u'llah	Maharishi Mahesh Yogi	Sect
Clear	Marcus Garvey	Theosophy
Cult	Millennium	Thetan
Eckankar	Operating Thetan (OT)	Transcendental Meditation (TM)
Elohim	Paul Twitchell	Unification Church
Engrams/e-meter	Raëlians	
Haile Selassie	Ras Tafari	

INTRODUCTION

The term new religious movements (NRM) was coined in the 1960s. The first challenge to address when discussing NRM is to define them. How new is new? In the scheme of world religions many of which are thousands of years old, a religion like Islam that began in the sixth century CE can seem new. However, the religions we will include in our study have all begun in the last three hundred years or so. In Chapter 1, we discussed the challenge of defining religion. The same dilemma applies here when looking at NRM.

Is **scientology** a NRM or is it applied psychology? Is the Church of the Flying Spaghetti Monster a serious movement or is it a satire on the human need for religion? Emerging traditions are harder to characterize than more established ones because they often do not have the structures and institutions in place that are commonly associated with religious traditions.

The second challenge is how to classify them. Sociologically, these movements have often been characterized as either sects or cults. A **sect** is defined as a subgroup of a larger tradition. For instance, Methodists are a sect of Christianity. Zen is a sect of Buddhism. Shi'a is a sect of Islam. The second term is a more problematic and comes with a lot of baggage. When one hears the word "**cult**," the tendency is to think of a group led by a charismatic leader who isolates and brainwashes his/her followers to ulti- mately destroy them. Images of Jim Jones in Guyana, the burning compound of the Branch Davidians in Waco, and the followers of Heaven's Gate who committed suicide to meet a spaceship in the tail of the Hale-Bopp comet often come to mind. Sociologically, however, a **cult** is a movement that centers around a single person or deity and represents a distinct break from a prevailing tradition. In the soci- ological sense, Christianity can be defined as a cult. It centers around the teachings of Jesus Christ and represents a distinct break from the Judaism of its day. In the same way, Buddhism is a cult that centers around the teachings of the Buddha and represents a distinct break from the Hinduism of its day. However, because of the negative associations with the word "cult," the term new religious movements is used to describe both cults and sects that have developed in the last several hundred years.

Furthermore, many movements resist characterization as either a sect or cult in that they are not specifically related to a major religious tradition; and therefore, they don't fit the classic definitions.

THE SOCIAL CLIMATE IN WHICH NRM DEVELOP AND THRIVE

Times of rapid social change are often conducive to the development of NRM. In the period since World War II, thousands of new religious groups have sprung up around the world. NRM are generally met with resistance from previously organized religions. Many of the major world religions were once new and resisted by entrenched religions (i.e., Buddhism, Christianity, Islam, and Sikhism). Religious freedom is highly desired for NRM to take off, but it is not essential. Many movements thrive despite persecution or harassment from the established religions or government systems.

Technology, particularly the Internet, has greatly enhanced every religion's efforts to get the word out about their movement. Not too many years ago, if people had a message to share, they had to do so by word of mouth or travelling great distances. Today the message can be spread rapidly through the Internet and online networks. As the printing press facilitated the Protestant Reformation, the Internet and social media have transformed religion in the twenty-first century.

NRM spring up all the time. Some are a blip on the screen of history and others move from trend to tradition. What factors enable a religious movement to outlast the death of its founder? Mary Pat Fisher in her book, *Living Religions*, proposed some of the following criteria:

- Does it have a balance between new ideas and the comforts of familiar ideas?
- Does it have a sufficient organizational framework so that leadership is clear after the death of the founder?
- Does the social setting support or encourage new movements? Have the established religions become stale and lifeless?

◆ Are young people joining the movement? Does the movement satisfy spiritual needs? Do the teachings lead to transformation?

◆ Is the founder a person of deep and genuine faith? Can the founder or other leadership within the movement convey the message in a clear and compelling way?[1]

Some assume NRM require a sacred text and a large number of followers in order to succeed and become established. However, this is not always the case. A sacred text is not necessary as long as the teachings are clearly presented and they resonate with the life practices of followers. Furthermore, large numbers of followers are not critical as long as people continue to join the movement consistently over the years.

Countless NRM have developed and will develop in the coming years. In this chapter, we will focus on a sampling of new movements. Some are emerging and others have become more established. Some authors categorize the movements by theme (i.e., self-improvement, millennial, etc.); however, the movements tend to easily overlap. Some movements focus on the coming of a millennium, a period of peace and justice, a time when the world is made right and those who have been oppressed are rewarded. Other movements center around some form of healing, be it physical, spiritual, mental, or emotional. For the sake of order, the movements in this chapter are simply arranged alphabetically.

BAHA'I

Baha'i is one of the newest world religions. It was founded in Persia (modern day Iran) in the mid-1800s. As a monotheistic faith, it challenged Islam's assertion that Muhammad was the final prophet. The founders of Baha'i claimed to have a new message to share with God's people through the prophet Baha'u'llah; and, this assertion led to persecution of the early followers of the movement. Baha'i spread from the Middle East to India and finally to the United States.

Early History

In Iran in 1844, a young merchant received a divine revelation that a prophet was soon coming who would announce a message of peace and justice. The young merchant became known as The Báb, a term meaning, "the Gate," in Arabic. It wasn't long before he had attracted a small group of followers drawing the attention of some Muslim clerics. For them, his message was heretical because the last prophet, Muhammad, had already come; there could be no other. The Báb and some of his followers were jailed. Despite imprisonment, his following grew and included the son of a wealthy minister, a young man named, Mirza Husayn-'Alí. Alí later became known as Baha'u'llah, which means "the Glory of God" in Arabic. In 1850, as his followers grew in number, The Báb was executed. Two years later, Baha'u'llah was accused of trying to assassinate the Shah. Baha'u'llah gave himself up to authorities and was taken to the "Black Pit," an infamous dungeon prison. It was while in prison that Baha'u'llah received his first revelation from God. Baha'u'llah was exiled from Iran after four months in the "Black Pit." He went from Iran to Baghdad with his family. During his time in Iraq, he wrote three of his most important writings; and, the followers of the faith The Báb formed continued to grow. In 1863, just before he was forced to flee from Baghdad to Constantinople, Baha'u'llah announced that he was the messenger The Báb had predicted would come. From Constantinople, he and his followers were banished to the

[1] List adapted from Mary Pat Fisher, *Living Religions*, 9th ed. (Pearson, 2014).

frigid city of Adrianople in the middle of winter. For the next seven years, he was moved from place to place, imprisoned, and unable to freely go where he wished. Finally, in 1870, he was given some freedom to move about and meet with his followers.

During the formative years of the movement, many of the followers of The Báb were persecuted and imprisoned. Despite this, Baha'u'llah encouraged his followers to travel to other countries to share the faith. By the time of Baha'u'llah's death in 1892, the Baha'i faith had spread to numerous countries throughout the Middle East and Asia and had attracted the attention of Western spiritual seekers. Thorton Chase, an American from Chicago, established a study group in that city as early as 1893.[2] Before death, Baha'u'llah appointed his oldest son, 'Abdu'l-Bahá, as his successor in a written statement to avoid any controversy over succession that may result after his death.

Beliefs and Sacred Texts

Baha'i is a monotheistic tradition that emphasizes unity and the essential oneness of religion. The founders of all the major religions as well as indigenous faiths are honored and viewed as reflections of God's love and concern for humankind. The sacred texts of the movement are the writings of The Báb, Baha'u'llah, 'Abdu'l-Bahá, and Shoghi Effendi (grandson of 'Abdu'l-Bahá), as well as the pronouncements of the Baha'i Universal House of Justice.[3] However, prayers and scriptures of other faiths are utilized in services and honored as sacred.

Central to the beliefs of Baha'i are equality and justice. The Universal House of Justice was formed in 1963 to provide leadership to the movement after the unexpected death of Shoghi Effendi in 1957. During the six years between Effendi's death and the election of the nine members of the Universal House of Justice, a group of "Hands of the Cause" leaders were appointed by Effendi to help carry out his objectives, and to hold the faith together. The equality of men and women is an important aspect of this emphasis on justice as is the pursuit of peace, human rights, and a reduction in economic disparity between rich and poor. Baha'is believe that religion should unify and not divide people. People are viewed as spiritual beings who need to be liberated from ignorance by the teachings of prophets who call them to faithfulness to God and justice toward others. One historic teaching that is causing issues in the Baha'i community today is the issue of homosexuality. Historically, homosexuality was viewed as immoral, which has led to much angst in the Lesbian, Gay, Bisexual and Transgendered (LGBT) Baha'i community. The Baha'i faith strongly emphasizes living out the faith through practice.

Rituals and Symbols

Central to Baha'i devotion to God are the practices of prayer and meditation. Baha'u'llah advocated prayer at least three times a day and wrote three prayers to be used on a regular basis. A brief prayer is recited at noon. In addition, a prayer that is a little longer is provided for the three daily prayers. As in Islam, bodily movements match the various parts of the prayer. A longer prayer is to be recited once each day.[4]

---

[2] http://www.bahai-encyclopedia-project.org/index.php?option=com_content&view=article&id=46:chase-thornton-18471 912&catid=37:biography.

[3] To read the authoritative texts of Baha'i visit, http://www.bahai.org/library/authoritative-texts/.

[4] To read the three obligatory prayers, see http://www.bahai.org/documents/bahaullah/obligatory-prayers.

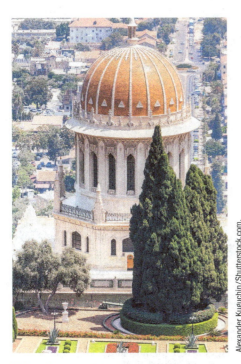

Figure 1   The Bab Shrine in Haifa, Israel.

Read the obligatory prayers found at http://www.bahai.org/documents/bahaullah/obligatory-prayers. Was there anything in particular that caught your attention? What characteristics of God do you notice in the prayers? What characteristics of human beings are evident?

_____

_____

_____

_____

_____

Fasting is also a part of Baha'i spiritual discipline. A nineteen-day fast from sunup to sundown is observed yearly between March 2 and 20. The period of fasting comes just around the time of the Baha'i New Year (Nowruz) and is observed as a time of spiritual growth and worship. Nowruz is the Persian New Year and is celebrated by Bahais, Zoroastrians, and other faiths of the Iranian people.

Devotional gatherings of prayer, readings of the sacred texts, discussion, and worship often take place in people's homes. In addition, some communities have a building that serves as a meeting place and community center. Baha'i temples are located in various places throughout the world, with the largest and most sacred one in Haifa, Israel (Figure 1). This temple is also a shrine to The Báb and a site of pilgrimage for many Baha'is. There are no clergy in Baha'i. Anyone in the community can participate in leading devotional services and prayers.

Working for justice, peace, and the alleviation of suffering is another major component of Baha'i spirituality. Baha'is view the work that is done to earn a living as an opportunity for service to others. Moreover, community service involves meeting the needs of others through providing health care, food, shelter, and so on, to those who are in need.

The two most prominent Baha'i symbols are the nine-pointed star and the "Greatest Name." Nine is viewed as the number of completeness; it is also the number of years between The Bab's foretelling of the messenger and Baha'u'llah's first revelation while in prison. Furthermore, Baha'i temples are often built with nine sides and the word *Baha* in Arabic represents the number nine. The Greatest Name symbol is the phrase "Ya Baha'ul Abha" in Arabic, meaning "O glory of the All-Glorious." The shape of the calligraphy is reminiscent of a boat and speaks to God's ability to preserve and sustain humankind in the midst of life's struggles.[5] (Figure 2)

Figure 2   The Greatest Name Symbol.

[5] Maya Bonhoff, "What Do Baha'i Symbols Mean," April 9, 2014, http://bahaiteachings.org/what-do-the-bahai-symbols-mean.

Baha'i in the United States

Around the world, in 2010, about five million people practiced Baha'i[6]; and, major population centers for Baha'i include such diverse places as India, the United States, and Kenya. As noted earlier in the chapter, from the early days of the movement, interest in the faith could be found in the United States. Thornton Chase founded a Baha'i study group in Chicago in 1893. In 1899, Kate Ives became the first Baha'i believer in Boston and a Baha'i school was founded in Maine.[7] In 1953, the Baha'i temple in Wilmette, Illinois, was completed. It is one of seven Baha'i temples worldwide and the only one in North America (Figure 3) According to the Office of Communications of the US Baha'i National Center, there are about 176,000 followers in the United States.

Source: Stephanie Curran, December 2018.

Figure 3   Baha'i Temple in Wilmette, Illinois, Completed in 1953.

CAO DAI

Cao Dai, like Baha'i, is a movement that seeks to unite people of diverse religious traditions. Cao Dai was founded in Vietnam in 1926 with a revelation from God that all religions worship the same Supreme Being. In 1919, Ngo Van Chieu received a vision of the One God, Cao Dai. Cao Dai literally means, "roofless tower." Before this experience, Chieu practiced Daoism. In the vision, God revealed the symbol of Cao Dai, an all-seeing eye, to Chieu and impressed on him the importance of sharing the message of love and unity with the world. Then, in 1925, three Vietnamese men gathered to consult the spirits. One of the spirits who spoke to them was AAA who revealed to them that God wanted them to found a religion. The spirit directed these men and several others to visit Chieu, and the movement was born. A hierarchy and system of leadership transition was set up. The Cao Dai Temple was built in Tay Ninh beginning in 1933 and reached completion in 1955. The quest for unity can be seen in the structure of the "Holy See," as the temple in Tay Ninh is called (Figure 4). Symbols from Buddhism, Christianity, Hinduism, and Islam are all on spires rising from the temple.

The two paths for practicing this faith are an outer and an inner practice. The outer practice involves moral goodness and worship in the temple while maintaining life in the world (marrying, working, etc.). The inner practice involves cultivating the true self and can be done alone. The movement has roots in Spiritism (the receiving of messages through the spirits) and continues to value this method of

---

[6] http://www.pewforum.org/2015/04/02/other-religions/.

[7] http://pluralism.org/timeline/bahai-in-boston/.

revelation. The ultimate goal of spiritual practice is to be released from the cycle of birth, death, and rebirth and be reunited with God. Members also promote peace, vegetarianism, and harmony between religions. They do not seek converts. The religious hierarchy in the church mirrors, to some extent, the organizational hierarchy of the Catholic Church. The movement has also been greatly influenced by Daoism, Confucianism, and Buddhism. A wide variety of saints from around the world including Joan of Arc and Shakespeare are honored as well. Prayers at the temple take place at 6:00 a.m., noon, 6:00 p.m., and midnight.

Figure 4   Cao Dai Temple and the symbolic One Eye in Tay Ninh, Vietnam.

The faith experienced great persecution over the years in Vietnam, but has continued to grow and spread. It is estimated that there are about six million followers worldwide and that about half of those are in Vietnam.[8] Several Cao Dai temples have been built across the United States including California, Houston, and New Orleans.

ECKANKAR

Eckankar was founded by Paul Twitchell in 1965. It is rooted in the Radhasoami (or Sant Mat) movement of living gurus that came out of India in the 1800s. Eckankar is understood to be a path to oneness with God through spiritual practices, including dreams and soul travel. Twitchell referred to it as "God Science" and identified five principles in soul travel including: the soul is individual and able to move in various universes, the soul works through wave lengths and sound rays, the soul has a "full range of perceptions similar to the physical senses but at a higher vibration," and the Soul can "know and understand all things … and dwell in Total Awareness."[9] ECK is the Divine Spirit made up of light and sound. ECK cleanses the soul of karma and fills it with love for all living things. HU is the sacred sound of God. The word is sung as a means of experiencing God.[10] The goal of the practice is to become a coworker with God, which is the essence of the name, Eckankar. Through the spiritual exercises outlined by the movement, practitioners can achieve a heightened state of soul consciousness and liberation from the cycle of rebirth in a single lifetime. The current leader of the movement is Harold Klemp; and the headquarters of the movement and the temple of ECK are located in Chanhassen, Minnesota.

[8] Mike Tolson, "From 'Nothingness' to the Largest of its Kind," *Houston Chronicle*, September 6, 2015, http://www.houstonchronicle.com/news/houston-texas/houston/article/From-nothingness-to-largest-of-its-kind-in-6488654.php.
[9] Paul Twitchell, *Eckankar: Compiled Writings*, vol. 1 (San Diego: Illuminated Way Press, 1975), p. 130.
[10] To listen to HU, see http://www.eckankar.org/hu.html.

INTERNATIONAL SOCIETY OF KRISHNA CONSCIOUSNESS

The International Society for Krishna Consciousness, or ISKCON, was founded by A.C. Bhaktivedanta Swami Prabhupada in 1966 in New York City. It is also known as the Hare Krishna movement because of its devotion to Krishna. Members practice bhakti (devotion) at home as well as in temples around the world. In ISKCON, God has form. Meditation, particularly using the Hare Krishna, Hare Rama mantra, is an important spiritual practice. Devotees also practice yoga and devotional singing, **kirtan**.[11] ISKCON shares a belief in karma and reincarnation with religious traditions founded in India. The primary texts are the *Bhagavad Gita* and the writings of Swami Prabhupada. Followers practice nonviolence and vegetarianism. Some followers live together in farming communities, or eco-villages, around the world. In the United States, some of these communities are located in Mississippi and

Pennsylvania.[12] ISKCON temples often host festivals, such as the Holi festival in Washington, DC.[13] George Harrison of the Beatles is probably its most famous follower; and, the mantra is immortalized in the Beatles' song, *My Sweet Lord*. Since the 1980s, the movement has been primarily composed of Indian followers but in recent years, a renewed interest has been evident among non-Indians. The movement Krishna West was founded by Howard Resnick to help spread the faith among Westerners. Estimates of the number of U.S. followers varies wildly from 10,000 to nearly a million (Figure 5).

Figure 5   Hare Krishna Followers in New York City, September 2014.

Kaesler Media/Shutterstock.com.

JEDIISM

This movement is indeed serious and has moved beyond fandom to an organized, global community with members in the United Kingdom, Canada, Australia, New Zealand, and the United States. In the Maryland/Virginia area, a meet-up group has been formed for followers of the Jedi philosophy. It is not a Star Wars fan club and doesn't involve reenactments. Jediism is based on the force, the energy underlying the universe; but, it is not the worship of Star Wars or George Lucas. The Temple of the Order of the Jedi has a creed based on the Prayer of St. Francis; it has a code of behavior, as well as a series of sixteen beliefs and twenty-one maxims.[14] Daniel Jones is credited with founding the Jedi Church in 2007 in the United Kingdom.[15] The faith is nontheistic and based on the idea that life is sacred. They hold that soci-

---

[11] To listen to a kirtan, or devotional chant, go to https://www.iskconmysore.org/audio/.

[12] The website for the community in Pennsylvania is http://www.gitanagari.org/ in case you would like to explore some of the events and resources the community offers.

[13] For information on this festival, see https://holidc.com/.

[14] For the full description of these elements, see https://www.templeofthejediorder.org/doctrine-of-the-order.

[15] http://www.bbc.com/news/magazine-29753530.

ety should be rooted in reason and compassion; and as such as such, there is no disconnection between religion and science in Jediism. A hierarchy of membership exists from those who simply express interest to Jedi Knights and leaders of the Jedi Council. When becoming a Jedi, a person may choose to make a simple oath:

> **"I profess before all my fellow Jedi that I, [name] born [dd/mm/yyyy], without reservation, choose the Jedi path with all its duties and responsibilities. I promise to uphold the Jedi teachings, and to live a life worthy of a Jedi."[16]**

Jediism is largely an individual practice with meditation[17] being the most common spiritual exercise. however, communities of those who practice Jediism are becoming more commonplace where people gather together for discussion and service to others.

MAHIKARI

Mahikari began in Japan in 1959 and has spread throughout the world. Yoshikazu Okada founded the movement after receiving a revelation from God. His followers later gave him the title, Sukuinushisama, "Great Savior." Leadership has passed down through Okada's adopted daughter and grandson, Ko-o Okada, who is the current leader of the movement. The movement focuses on the Divine Light which purifies and heals. This divine light or energy is given and received through the hands. This NRM is described as a means of spiritual growth and enrichment rather than a religion. After joining the movement, followers go on a three-day training session. At the end, they are given an Omitama, or amulet, which is said to protect the wearer with a halo of light.[18] Mahikari centers of spiritual development are located throughout the world including New York and Washington, DC.

PASTAFARIANISM

The Church of the Flying Spaghetti Monster (FSM) began in 2005 as a satire inspired by the decision of a Kansas school board to give equal time to teaching intelligent design in the classroom. Bobby Henderson brought the church into the public eye by writing an open letter calling on the school board to allow his theories of the origin of the world and his data regarding the correlation between the increase in the Earth's temperature and the decline of pirate to be taught in the classroom.[19] The Pastafarian deity is the FSM, also known as His Noodly Appendage. The sacred text, written by Bobby Henderson, is *The Gospel of the Flying Spaghetti Monster*. However, an additional book has also been written called, *The Loose Canon*, which contains the writings of followers of FSM. To convert to the church, one slurps a long spaghetti noodle cooked al dente in one quick motion.[20]

---

[16] https://www.templeofthejediorder.org/component/content/article/40-information/2078-the-oaths-of-temple-of-the-jedi-order.

[17] For a discussion of meditation from a Jedi perspective, see http://thejediismway.tripod.com/meditation.html.

[18] Jackie Fowler,. "Mahikari" https://wrldrels.org/2016/10/08/sukyo-mahikari/.

[19] http://www.venganza.org/about/open-letter/.

[20] http://spaghettimonster.com/church-of-the-flying-spaghetti-monster-founded/the-gospel-of-the-flying-spaghetti-monster/.

Church members can be identified by the characteristic colander on their heads (Figure 6). Some have received permission to wear the colander for driver's license photos and even in the workplace. A town council member in New York was sworn into office in 2014 wearing the FSM headgear.[21] From its origins as satire, it has become a sacred community for faithful skeptics around the world. It should be noted that this is not the only movement of skeptics who have drawn inspiration from food. The Church of Bacon is another movement with a similar mission.[22]

Figure 6   Pastafarians with Colanders on Their Heads Play in a Parade in Brussels, May 2010.

☯ Explore the websites related to the Church of the FSM. What do you think draws people to this movement? Why do you think organizations of skeptics are forming?

_____

_____

_____

_____

_____

RAËLISM

On his way to work one morning in 1973, Claude Vorilhon, felt compelled to take a detour to the Volcano Nature Park in southern France. While there, he saw a bright light which, he says, was lowering down from the sky. At the base of the unidentified flying object (UFO), a staircase emerged, and a small man came out to give Vorilhon a revelation of the religion of the **Elohim**. Vorilhon took on the name Raël and founded an NRM. The Elohim are "highly advanced extraterrestrial scientists who created life on Earth."[23] The Elohim are said to have created human beings from their DNA and placed them on Earth. While on earth, human beings must choose between nuclear annihilation and awakening our planetary consciousness.[24] Raël opposes war, promotes tolerance, and advocates human cloning. Moreover, Raël believes that the purpose of cloning is to bring back people who have committed atrocious acts and have gone largely unpunished. By re-creating them, these criminals can be brought to

---

[21] https://www.independent.co.uk/news/world/americas/pastafarian-minister-christopher-schaeffer-is-sworn-into-new-york-town-council-9044607.html

[22] To learn more about the Church of Bacon, see http://www.unitedchurchofbacon.org/

[23] Claude Vorilhon, "Elohim Embassy" https://www.rael.org/embassy.

[24] Susan Palmer, "The Raëlian Movement: Concocting Controversy, Seeking Social Legitimacy," *Controversial New Religions*, ed. by James Lewis and Jesper Petersen (Oxford, 2005), p. 374.

justice. Raëlians are hoping to build an embassy in Israel to welcome the Elohim back to Earth sometime between now and 2035. If human beings have created a more peaceful world by the time the Elohim come back, then the Elohim will impart the knowledge they have gathered to humans on Earth.

RASTAFARIANISM

Rastafarianism is a black power movement that began in the early 1900s in Jamaica. The movement was inspired by Jamaican independence, Pan-Africanism, and Ethiopianism. Ethiopia is one of the only African nations that remained a sovereign nation and did not come under colonial rule. It also has a rich history as an empire and is seen as the cradle of the African race and identity. Marcus Garvey, an early influence on the movement, is said to have predicted that when a black king is crowned in Africa, the day of redemption for the black community was close at hand. In 1930, when Ras Tafari Makonnen was crowned Emperor of Ethiopia and given the title of "Haile Selassie I, King of Kings, Lord of Lords, and Conquering Lion of the Tribe of Judah,"[25] many believed this prophecy had reached its fulfillment.

Some, including Leonard P. Howell, an early leader of the movement, believed Haile Selassie I was the incarnation of God. The fact that the emperor did not see himself as such, only added to the mystique that surrounded him. Rastafarianism is difficult to characterize. Some see it as a separatist movement unrelated to Christianity and others see it as a reform movement within Christianity. Rastas draw inspiration from the themes of liberation and redemption found in the Bible, particularly in the figures of Moses and Elijah. Rastafarians refer to the forces of oppression as Babylon and seek liberation from all that would hold them back. Ethiopia is understood as Zion, the Promised Land. In addition to the Bible, other texts that form a foundation of the faith are *The Promised Key* and *The Living Testament of Rasta-for-I*. God is in each Rasta which is the belief that forms the core of the I-and-I philosophy of Rastafarianism. I and I is used in place of "we," and language is seen as key to expressing Rasta belief. Oppression is referred to in Rasta circles as "downpression" pointing to the way policies and idea press down people. Rastas also speak of "overstanding" rather than understanding as overstanding represents increasing in wisdom.[26]

Figure 7 Rastafarian Drummer Celebrating What Would Have Been Bob Marley's 68th Birthday in Kingston, Jamaica in 2013.

Living naturally is characteristic of Rasta practice. Dreadlocks are a common symbol and are rooted in the Nazarite vow of not cutting hair found in Numbers 6:5. This idea of living naturally is called I-tal and also influences diet. Rastas avoid alcohol and caffeine; many are vegetarian, and most eat food in as close to its raw state as possible. Rastas gather for reasoning sessions,

---

[25] http://smithsonianeducation.org/migrations/rasta/rasessay.html.
[26] See this link, https://jahworks.org/adjua_dubb/rastafari-way-of-life/#.XaJZyudKhp8, for a good discussion of Rasta history, belief, language and structure.

drumming, and meditation. Some utilize "ganja," the holy herb, as a sacrament in these gatherings. Both the practice of communal smoking of marijuana and the wearing of dreadlocks may have also been influenced by the holy men, **sadhus**, of India. East Indians came as indentured laborers to Jamaica in the 1830s and probably influenced some Rastafarian practices. A discussion of Rastafarianism without reference to music would be like pancakes without syrup. Reggae music and the work of Bob Marley had a strong impact on the spread of Rastafarianism. Many of Bob Marley's lyrics speak of Rastafarian themes such as Babylon, redemption[27], exodus, and liberation.

SATANISM, THE CHURCH OF SATAN

When most people hear the words Church of Satan, they are sure it must be about worshipping the devil and sacrificing small animals. With a name like that, it must be evil, right? Actually, like many things, it isn't exactly what it seems. "Satanic groups are composed of ordinary people interested in religious and philosophical matters, not evil monsters or ignorant simpletons."[28] They seek to explore religious questions in a modern framework. They are closely related to Self-spirituality in that they view the Self as sacred and seek to explore our "authentic nature."[29] Satan, particularly as visualized as the serpent in the Garden of Eden, opened Adam and Eve's eyes to their true nature and an exploration of the knowledge of good and evil. For Satanists, this knowledge is to be prized. Modern Satanism does not involve worship of any deity but rather seeks to elevate the Self and its true nature. Different types of Satanism can be found. Rational Satanists focus on philosophy and science. Followers of Aleister Crowley and others seek an esoteric path focused on mysticism and **magick** for the benefit of the individual.

Anton LaVey (Howard Stanton Levey) is often credited as being the founder of Modern Satanism. He created the Church of Satan in San Francisco in 1966 and published *The Satanic Bible* in 1969. LaVey celebrated human desire and an elemental energy rooted in the earth. He worked the carnival as a musician, a hypnotist, and a magician's assistant. He knew how to create a show and publicize his views. An interesting element of the "church" he created is that it mirrors Christianity and other established religions in terms of organization and structure. As a result of disagreements over practice and structure, many splinter groups have formed off of the original Church of Satan including the Temple of Set.

An overview of the *Nine Satanic Statements*, the *Eleven Rules of Satanism*, and the *Satanic Sins* offers a view of the philosophical and moral framework of Satanism. The Satanic Statements are an elevation of personal gratification, having one's eyes open to the true nature of humanity, and offering kindness to the deserving. The Eleven Rules of the Earth and the Satanic Sins are guidelines for behavior. Of the eleven rules, two involve not causing harm to children or animals; and, two deal with treating others as they treat you (not treating others as you want to be treated, but rather treating others as they have treated you). Vengeance is permissible within limits. Furthermore, advice or help is not to be given unless it is asked for. One of the most serious of the Nine Satanic Sins is stupidity, people blindly believing what they are told. Other "sins" include thinking you are better than you are, projecting your expectations on others, deceiving yourself, a lack of appreciation for beauty, and going along with the crowd.

---

[27] Click on link, http://www.metrolyrics.com/redemption-song-lyrics-bob-marley.html, to view the lyrics to Bob Marley's, *Redemption Song*.

[28] Jesper Aagaard Petersen, "Modern Satanism," *Controversial New Religions* (Oxford, 2005), p. 424.

[29] Ibid., 425.

❂ Explore the opening page of the Church of Satan's website as well as the Satanic Statements, Sins, and Guidelines. What struck you in your reading? What draws people to this movement? How does the movement differ from other religions discussed in class?

_____

_____

_____

_____

_____

SCIENTOLOGY

The Church of Scientology was founded by Lafayette **Ron Hubbard** in the 1950s. It is based on the philosophy of mental, emotional, and physical healing he outlined in his book, *Dianetics: The Original Thesis*. He called his movement an "applied religious philosophy." Hubbard asserts there are three parts of a person: the body, the mind, and the spirit (**thetan**). The **thetan**, or spirit, is held back by **engrams**, which are negative thoughts and emotions that stem from our subconscious mind. To become **clear** of these engrams, a person goes through a process called **auditing** to identify and remove these engrams. A device, called an **e-meter**, is used to measure and identify these engrams, then a trained **auditor** helps the individual process and become free of these negative thoughts and emotions that block the spirit. The path to becoming an **Operating Thetan (OT)** is called the Bridge to Total Freedom. Each level requires various courses, auditing, and training sessions. According to Scientology, a person has two minds: the analytical mind and the reactive mind. When a person becomes clear, they operate out of their analytical mind rather than reacting unconsciously to people and situations.

Hubbard's father served overseas in the Navy leading L.Ron to spend quite a bit of time in India and China as a young person. He was influenced by Eastern views of karma and reincarnation which also made it into his religious philosophy. Scientology holds no specific view of God and leaves the belief in God up to the individual. Human beings are understood to be basically good and capable of amazing things when they are free from negativity and all that would hold them back.

The 1950s and 1960s saw the rise of an antipsychiatry movement. Hubbard was a part of this movement, and the Church of Scientology continues to be a vocal critic of psychiatry. Scientology, too, has been the subject of much

Figure 8　Headquarters Building for the Church of Scientology in New York City.

criticism for its secrecy, commercialism, and unorthodox views. A 2015 Emmy Award winning documentary, *Going Clear*, produced by HBO exposes some of the unflattering aspects of Scientology through the eyes of former members of the church. However, the Church of Scientology continues to spread the message and build around the world including new centers in Tokyo and Milan in 2015. The actual number of Scientologists is hard to find, but a 2008 American Religious Identification Survey put the number in the United States at around 25,000 (Figure 8). The 2011 census in the United Kingdom showed that there are 2,418 self-identified Scientologists compared to 176,632 who identified as Jedi Knights.[30]

THEOSOPHY

The term **theosophy** means the exploration of divine wisdom. The Theosophical Society was brought into being by Madame **Helena Blavatsky** in New York City in 1875. Along with her colleagues, Henry Steel Olcott and William Quan Judge, she created a study group exploring the connection between Eastern and Western religious and philosophical traditions. Madame Blavatsky and Henry Steel Olcott moved to India in 1879 to spread their thoughts and ideas. Olcott was the first president of the Theosophical Society. William Quan Judge stayed and continued their work in the United States. The movement also influenced other esoteric groups such

Figure 9   Memorial to Henry Steel Olcott at his cremation site Tamil Nadu, India.

as the Anthroposophical Society, the Rosicrucians, and the Hermetic Order of the Golden Dawn.

Blavatsky wrote several important texts including *The Secret Doctrine* published in 1875 and *The Key to Theosophy* in 1889. The Theosophical Society stresses the search for Truth and the common ethical foundations that inform most of the major world religions, particularly the emphasis on love. The practice further asserts the unity of religion, philosophy, and science. The Inner Self of all human beings is Divine. The key to spiritual practice is to realize the divine nature within and to nurture it. The belief in karma and the view of human beings as made up of seven "bodies" is deeply rooted in Indian religious traditions. In addition, the teaching of Theosophy draws on the ideas of reincarnation and meditation from Eastern traditions, with meditation serving as the key spiritual practice.

It is difficult to find statistics on the number of followers of Theosophy. The Theosophical Society in America attests to 110 study circles around the country and reports the international organization to be present in seventy countries.[31]

---

[30] Statistics from a 2015 article in *The Atlantic* magazine, http://www.theatlantic.com/entertainment/archive/2015/03/its-not-easy-being-scientology/388634/.

[31] Numbers found at https://www.theosophical.org/about/about-the-society.

TRANSCENDENTAL MEDITATION

Transcendental Meditation (TM) was founded by **Maharishi Mahesh Yogi**. Maharishi Mahesh Yogi was a student of a guru in India, Brahmananda Saraswati, who developed the meditation technique. Before the guru died in 1953, he gave Maharishi Mahesh Yogi the task of spreading the technique around the world. He was very successful in this endeavor even teaching The Beatles this method. Maharishi Mahesh Yogi died in 2008, but the technique itself is alive and well (Figure 10).

Figure 10 Maharishi Mahesh Yogi Ashram in Rishikesh, India, visited by The Beatles.

The website of the movement asserts it is not a religion but a technique. The meditation practice is performed is for twenty minutes twice a day. The practice is taught by a trained instructor who gives the student a mantra that is suited specifically for that individual. The mantras are not words, but ancient Vedic sounds. The vibration of the sounds quiets the mind and brings healing to the spirit. Monetary charges are associated with learning the techniques, and charities have been set up to help fund the courses.[32] During the 1970s and 1980s, the movement splintered and seemed to be on its way out; however, it is making a comeback. In recent years, the technique has received a lot of attention because of various research studies conducted on its effectiveness and the endorsement of the practice by some celebrities and chief executive officers.[33]

UNIFICATION CHURCH

The **Unification Church** was founded by **Rev. Sun Myung Moon** and his wife in 1954 in South Korea. It is formally known as Family Federation for World Peace and Unification (FFWPU) and is based on Moon's writings, *The Divine Principle*. According to *The Divine Principle*, God has a plan of three blessings for all people. The first is to be fruitful, this involves developing integrity and moral goodness in the context of a loving home. God is viewed as a loving parent who helps parents carry out the task of raising children to become children of God. From this first blessing, stems the second which is to marry and begin a family when an individual reaches adulthood. The third blessing is to serve as caretakers of the earth and its resources while promoting peace among nations.[34]

Rev. Moon believes that Jesus was not able to finish the work that he started as the new Adam because he did not marry. Rev. Moon teaches that he and his wife are finishing the work that Jesus started. The church is known for its facilitated marriages and large wedding ceremonies held each year. In February 2016, 3,000 couples participated in the ceremony at Cheong Shim Peace World Center in Gapyeong, about 37 miles outside of Seoul. An additional 12,000 couples participated via satellite around the

---

[32] An example of this is The Meditation Trust in the UK. http://www.meditationtrust.com/.

[33] To read more about this movement and recent publicity, https://dianerehm.org/shows/2016-05-17/mindfulness-and-trascendental-meditation-why-these-practices-are-having-a-moment.

[34] For a deeper discussion of the Three Blessings, see http://dplife.info/blog/view/category/dp-insights/.

world. Rev. Moon died in 2012 at the age of ninety-two. His wife, Han Hak-ja, continues to perform the annual ceremony. Moon also founded *The Washington Times* newspaper and owned a hotel and video production center in Washington, DC. Membership numbers are difficult to determine. The church claims three million members worldwide, but outside groups place the numbers much lower than that.

UNITARIAN UNIVERSALISM AND THE UNITY MOVEMENT

Unitarian Universalism (UU) and The Unity Movement are often confused. Both movements affirm the equality of all people and that the search for truth takes many forms. Neither movement has a set creed or doctrine that its members must affirm. Both movements draw from a variety of traditions in their quest to make the world a more peaceful, just and free place. Both movements are committed to providing a safe and open environment for the LGBT community. At the same time, the movements are not identical; each has its own unique history and focus.

UU grew out the 1961 merger of two religious organizations: The Universalist Church of America and American Unitarian Association. Members of UU come from all religions as well as atheists, agnostics, and skeptics. Though there is no creed or doctrine, Unitarian Universalists affirm seven core principles:

◆ The inherent worth and dignity of every person.
◆ Justice, equity, and compassion in human relations.
◆ Acceptance of one another and encouragement to spiritual growth in congregations.
◆ A free and responsible search for truth and meaning.
◆ The right of conscience and the use of the democratic process within congregations and in society at large.
◆ The goal of world community with peace, liberty, and justice for all.
◆ Respect for the interdependent web of all existence of which we are a part.[35]

Unitarian churches also affirm six sources of truth including direct experience, the wisdom writings of the world's religions and those of the earth-centered religious traditions, among others. The local Unitarian Church in Frederick, Maryland, shares space with a Reform synagogue and serves as the meeting place for a several spiritual practice groups with focuses such as Buddhist, Pagan, and Jewish.

The Unity Movement was founded by Charles and Myrtle Fillmore in 1890 when they convened a prayer group that later came to be called Silent Unity. The next year they began publishing Unity magazine. The Unity movement has a stronger Christian focus but still values spiritual practices from all traditions, such as drumming and meditation, to help connect individuals to the presence of God. The Unity Movement has five basic principles:

◆ God is the source and creator of all. There is no other enduring power. God is good and present everywhere.
◆ We are spiritual beings, created in God's image. The spirit of God lives within each person; therefore, all people are inherently good.

---

[35] http://www.uua.org/beliefs/what-we-believe/principles.

◆ We create our life experiences through our way of thinking.

◆ There is power in affirmative prayer, which we believe increases our awareness of God.

◆ Knowledge of these spiritual principles is not enough. We must live them.[36]

The practice of affirmative prayer is central to Unity. In this form of prayer, the person praying does not make requests but rather verbalizes and visualizes positive outcomes.

☯ Only a sampling of NRM is explored in this chapter and those covered are summarized rather than offering a lot of depth and detail. What movements most interested you? What questions do you still have? Find one new religious movement not covered in this chapter and provide a little background on this movement to share with the class.

_____

_____

_____

_____

_____

_____

WEB RESOURCES FOR FURTHER STUDY

https://www.bahai.org/—The official website of the Baha'i faith includes history, translations of sacred texts, and numerous articles by Baha'i leaders.

http://bahaiteachings.org/—A website with many resources on the Baha'i faith.

http://caodai.org/—The home page of Cao Dai including information on its history, faith and practice.

http://www.churchofsatan.com/index.php—The official website of the Church of Satan. A reading of the opening page of the site gives a good overview of what Modern Satanism is about.

https://www.eckankar.org/—The homepage of Eckankar and a resource on the history, teachings, and spiritual practices of the movement.

http://www.elohimembassy.org/—Website promoting the Raëlian vision of an Elohim Embassy to prepare the world for the return of the Elohim.

http://www.krishna.com/—The official website for ISKCON includes resources, information on temple locations, beliefs and practices.

http://jahworks.org/adjua_dubb/rastafari-way-of-life/#.WaMQhJOGNfQ—A good article summarizing the beliefs and practices of Rastafarianism.

---

[36] http://www.unity.org/about-us/our-philosophy.

http://krishnawest.com/—An ISKCON organization founded by Howard Resnick to promote Western practice of ISKCON. This site offers resources about ISKCON and the study of the Bhagavad Gita.

https://www.rael.org/home—A website for the Raëlian message along with a link to the latest Raëlian news.

http://www.scientology.org/—The official website of the Church of Scientology with information on Hubbard and the church's key practices and beliefs.

http://www.sukyomahikari.org/—The official homepage of Mahikari in North America. It offers information about the origin of the movement, its beliefs and practices.

https://www.templeofthejediorder.org/—One of several Jedi websites. This site offers doctrine, sermons, and a forum for discussion.

http://thejediismway.tripod.com/index.html—A website with information on the Jedi faith including beliefs, meditation practices and a Jedi symbol.

https://www.theosophical.org/—The website of the Theosophical Society in North America offers articles on Theosophy and the organization's programs.

http://theosophy.org/—An online library of the writings of some of the leaders of Theosophy.

https://www.tm.org—This site discusses the TM technique and has articles about the practice and its founder.

http://www.unity.org/—The main website for the Unity Church includes information on the history, beliefs and spiritual practices of this movement.

http://www.uua.org/—The official website of the Unitarian Universalists Association with a wealth of information on history, beliefs and practices.

https://wrldrels.org/wrsp-index/—Excellent resource with brief profiles of many religious movements.

Appendix

RELIGIOUS SITE VISIT WORKSHEET

Date: _____

Name of site visited:

_____

Address:

_____

Briefly describe your impressions of the sacred space (may include building, grounds, any statuary or artwork, etc.).

_____

_____

_____

_____

What symbols or sacred texts do you notice? How are they used?

_____

_____

_____

Summarize the experience. What did you see? What was said? What caught your attention? Was there are a central theme that stood out to you?

_____

_____

_____

_____

_____

_____

_____

_____

What key terms from the course come to mind?

_____

_____

_____

What do you notice about how the religious tradition/faith is lived out?

_____

_____

_____

What questions would you like to ask?

_____

_____

_____

_____

Questions for reflection: What did you learn from the experience? What surprised you or challenged preconceptions? What similarities or differences did you notice from other religions you have experienced/studied? _____

_____

_____

_____

_____

_____

SAMPLE INTERVIEW QUESTIONS

Following are some questions to consider when interviewing someone of another faith:

1. Were you born into this faith or did you choose it later in life? If you chose the faith later, what drew you to it? If you were born into it, what keeps you practicing it?
2. What is the earliest memory you have of your faith?
3. What holidays/festivals do you celebrate? What is your favorite tradition?
4. What do you see as the central beliefs/practices of your faith?
5. What writings/stories of the faith are important to you?
6. What do you wish people knew about your religion? What misconceptions do you think others have?
7. Are there any aspects of your faith that are hard for you to follow?
8. What impact does your faith have on your daily life?

Glossary

Abraham – the patriarch of Judaism, Christianity, and Islam who entered into a covenant with God.

Abu Bakr – the close friend of Prophet Muhammad and the first Sunni Caliph.

Adhan – the call to prayer in Islam.

Advent – season of the Christian year marked by preparation for the birth of Christ.

Agni – the Hindu god of fire.

Agnosticism – the belief that if there is a divine reality, there is no way for human beings to know it.

Ahimsa – nonviolence or noninjury.

Ajiva – the material world in Jainism.

Ali – the son-in-law of Prophet Muhammad and the first Shi'ite Imam.

Allah – God in Arabic, literally "the only One to be worshipped."

Amaterasu – the sun goddess in Japanese mythology.

Amida Buddha (Amitabha) – the Buddha of Boundless Light.

Amrit – sacred nectar.

Analects – the collection of the sayings of Confucius.

Anatman (Anatta) – the Buddhist doctrine of the non-Self, or the impermanence of the Self.

Ancestor Reverence – the honoring of ancestors accompanied by the belief that they still have influence on the living.

Anekantwad – the Jain view of the relative nature of truth; the recognition that there are a variety of viewpoints.

Angra Mainyu – the evil aspect of divine energy in Zoroastrianism.

Anicca – the doctrine of impermanence in Buddhism.

Animism – the belief that all living things are imbued with spirit and are spiritually interconnected.

Anthropomorphism – giving a deity or supernatural being human characteristics.

Aparigraha – the virtue of nonattachment or non-possessiveness

Apocrypha – collection of texts included in the Septuagint and therefore also in the Christian Old Testament, but later removed by Luther as writings useful for study but not canonical.

Atheism – the denial of the existence of any deity or supernatural reality outside the physical world.

Atman – the essence of Brahman in all living things, not an individualized soul but a sacred essence.

Baptism – a sacrament of cleansing and initiation in the Christian Church involving water.

Beatitudes – a statement of blessings found in the first verses of the Sermon on the Mount in Matthew 5.

Bhakti Yoga – the path of devotion in Hinduism, generally characterized through worship.

Bodhisattva – an enlightened being who chooses not to enter nirvana in order to help others achieve enlightenment.

Brahma – Hindu god of creation.

Brahman – the Supreme Reality, the One sacred essence without form or name.

Brahmin – the priestly caste in Hinduism.

Buddha – the Awake or Enlightened One.

Butsudan – a Japanese Buddhist household shrine.

Cargo Cults – Religious traditions in the South Pacific that originated from contact with the West and have a messianic belief in the promise of material success.

Caste – the Hindu system of social class that dictated all aspects of a person's life including occupation, diet, and social relationships.

Chanunpa – ceremonial pipe used in Native American tradition.

Circumcision – the sign of the covenant between God and Abraham.

Clear – In Scientology, the state of being free from engrams and able to operate out of the analytical mind.

Code – is the component of religion involving expectations for behavior, guidelines for conduct, dress, etc. in a religious tradition.

Constantine – Roman emperor who made Christianity the official religion of the Roman Empire in 313 CE.

Consubstantiation – the Lutheran view of the Eucharist which views the bread and wine as both literally and symbolically the body and blood of Christ.

Coven – small group of pagans who practice together.

Covenant – an agreement between two parties; in Judaism, God makes a covenant with Abraham and later with the whole Hebrew people at Mt. Sinai.

Creed – the basic beliefs of a religious tradition; can include sacred narratives, religious texts, creedal statements, etc.

Cult – sociologically, a movement centered around a specific teaching or deity representing a break from a larger religious tradition.

Cultus – ritual and community life in a religious tradition; this can include festivals, sacred practices, sacred sites, and symbols, etc.

Dakini – literally, "sky dancers," embodiments of female deities or spirits.

Dao (Tao) – the Nameless Force or Way in Daoism.

Daodejing – sacred text of Daoism, "The Classic of the Way and Its Power."

Darsan – a visual connection between people and the Sacred; seeing and being seen by the Divine.

De – virtue or moral power in Daoism.

Dharma – In Hinduism, the idea of sacred duty; in Buddhism, the teachings of the Buddha.

Diaspora – the scattering of a people, particularly the scattering of the Jewish people after the Exile.

Digambara – "Sky clad" sect of Jainism, the strictest of the two major sects.

Diksha – initiation ritual in Jainism for becoming a monk or nun.

Divination – the act of discerning the will of the spirits or determining the proper course of action in a given situation.

Diwali – the festival of lights celebrated by Hindus, Jains, and Sikhs.

Dreaming – the period of creation in Aboriginal religion, as well as the realm of ancestors and spirits.

Dukkha – the reality of dissatisfaction or suffering.

Durga – the goddess of righteousness in Hinduism.

Ecumenism – cooperation and dialogue between different branches of the same religion.

Ema – a small plaque in Shinto on which a prayer or wish is written.

Engram – a negative thought or emotion in Scientology.

Epiphany – a revelation or manifestation; in the Christian liturgical calendar, the celebration of the coming of the wise men.

Epistles – letters to churches in Christianity.

Eucharist – a sacrament usually involving bread or wine that re-enacts the Last Supper of Jesus and his disciples.

Exclusivism – the belief that one's own religious tradition is the only true faith. This perspective often emphasizes dialogue only for the purpose of conversion.

Exile – the period in Jewish history beginning in 586 BCE, when the Babylonians destroyed the Temple in Jerusalem and forced many of the Jewish community into exile in Babylon.

Exodus – the period in Jewish history when Moses led the Hebrew people out of slavery in Egypt.

Fasting – the sacred act of abstaining from food for a specific period of time to promote spiritual growth and discipline.

Fatima – the daughter of Muhammad and Khadijah and wife of Ali.

Feng Shui – working with energy to create a harmonious space.

Fetish – a charm or symbol that brings good fortune or wards off evil.

Filioque – the belief in Catholicism that the Holy Spirit issues from both God, the Father, and Jesus, the Son.

Gabriel – an angel in Christianity and Islam. In Islam, it is the angel who revealed the Qur'an to Muhammad.

Ganesh (Ganesha) – the elephant-headed Hindu god, the remover of obstacles and the god of good fortune.

Ganja – the holy herb, marijuana, in Rastafarianism.

Gathas – sacred texts in Zoroastrianism.

Gospel – literally, good news. Accounts of the life and ministry of Jesus.

Gurdwara – place of worship for Sikhs.

Hadith – the traditions, sayings of and stories about the Prophet Muhammad in Islam.

Hafiz – a Sufi poet.

Hajj – the pilgrimage to Mecca a faithful Muslim should make once in a lifetime if physically and financially able.

Halal – that which is permissible in Islam.

Hanukkah – the Jewish feast of dedication after the Maccabees drove the army of Antiochus Epiphanes from the temple.

Harae – purification rituals in Shinto.

Haraigushi – a wooden stick with white strips of paper or hemp used in Shinto purification rituals.

Haram – that which is forbidden in Islam.

Hatsumode – the first shrine visit of the New Year in Shinto.

Henotheism – a system of belief in which there is one deity that has a greater status than all the others.

Hijab – modest dress in Islam; may also be used to refer specifically to the head scarf.

Hijrah – the flight of Muhammad and his followers from Mecca to Medina in 622 CE. It is from this year that Muslims date their calendar.

Icons – images of Christ and the saints in the Orthodox tradition used as a visual focal point during prayer.

Id-al-Adha – the Feast of Sacrifice that takes place at the end of the month of pilgrimage in Islam.

Id-al-Fitr – the feast commemorating the end of the month of fasting in Islam.

Iftar – the meal at the end of each day during Ramadan that breaks the fast.

Imam – a scholar of the Qur'an and religious leader in Islam in Shi'ite Islam, it may also refer to the first leaders of the Shi'ite community after the death of Muhammad.

Imitative Magic – rituals that enact a desired result (i.e., rain dance)

Immaculate Conception – the belief that Mary was without original sin.

Immanent – the divine manifested in the created world.

Incarnation – the divine taking human or human-like form.

Inclusivism – the view that all religions can be viewed from the same lens and have the same goal. This view often downplays the differences between religions.

Indra – the lord of heaven and the god of thunder in Hinduism; prominent during the Vedic period.

Interfaith Movement – the movement to promote dialogue, respect, understanding, and cooperation between people of differing religions.

Isaac – Abraham's second son, born of Sarah. It is through Isaac that Judaism and Christianity trace their lineage.

Ishmael – Abraham's firstborn son, born of Hagar. It is through Ishmael that Islam traces its lineage.

Islam – peaceful submission to the will of God.

Izanagi – the male kami of creation in Japanese religion.

Izanami – the female kami of creation in Japanese religion.

Japji – the opening hymn of the Sikh sacred text used daily in prayer.

Jihad – struggle or striving; most specifically the struggle to do what is right and faithful.

Jina – one who has conquered, or reached enlightenment, in Jainism.

Jinn – a spirit who is able to take human and nonhuman form; may be a submissive or nonsubmissive being.

Jiva – the spiritual essence in Jainism.

Jnana Yoga – the Hindu spiritual pathway of knowledge or wisdom.

Ka'bah – the sacred building in Mecca said to have been built by Abraham. The site of pilgrimage.

Kabbala – the mystical texts in Judaism including passages about dream interpretation, numerology, predictions of the coming of the Messiah, etc.

Kachera – undergarment worn by members of the Sikh Khalsa.

Kalachakra – the world cycle in Jainism represented as a wheel with 12 spokes.

Kali – the destroyer aspect of the mother goddess in Hinduism.

Kami – the sacred manifest in everything including nature, deities, and creativity.

Kamidana – a Shinto household shrine or altar.

Kami-no-michi – Japanese term for Shinto, meaning the way of the sacred.

Kangha – a comb worn by members of the Sikh Khalsa.

Kannagara – harmony with nature in Shinto.

Kara – steel or iron bracelet worn by members of the Sikh Khalsa.

Karah Prasad – a sweet, blessed by the Guru and served at Sikh services.

Karma – actions and the fruits or consequences of action.

Karma Yoga – the spiritual pathway of selfless service in Hinduism.

Kesh – uncut hair; members of the Sikh Khalsa do not cut any of the hair on their bodies.

Khadijah – the first wife of the Prophet Muhammad.

Khalsa – the community of baptized Sikhs established first by Guru Gobind Singh.

Khanda – the symbol of the Sikh faith.

Ki – spiritual energy in Shinto.

Kirpan – dagger or small sword worn by members of the Sikh Khalsa.

Kirtan – the practice of devotional singing.

Koan – riddle used in Zen Buddhism to facilitate transcending reason.

Kojiki – "records of ancient matters"; one of the two major collections of Japanese mythology.

Kosher – ritually pure and fit for consumption in Judaism.

Krishna – an incarnation of the Hindu god, Vishnu and the teacher of Arjuna, the warrior, in the Bhagavad Gita.

Kufr – a serious sin in Islam; usually translated as "ingratitude" or "unbelief."

Kundalini – a form of yoga that focuses on opening up chakras, or fields of energy.

Kwanzaa – a week-long celebration of African American culture and values, rooted in an indigenous African festival.

Lakshmi – also known as Sri; she is the goddess of wealth and good fortune and the consort of Vishnu.

Lama – teacher-monk in Tibetan Buddhism.

Langar – community meal served by Sikhs to anyone who wishes to eat.

Lent – A forty-day period of preparation for the death and resurrection of Christ.

Li – doing the right thing in a given situation as well as proper rituals for ancestors and spirits.

Liturgy – literally "the work of the people"; the order of service in Christian worship.

Loka – vast, finite, eternal space; the universe in Jainism.

Mabon – Autumn Equinox.

Magic (Magick) – the ability to bring about change through ritual or the directing of energy.

Mahadevi – the Great Mother Goddess in Hinduism.

Mahavira – Great Hero, the title given to Nadaputta Vardhamana, the 24th Jain Tirthankara.

Mandala – a visual representation of the universe used in meditation.

Mandir – a Hindu temple.

Manifestation – the divine taking nonhuman form.

Mantra – repetitive sound or phrase used in meditation or worship.

Mara – the lord of desire in Buddhism.

Matsuri – a Japanese festival.

Menorah – candelabra used in Jewish worship.

Miko – female attendants at a Shinto shrine.

Mikoshi – a portable shrine for the kami.

Mikva – water baptism in Judaism for ritual purification.

Millennium – an era of peace and justice when the oppressed/faithful are rewarded and the evildoers punished.

Minaret – the tower from which the call to prayer is broadcast in Islam.

Minyan – the minimum number of 10 Jewish people (traditionally males) needed to form a synagogue.

Misogi – the Shinto ritual of purification that takes place in running water, such as a waterfall.

Moksha – liberation, freedom from the cycle of birth, death and rebirth.

Monotheism – the belief in one god or goddess.

Mudra – hand gestures used in meditation as well as dance.

Muezzin – the person who calls people to prayer in Islam.

Muslim – one who faithfully submits to the will of God, a follower of Islam.

Musubi – the power of creation which originates from the kami.

Myth – a sacred narrative.

Nam simaran – the devotional practice of repeating the Divine Name in Sikhism.

Nihon Shoki (Nihongi) – "chronicles of Japan"; one of the two collections of Japanese mythology.

Nirvana – literally "the extinguishing of a flame due to lack of fuel"; enlightenment, a state of equanimity and peace, devoid of desire.

Nontheistic – a religious or philosophical system based on a worldview and practice used to achieve one's spiritual goals rather than on a personal relationship with a divine being.

Nowruz – Persian New Year.

Ofuda – an amulet on a Shinto home shrine to absorb evil spirits.

Ordinary Time – the period in the Christian liturgical year that falls between seasons and marks the life and ministry of Jesus.

Original Sin – the belief in some traditions of Christianity that human beings are born with the guilt of Adam and Eve.

Orisha – gods or spirits in West African religious traditions.

Ostara – the Spring Equinox, a celebration of fertility and new life.

Pandit – common way to address a Hindu priest indicating he is a scholar of the Vedas.

Pantheism – the belief that God is everything and everything is God.

Papal Infallibility – the doctrine that when the Pope speaks "ex cathedra," or from the office of Pope his words are without error. This has only occurred twice in history.

Parables – teaching stories from ordinary life used by Jesus, often to describe the kingdom of God.

Param Brahma – the One Supreme Lord in Hinduism.

Parvati – the gentle aspect of the mother goddess in Hinduism; she is the consort of Shiva.

Passover – the Jewish festival celebrating the Exodus from Egypt when the angel of death passed over the homes of the Hebrews.

Patriarch – a bishop in the Orthodox tradition.

Pentecost – the Christian festival marking the gift of the Holy Spirit; sometimes called the "birthday of the church."

Peyote – a button-shaped cactus that is a sacrament in the Native American Church.

Pluralism – the building of working relationships based on respect and knowledge between individuals or groups who do not share the same religious/spiritual perspective.

Polytheism – the belief in multiple deities, or multiple manifestations of one divine essence.

Pope – Bishop of Rome; head of the Roman Catholic Church.

Popol Vu – Mayan creation narrative.

Profane – ordinary; pertaining to the material world.

Puja – Hindu worship which can take place in the home, at a temple or on pilgrimage.

Purgatory – in Roman Catholicism, a place of purification for the consequences of sin before entering into heaven.

Purim – the Jewish festival celebrating the story of Esther and the sparing of the Jewish people from massacre during the Persian Empire.

Qi – energy that flows through the universe manifesting in two complementary forces, yin and yang.

Qibla – a marking that points the direction of prayer in Islam.

Rabbi – a Jewish teacher and scholar of the Torah and Talmud.

Rabi'a – a female Sufi poet from Iraq.

Raja Yoga – the Hindu spiritual path of meditation.

Ramadan – the month in the Islamic calendar when Muhammad received his first revelation; it is a month of fasting from dawn to sunset.

Ren – the Confucian virtue of human-heartedness or benevolence.

Rig Veda – the oldest of the Hindu sacred texts, said to be the inspired word given to the rishis, or sages. Dates to around 2000 BCE.

Rites of passage – rituals that mark significant life events; such as, birth, puberty, marriage, and death.

Ritual – repetitive actions and/or words that enable individuals or communities to connect with the sacred.

Rosary – a form of prayer in Christianity using beads to mark the sequence and number of prayers.

Rosh Hashanah – the celebration of the Jewish New Year.

Sabbath – day of worship and rest; in Judaism, it begins at sundown on Friday and ends at sundown on Saturday.

Sacrament – A ritual that connects one to or opens one up to the sacred; a means of grace in Christian traditions.

Sallekhana – ritual fast until death in Jainism.

Samhain – Pagan New Year, a time to celebrate ancestors and also a good time for divination.

Samsara – the cycle of birth, death and rebirth; reincarnation.

Sanatana Dharma – the Indian name for Hinduism; meaning, the Eternal Religion, or Eternal Truth

Sangha – the Buddhist community of monks and nuns.

Sants – a group of Hindu and Muslim mystics who influenced the development of Sikhism.

Saraswati – the Hindu goddess of art and learning; and the consort of Brahma.

Sat – Truth, a title for God in Sikhism.

Satori – the term for enlightenment in Zen Buddhism.

Sect – a subgroup of a larger tradition.

Seder – during Passover, the meal and ritual retelling of the story of the Exodus.

Sema – a form of circle dance in the Mevlevi order of Sufis.

Sermon on the Mount – Matthew 5–7; the ethical core of Jesus' teachings in Christianity.

Shahadah – the central statement of faith in Islam, used daily in prayer and the confession by which one becomes a Muslim.

Shakti – the power of energy and creativity manifest in the goddess.

Shaman – a spiritual specialist who serves an intermediary and can will his or her spirit to leave the body and travel to upper and lower spirit worlds.

Shangdi – the Lord of Heaven in Chinese religion.

Shavuot – also known as Pentecost, the Jewish festival honoring the giving of the law at Mt. Sinai.

Shema – the central prayer in Judaism found in Deuteronomy 6: 4–5; means "Hear" in Hebrew and is the first word of the actual prayer.

Shimenawa – a straw rope hung over shrines, homes, and other sacred spaces in Japan.

Shirk – the sin of idolatry in Islam.

Shiva – the Hindu god of death, destruction, and reproduction

Shopping Cart or Eclectic Spirituality – an individual approach of combining practices or beliefs from more than one religious tradition to form one's own spiritual practice.

Shu – the Confucian virtue of reciprocity, "do not do to others what you would not wish done to yourself."

Sikh – a disciple or seeker

Sin – disobedience to God in Judaism, Christianity, and Islam, may result from actions or inaction.

Smudging – the practice of using smoke from various plants to bring about healing.

Spenta Mainyu – the good energy of the sacred in Zoroastrianism.

Spirituality – the way in which an individual connects to the holy. Spirituality is often contrasted with religion by emphasizing it as more individual and noninstitutional than religion.

Stupas – symbols of enlightenment in Buddhism that often hold relics.

Sufism – the mystical tradition of Islam.

Sukkot – the festival of booths, a Jewish festival commemorating the period of wandering in the wilderness.

Sunyata – the doctrine of emptiness in Buddhism.

Surah – a chapter in the Qur'an.

Sutras – wisdom writings in Buddhism, such as the Diamond Sutra or the Lotus Sutra.

Svetambaras – literally "white clad," a sect of Jainism in which the monks and nuns wear white robes.

Synagogue – a place of fellowship, study, and prayer in Judaism.

Taboo – a behavior that offends the gods or spirits or violates a code in religious traditions.

T'ai chi ch'uan (Taiji quan) – Daoist practice/exercise focused on balance, harmony, and the breath.

Talmud – commentary and interpretation of the Torah, the second most important text in Judaism. It is made up of two parts: the Mishnah and the Gemara.

Tanakh – the Hebrew Bible, an acronym formed from the first letter in Hebrew of each of the three sections of the Bible: Torah, Nevi'im (Prophets), and Ketuvim (writings).

T'fillin – the small boxes worn on the forehead and the arm by Jewish males during prayer; they are reminders of the Shema, the central prayer of Judaism.

Theistic – religious traditions that emphasize a personal relationship with a divine being(s).

Theosophy – a new religious movement that focuses on seeking "Divine wisdom."

Thetan – the spirit of a person in Scientology.

Tian – heaven in Chinese religion.

Tirthankaras – literally "ford makers," the 24 enlightened teachers in Jainism.

Tonks – places of meditation marking where someone has reached enlightenment.

Torah – the first five books of the Hebrew Bible, the Law of Moses.

Torii – sacred gate marking the entrance to a Shinto shrine.

Totem – an animal or plant spirit helper for a family or community that provides identity and protection.

Touro Synagogue – the longest standing Jewish synagogue in the United States. It opened in 1763.

Transcendence – the aspect of the sacred that is separate or removed from the created world.

Transubstantiation – the belief that when blessed the bread and the wine transform into the body and blood of Christ.

Trickster – a spirit who may take animal form who often teaches a lesson through bad behavior and/or humor.

Trimurti – the triad of Hindu Gods: Brahma, Vishnu, and Shiva.

Trinity – Christian doctrine of the relationship among God, Jesus, and the Holy Spirit, God in three persons.

Triple Gem – the statement of "faith" in Buddhism; "I take refuge in the Buddha; I take refuge in the Dharma; I take refuge in the Sangha."

Tsumi – ritual impurity in Shinto.

Tulku – a reincarnated lama in Tibetan Buddhism.

Ummah – the community in Sunni Islam.

Upanayana – the sacred thread ceremony in which young Hindus are initiated into the study of the Vedas.

Upanishads – philosophical writings of Hinduism.

Vedas – collection of sacred texts in Hinduism.

Vishnu – the Hindu god known as the God of Benevolence, the Preserver. He takes various forms to call people to goodness.

Vision Quest – a Native American rite of passage in which a young person goes out into the wilderness to fast and await a vision, new name or vocation.

World's Parliament of Religions – an interfaith gathering. The first one opened September 11, 1893 in Chicago during the World's Fair.

Wudu – ablutions, or washing, before prayer in Islam.

Wu Wei – "doing by not doing"; going with the flow or not acting in conflict with the Dao.

Xiao – filial piety, the virtue of caring for family.

Yamas – ethical principles in Hinduism and Jainism.

Yarmulke – also known as the kippah, the small cap worn by Jewish males.

Yang – the bright, assertive male aspect of energy.

YHWH – the sacred name of God in Judaism, also called the tetragrammaton.

Yi – right conduct in Confucianism.

Yin – the dark, receptive, female aspect of energy.

Yoga – a term for the spiritual pathways by which Hindus seek union with the Sacred; the word literally means "yoke" or "union."

Yom Haatzma-ut – the May 14th celebration of Israel becoming a sovereign state after World War II.

Yom Hashoah – a service in memory of those lost during the Holocaust.

Yom Kippur – the most sacred day of the year in Judaism, the Day of Atonement.

Yule – the celebration of the Winter Solstice.

Zakat – the tithe in Islam that goes to those who are in need; 2.5% of one's wealth beyond that which is needed to live.

Zarathustra – founder of Zoroastrianism.

Zazen – sitting meditation in Zen Buddhism.

Zhong – Confucian virtue of loyalty.

Zionism – the movement to reestablish a Jewish homeland in Israel.

Index